S. H. IRVINE

METHUEN'S
MANUALS OF MODERN PSYCHOLOGY

General Editor C. A. Mace 1946–68

H. J. Butcher 1968–

Intelligence and Cultural Environment

Intelligence and Cultural Environment

PHILIP E. VERNON

Professor of Educational Psychology and Senior Research
Consultant, University of Calgary, Alberta:
Emeritus Professor of Psychology, University of London,
Institute of Education

METHUEN & CO LTD
11 NEW FETTER LANE LONDON EC4

First published 1969
© 1969 by Philip E. Vernon
Printed and bound in Great Britain
by Butler & Tanner Ltd, Frome and London
SBN 416 12120 9

Distributed in the U.S.A.
by Barnes & Noble Inc.

Contents

PART IV

Studies in Britain

PART V

Cross-Cultural Studies

PART VI

Summary and Implications

Acknowledgments

This book is dedicated to my wife Dorothy, who for over 20 years has accompanied and supported me in my psychological and educational activities, and who bore the brunt of the mental testing described below.

Probably it would never have been written if my interest in education and child development in many parts of the world had not been stimulated by the British Council's enlightened policy of sending lecturers in psychology (among other subjects) to all quarters of the globe. Under the Council's auspices we have spent considerable periods in Australia, New Zealand, Lebanon, Jordan, Greece, Tanzania, Mexico, Colombia, Ecuador, Peru and Venezuela.

Next I wish to acknowledge most gratefully the financial support given by the Association for the Aid of Crippled Children, in New York, whose interests extend to children handicapped in mental as well as in physical development. By means of their grant, and through the willingness of the University of London Institute of Education to arrange leave of absence, we were able to carry out studies in Jamaica, Canada, East Africa and the Hebrides and elsewhere in the UK. I particularly enjoyed the stimulating interest of the Association's Assistant Director, Dr Stephen Richardson. This book represents, in fact, my final Report to the Association. I would also thank Mr B. Thorsteinsson of the Education Division of the Department of Northern Affairs and Natural Resources in Ottawa for arranging our trip to the Arctic and for a grant towards expenses.

So many Directors of Education, Head teachers or Principals of schools and their staffs, and members of Departments of Education in universities where I worked, have helped that it would take too long to name them individually; but I am sincerely grateful. The following, who carried out the interviewing of the boys on our field trips, must be specially mentioned: Dr L. H. E. Reid and Mrs J. Figueroa (University of the West Indies); Miss Sheila Cumming (Glasgow Child Guidance Service); Mr J. Hawkes (Counselor, University of Calgary); Miss Dawn Potter (Teacher-at-large, N.W. Territories, Canada); Mr J. Igaga (Makerere University College, Uganda), and Mr Mwalongo (Inspector, Ministry of Education, Dar es Salaam).

The Chart on p. 35 is reproduced with the permission of its author, Prof. J. Cravioto, Hospital Infantile de Mexico; and the picture on

p. 43 by permission of Dr W. Hudson and the National Institute for Personnel Research, Johannesburg. Dr P. A. Schwarz's principles of test administration and construction in developing nations appear in Chapter 16 by permission of the American Institute for Research.

PART I
Current Conceptions of Intelligence

I

Introduction

Results from tests of general ability and so-called verbal intelligence can be utilized not to cast aspersions upon less civilized peoples or to heap praise upon the more civilized but to establish differences between societies living under different conditions and hence favoring some kinds of knowledge and some ways of living rather than others (L. W. Doob, *Becoming More Civilized: A Psychological Exploration*, 1960, p. 173).

Psychology, according to some of its critics, consists either of platitudes which everyone knows already, or else of technical trivialities and statistics which nobody wants to know. This is unfair, but perhaps it could be applied to this book, which first of all discusses some problems of mankind that are too complicated for any scientific solution to be possible, and then presents a lot of detailed test results whose relevance and interpretation may strike the reader as dubious.

We start with a glaring platitude, namely that people differ in their abilities and achievements. Within any one country such as England, some people become wealthy executives, others seem unable to rise above the level of unskilled labourers. Some progress rapidly and brilliantly through school and university to a professional career, many others fall by the wayside. Some are rewarded by life because their own capabilities and efforts bear fruit, or through the influence of others or often just because they are lucky, and many are punished because of their weaknesses or through circumstances over which they have no control. Apart from overall success or failure, there are tremendous varieties of talent as between artists, scientists, political leaders and administrators, sportsmen and skilled artisans. Many who are outstanding in one direction are hopeless in others, and there are many who probably never find their niche – the square pegs in round holes. We all realise, of course, that a man's temperament, character and inclinations are at least as important in determining these outcomes as the abilities that he is born with or acquires, and that in practice capacity and motivation are always mixed up. However, it is much easier to observe and measure what a child or adult *can* do than it is to find out *why* he does it. Hence we intend to concentrate on the former – the cognitive characteristics of man, while not forgetting the latter – the orectic aspects.

Within any nation there are many distinguishable subgroups or cultures which clearly differ not only in dress, habits, speech, types of occupation, moral and political attitudes, but also in abilities. Social class differences are pervasive in western societies, and even in such differently organised societies as USSR and India there are differences of wealth and privilege – the haves and the have-nots. Usually the children of the haves are brought up under more favourable conditions and, whether for this or for other reasons, they are more likely to do well at school and to enter the higher-grade careers. Many countries besides England, notably the United States, have their minorities – people of different race, colour or language, who are incompletely assimilated into the community, perhaps discriminated against, and who tend to fall at the bottom end of the scale of achievement. Obviously too there are wide differences within classes or other subgroups: many upper or middle-class children are stupid and many working class children, including negroes within a white community, are upwardly mobile. Indeed a major contribution of psychology has been to bring out the extent of overlapping – that 10 per cent or more of American negroes score better on intelligence tests than the average American white. In Britain, parents who work in semiskilled occupations actually produce a rather bigger *total* of bright children than professional-executive parents, since the former constitute a very large group, and the latter a relatively small group. But this does not alter the fact that the higher-class parents have an enormously greater *proportion* of able children who do well educationally and vocationally than the lower classes; their chances in life are vastly better.*

In this second half of the twentieth century there is an ever-increasing need for brain workers, accompanied by decreasing opportunities for manual workers. Previously the western world depended so greatly on hewers of wood and drawers of water that many labourers, farmers and individual craftsmen could achieve a reasonably satisfying life. They were not rich, but their essential needs were met and they could take some pride in their jobs. In our more complex civilisation, particularly with the onset of automation, the 'lower classes' may in fact be better

---

* See J. L. Gray; Anastasi 1958; Vernon 1960.
Note that references to the bibliography are made by date when an author has made two or more contributions. But if only a single book or article is cited, dates are often omitted in order to simplify the text or to avoid footnotes.

off, but they are even less secure, and more aware of the disparities between their lot and that of the more able, the better educated and more favoured. Moreover it has been pointed out that the traditional methods of education and training are inadequate for the modern world. It is not enough to acquire a certain amount of information at school and pick up occupational skills on the job. The successful individual needs to be trained to solve problems, to adapt to new situations; in other words he must be more intelligent (cf. Bloom, Davis and Hess).

Differences between nations are still more striking, and here too, while we recognise qualitative differences in type of economy and culture, between the Indian, African, Arab and Polynesian for example, we also naturally tend to grade them on a scale of wealth and technological advancement, of more and less civilised or – in our attempts to be more sympathetic and less self-satisfied – we talk of the developed and the underdeveloped. It is only too clear that such inequalities between nations are increasing, despite financial and technical assistance from the haves to the have-nots. In the former there is an upward spiral: their wealth and technology make possible the production of a better-educated population with higher standards of living, and of more scientists and engineers who improve the technology still further. Whereas in the latter there is a vicious circle of poor or unexploited natural resources, primitive skills and conservative attitudes, under-nourishment, disease and overpopulation, poor education and consequent under-production of able and intelligent men who could lead them out of the slough. Most developing countries are doing their best to break this circle at many points; but certainly one of the most fundamental difficulties, being tackled most urgently, is the lack of trained and trainable personnel to provide the professionals, teachers, commercial and political leaders, and technicians, without whom economic viability is unattainable. They no longer wish to, nor can afford to, depend on administrators, advisers and educationists borrowed from the western nations, and indeed often attribute their present backwardness to previous exploitation by the whites and to the shortcomings of benevolent colonialism.

The nineteenth and early twentieth centuries were content to accept:

'The rich man at his table, the poor man at his gate,
God made them high and lowly, and ordered their estate,'

or to ascribe low achievement and consequent poverty to innate inferiority of intelligence and temperament. In England there was strong opposition to the notion of educating the masses; and when it was first introduced it was cheap and meagre (cf. Vernon, 1957b). The incapacity of more 'primitive' races ever to govern themselves effectively or to achieve a western-type education and civilisation is still widely voiced in South Africa, Rhodesia and occasionally in parts of the USA. But the mid-twentieth century has developed a conscience about the underdog, both at home and abroad, and in any case the underdog's demands for a better deal have become too clamant to be ignored. Thus we find in almost every country a ferment of concern for the 'underprivileged', more drastic redistribution of wealth, and improved medical and social services and educational opportunities for those hitherto denied them.

Now where does the social scientist, and the psychologist in particular, come into all this ? The value of economic surveys and planning is obvious, and the social anthropologist's studies of the structure, customs and beliefs of different cultural groups must surely help us better to understand the developing countries and their difficulties. The sociologist and psychologist should not try to set themselves up as experts on the actual measures that can best be taken in relation to other countries, or on the social reforms needed within their own borders. These depend to far too great an extent on value judgments, prejudices and emotions, political, religious and economic considerations to be approached as purely scientific problems. What they can do, though, is to provide relevant facts – facts about the abilities and attitudes of the peoples concerned. They can survey and measure the effects of changes which either occur naturally over the course of time, or are arbitrarily introduced. They can study the nature of the processes underlying changes in individuals or in groups, how and when acculturation takes place, what stimulates or inhibits the growth of abilities, the acquisition of new attitudes, the arousal of group conflicts. Psychological theories of intelligence have altered very drastically since the 1920s, and this has led to a fresh interpretation of individual, social class and ethnic differences. Since psychologists are themselves human beings, their reasoning too is liable to bias in accordance with their particular sympathies; and as middle-class westerners they may misinterpret the psychology of the western working class or the African negro. But at least they are more aware of their liability to ethnocentrism. Much of what the writer has to say will appear politically or socially loaded; very probably he will, despite all his efforts, be accused of snobbery or racialism or both. That is the risk one must accept in trying to trace the implications of observations and measurements in this enormously complex and controversial area.

There is a particular advantage in studying individual differences, subgroup and major group (e.g. ethnic) differences simultaneously, since each raises similar problems and helps to illumine the others. For example it is profitable to investigate how far differences in school efficiency or teaching methods affect achievements in a number of English schools; but far greater contrasts, which may highlight these effects, will be found by cross-cultural comparisons. Sometimes an unusual ethnic group will provide the crucial case which confirms or contradicts a generalisation reached in one's own culture.*

Turning then to the present book: its major objective is to explore the environmental and other factors which hinder the development of abilities within underdeveloped countries or depressed minority groups. A good deal is already known of the conditions within developed western nations that stimulate intellectual growth, and those which prevent large sections of a community from realising their full potential. Part I examines the concept of intelligence, how far it is genetically determined, how it is built up during childhood, and whether we can talk meaningfully of a general ability or intelligence, especially when comparing different cultural groups. Part II surveys the experimental evidence relating to the main environmental influences on the growth of general intelligence and some other abilities, of nutrition, of stimulation or lack of it during childhood, of family, socioeconomic and school conditions, particularly in the UK and USA.

Such knowledge, combined with studies of underdeveloped countries as such, should enable us to help these countries towards technological progress. Already, by the adoption of psychological testing techniques which have proved their worth in the western nations, we can assist them in selecting their more able adults and children, those who are most likely to be trainable for skilled and clerical jobs, and those most likely to benefit from advanced education (cf. P. A. Schwarz). But it would be still more useful to discover what factors of diet and health, cultural tradition and family upbringing, schooling and job training, most require attention, if they are to produce sufficient highly skilled personnel for their needs. However, there are very serious technical problems in taking over tests from other cultures, or in constructing tests more suited to local conditions – the more so the more backward and illiterate the people concerned. Many social scientists would say that the kinds of test data that the present writer and others have collected are too superficial and too equivocal to be worthwhile. Part III deals mainly with such problems of the applicability of tests in different cultural groups.

* Cf. Price Williams, 1966. He cites as examples the variations in weaning practices, and in Oedipus formation, in different cultures.

Part IV describes the battery of tests assembled by the writer and the results obtained in the UK. A considerable assortment of tests of varied abilities was given to samples of boys aged around 11 years in England, Scotland (the Hebrides), Jamaica and Uganda, and to Eskimos and Indians in Canada, 375 in all. The samples were small, mostly 40s and 50s, since it seemed more useful to concentrate on individual testing in order to reduce misunderstandings between tester and testee, than to give group tests to larger and more representative groups. (There is plenty of room for both types of research.) While it would have been preferable to test at various ages, or to assess children growing up in each ethnic group over a considerable period, cross-sectional surveys at a particular age are more feasible. The age of 11 was chosen since, in all the countries visited, pupils have acquired a moderate facility with English and are approaching the end of their primary schooling. In most of the samples the mother tongue was not English but, with suitable precautions, it was not necessary to work through interpreters. Admittedly it would be far more difficult to extend such testing to ethnic groups in which English is not the main medium of school instruction. Only boys were included for two good reasons, first that having girls would have involved doubling the numbers and further complicated the analysis and interpretation; and secondly that there is a good deal of evidence from child studies (e.g. Schaefer and Bayley) that cause-effect relationships are on the whole more straightforward in the male sex. Girls seem to react more to the immediate social situation, hence it is more difficult to trace their present behaviour back to past experience.

Part V, then, gives a sketch of each of these overseas groups, attempting to analyse the main handicaps that affect the development of their abilities, and to link these observations with the observed test results. It is realised, of course, that this type of evidence does not prove causal relationships; but by comparing groups and subgroups with one another, as well as with English standards, it is hoped that some progress has been made. Throughout the emphasis is laid, not on whether some groups are generally superior or inferior to others, but on the patterns of scores on different tests which reflect their cultural characteristics. Moreover, within each group, assessments were obtained of important environmental variables, and these were correlated with the boys' test scores, so that 'within-group' differences could be considered alongside 'between-group' differences.

The final Part provides a general summary and a discussion of the main implications of the research.

II

Intelligence A, B and C

Discussions of the intelligence of different social classes or different ethnic groups have been, and still are, characterised by bitter controversy and misunderstandings, though we are beginning to realise at last that much of the trouble is due to people using the term intelligence in different senses. In the first place 'intelligence' conveys the meaning – innate capacity, something which the child inherits from his ancestors through the genes, and which determines the mental growth of which he is capable. It is educability as distinct from acquired knowledge or skills. But secondly we use the term 'intelligent' to refer to the child or adult who is clever, quick in the uptake, good at comprehending and reasoning, mentally efficient. Yet a third meaning for intelligence is Mental Age or IQ or score on one of the widely used intelligence tests. Each of these three concepts is, as we shall see, highly complex; but it will save a great deal of confusion if we agree to label them Intelligence A, B and C, respectively.

The distinction between Intelligence A and B was formulated by D. O. Hebb, and it corresponds to the geneticist's familiar distinction between the genotype and the phenotype. The genotype does refer to the genetic equipment of the individual (or group), his inherited potentialities for growth. But it can never be directly observed, let alone measured. It is an hypothesis, albeit one for which very convincing evidence can be produced. All we can observe is people's behaviour, whether they act, speak and think in a manner that we call intelligent. And this phenotype always depends on the interaction of the genes with the prenatal and postnatal environment. In other words we should not think of any gene or set of genes as producing any particular trait such as intelligence (not even skin colour or height); the trait exists only in so far as an appropriate environment favours its development. Thus the Intelligence B that we observe is not genetic; nor is it acquired in the sense of being trained or taught. It is the product of nature and nurture. There is nothing very revolutionary in this; just the same applies to, say, plants. To obtain a fine crop of wheat one needs not only good seed, but also appropriate moisture, temperature and manure to nourish its growth. Similarly the typical member of an ethnic group may be dull because of inferior genetic equipment, or through lack of mental nourishment, or both, and we cannot really tell which.

A futher complication must be mentioned, though it somewhat blurs the distinction, namely that genetic equipment is not the same as physiological or constitutional equipment. There is much evidence that conditions during pregnancy and parturition affect the development of the nervous system in the foetus and newborn. Gestational stress may be brought about in the mother by malnutrition or exposure to certain diseases, by heavy manual labour or by anxiety.* Thus a child may be born with a brain which is incapable of normal development, however good the environment, not because of defective genes but because of prenatal conditions, birth injury or anoxia. Equally, later in life, the plasticity of the brain in some way deteriorates, or it may be affected by disease or injury, and these reduce the effective Intelligence B, particularly the capacity for any further learning. Nevertheless we find it more convenient to retain Intelligence A for the genotype and to regard such physiological conditions as part of the environment which determines the growth or decline of Intelligence B.

Two further points should be made here about Intelligence B: first that it is not static or fixed for life. If a child's environment or education, or his personality, alter then his intelligence level, relative to that of his contemporaries, may rise or fall. However, when people are brought up in a reasonably standard environment, the correlations between measures of intelligence given some months, or even years, apart are in fact remarkably high. Secondly we must try to discard the idea that intelligence (i.e. Intelligence B) is a kind of universal faculty, a trait which is the same (apart from variations in amount) in all cultural groups. Clearly it develops differently in different physical and cultural environments. It should be regarded as a name for all the various cognitive skills which are developed in, and valued by, the group. In western civilisation it refers mainly to grasping relations and symbolic thinking, and this permeates to some extent all the abilities we show at school, at work, or in daily life. We naturally tend to evaluate the intelligence of other ethnic groups on the same criteria, though it would surely be more psychologically sound to recognise that such groups require, and stimulate, the growth of different mental as well as physical skills for coping with their particular environments, i.e. that they possess different intelligences.

* A useful survey is given by D. H. Stott.

The present writer suggested, in 1955, adding Intelligence C to Hebb's dichotomy because far too many people who ought to know better – psychologists and sociologists, as well as teachers and laymen – are apt to refer to test results as 'intelligence'. Now an intelligence test is no more than a sample of the kinds of skills we regard as intelligent. Being based on carefully chosen and standardised tasks, it is more scientific and objective than our everyday observations. But it is more circumscribed, and it may or may not correspond closely to what most people regard as intelligent or unintelligent behaviour and thinking. The Stanford–Binet test and its derivatives happen to sample the Intelligence B of western children very thoroughly, but many other tests which are useful for various purposes tap different combinations of abilities. Group verbal tests, non-verbal tests like the Progressive Matrices, or practical performance tests all measure something rather different, hence they cannot all represent the same general intelligence. They do inter-correlate fairly highly, but not perfectly because they are sampling different kinds of thinking. Moreover good or poor test performance depends on other factors besides the obvious content of the test, for example on whether or not it is speeded, whether the testees have come across similar items before or can fully understand the instructions, and so on.

As children grow up, measures either of general intelligence or other cognitive factors, seem to become even less representative of ability as judged by society – of vocational success, of cleverness, of well-informed and quick thinking, of wisdom and understanding in affairs of daily life, of creative productivity, even of achievement in higher education. L. Hudson points out that tests differentiate quite poorly between out-standingly able and more mediocre boys in highgrade secondary schools, or among university students. To a large extent this arises because, once differentiation begins at school and children cease to study a common curriculum, we are dealing with relatively selected or homogeneous groups; and our tests cannot discriminate as well within these groups. In the occupational field too we are chiefly concerned with rather narrow-range groups. The humdrum civil servant may score as high in Intelligence C as the brilliant scientist, artist or entrepreneur, yet all of these would still score much higher than most unskilled labourers. But the main difference is, surely, that the kinds of items in the Binet test are reasonably typical of children's thinking, particularly in the school situation, whereas the short multiple-choice items of the adult group test are too trivial and uninteresting to sample the richness and variety of adult thinking.

How far Intelligence C can serve as an index of Intelligence A is still a matter of disagreement among psychologists. In the 1920's many believed that the tests were measuring innate capacity. Hence when it was found that negroes in the United States, or slum children in England, or members of less advanced ethnic groups, obtained lower scores than those of the average white, it was easy to jump to the conclusion that the differences referred to in Chapter I were genetic in origin. Yet psychologists and sociologists were also among the first to point out that they might result from the poorer economic circumstances, lack of education and other handicaps in these groups. During the 20s and 30s innumerable studies were made of children brought up in favourable and unfavourable circumstances, of twins and foster children, which demonstrated the very considerable effects of environment on test performance, and which accorded with observed differences in Intelligence B. The work has been summarised many times,* and we will not do so again except to refer, in Part II, to some more recent contributions. In consequence the pendulum swung, probably too far, in the opposite direction. Thus in 1951 the expert consultants to UNESCO issued the famous declaration that: 'According to present knowledge there is no proof that the groups of mankind differ in their innate mental characteristics, whether in respect of intelligence or temperament. The scientific evidence indicates that the range of mental capacities in all ethnic groups is much the same.'

What they should have added is – there is also no proof that innate mental differences do not exist. For it is obvious that marked inborn physical differences exist, even between neighbouring cultures such as the Watutsi giants and the pygmies of Rwanda-Burundi; so it is perfectly possible that the genes underlying mental growth in different groups differ also. In any isolated group, a trait which is advantageous for survival and for procreation is likely to be bred in by natural selection or 'genetic drift'. This might apply, say, to resourcefulness among the Eskimos, or to an indolent temperament more suited to dwellers in a very hot climate. Whether abilities of the kind we call intelligent could similarly differentiate genetically seems more doubtful since their effects are not necessarily eugenic; the more intelligent members of a tribe, for example might be more liable to be killed off or to have smaller families. But the real point is that we can't prove it, because we can only observe the phenotype, not the genotype. Conceivably some day, microscopic examination of the brain cells, or the electro-encephalograph, might give a direct index, at least of constitutional intelligence. But at the moment there is no convincing evidence of any substantial correlation

* See Anastasi 1958; Vernon 1960; Wiseman 1964.

between EEG or other physiological measures and mental efficiency, except in pathological cases.* Moreover one must insist that intelligence doesn't exist until it has been shaped by environment, hence it is little use trying to predict it by tests or measurements which do not yield actual samples of mental functioning.

Alternatively someone might try the experiment of rearing, say, Eskimo babies in Central Africa and finding whether they grow up to be different in temperament and abilities from Africans (obviously it would be almost impossible to ensure that they were treated just like African babies). But at the moment we can only hazard the guess that there are some genetic differences involved in some of the mental differences between ethnic groups, though their influence is probably small relative to that of the tremendous cultural differences.

The evidence for genetic differences between individuals cannot be ignored, though it will not be detailed here. It includes: the small but significant correlations between the intelligence of foster children or orphans and that of their true parents who have *not* brought them up; the existence of larger differences of IQ between siblings in the same family than could reasonably be accounted for by differences of up-bringing; the regression towards the mean of the IQs of children of bright and dull parents; the extreme difficulty, in practice, of raising the IQs of dull children, however stimulating the environment; the inability of environmental differences to account for the greater part of the variance in measured intelligence; and the correlations found between children with different genetic resemblances, i.e. twins and siblings. As B. K. Eckland points out, a typical correlation for *identical twins* brought up *apart is* ·75, for *unrelated children* brought up *together* ·25 (or lower). Calculations from twin data by Burt and Burks appeared to prove that some 80 per cent of differences in intelligence should be attributed to hereditary factors, 20 per cent to environment. However, this conclusion is not acceptable, since it is based on populations living in the fairly homogeneous range of environments encountered in Britain or the USA. If we allow for the much wider range of environmental differences between western middle-cass families and African or Indian peasants or Australian aboriginals, the proportions would be more nearly 50–50 or even reversed. In fact it is not very meaningful to try to reach any general figure, since the genes and the environment are not separate

* Correlations between certain EEG indices and measured intelligence have indeed been claimed in recent researches. But even if confirmed, this does not necessarily mean that such indices reveal Intelligence A. To the present writer it seems just as likely that the development of Intelligence B brings about changes in neural connections and therefore affects the EEG.

factors whose contributions can be added; they are mixed up from conception onwards. We need to think in terms of an interacting system rather than of the conventional antithesis between heredity and environment.

Differences between subgroups such as social classes are not the same as differences between isolated groups, since there is considerable mobility from one class to another and much intermarriage across classes. A majority of sociologists appear to ignore the possibility of genetic differences between classes and to attribute Intelligence C, and therefore B, entirely to the circumstances in which the children are reared. But it is known that a high degree of assortative mating occurs, i.e. that husbands tend to choose wives of similar intelligence level to themselves; and Burt and Conway make a convincing case that this must lead to genetic differences between upper-middle and lower-class children.* This does not mean, of course, that environmental advantages and handicaps are not extremely important also in widening and maintaining differences between classes.

Jensen puts forward the novel conception that environment affects development mainly as a 'threshold variable'; it is extremely important in the lower ranges of ability, but above a certain minimum has little further effect; in other words it operates quite like diet in relation to physical growth. In evidence he points to the common tendency for IQ distributions to be positively skewed, suggesting that there are large numbers of children around 70 to 90 who should be scoring more highly. And he has carried out experiments in which middle-class children of below average IQ (presumably *not* environmentally handicapped) do less well at new learning tasks than lower-class children of the same IQ. Two criticisms might be raised: first these learning tasks cannot be taken to measure the lower-class child's 'real' learning potential, and secondly – superior environments surely do have somewhat greater effects than average ones. (Otherwise what are the benefits of higher secondary and university education other than vocational training?) But we can agree with his main implication that conventional intelligence tests probably give better indications of all-round learning ability in middle-class than in lower-class children.

* See Halsey; Burt and Conway; Eckland; and Jensen 1967.

III

Cognitive and Intellectual Growth

We are not entitled to say that hereditary factors produce particular characteristics; nevertheless we do see their effects in the orderly sequence of development in the human infant – the growth of the various organs before and after birth, the emergence of reflexes, sensory and motor capacities, later the changes of puberty. While this process of maturation is generated, as it were, from within, each stage develops from the preceding ones only under appropriate stimulation from the environment, and the stimulation needs to come at the right time. For example the development of vision depends on stimulation of the retina by light: if an ape is brought up in the dark for the first year of life, its retina is permanently impaired. Much the same principles appear to operate in mental development; speech, perception, intelligent thinking grow through a series of stages, though we will have to reconsider later the question of whether, likewise, there are critical periods of optimum sensitivity (Chapter XII).

What we can say is that man's capacities are not determined by his internal structure to the same extent as those of species lower in the evolutionary scale; they are built up in him to a greater extent through stimulation and learning. As Bruner (1964) puts it: 'We move, perceive and think in a fashion that depends upon techniques rather than upon wired-in arrangements in our nervous system.' Elsewhere (1965, 1966) he refers to these techniques as amplification systems – tools and skills that mankind has developed and through which he vastly extends the intricacy and power of his own perceptual and motor responses. Among the most important are language and symbolic thinking or reasoning. Moreover such systems are cumulative, since they can be passed on from one generation to the next, and further improved by the latter. This implies that man has by no means reached the limits of his capacities – either of his own reasoning or of the tools he produces to work for him. Indeed if we could put into practice what we already know about the conditions of upbringing that favour or impede mental growth, we could certainly increase the all-round effectiveness of man's thinking, and go some way to reduce the present differences between the retarded and more advanced groups and subgroups. Bruner believes that we are only at the beginning of establishing a scientifically based education, and J. McV. Hunt goes so far as to claim that by applying Piaget's theories of child development we could raise the intelligence of the average (western) child by an amount equivalent to 30 IQ points. Almost certainly this is an exaggeration, since experimental attempts to accelerate the attainment of the stages that Piaget describes have so far been notably unsuccessful and, as already mentioned, dull children tend to stay dull even with improved schooling.* Moreover, this would involve not merely an educational revolution, but incalculable social and emotional changes among parents.

Admittedly, though, we have been too apt in the past to stress hereditary limitations. Clearly there has been a marked rise in the average intellectual capacity of the British over the past 100 years, and a much more spectacular one in Soviet Russia over the past 50. Whether there has also been a rise at the top end of the scale, i.e. in the production of men of outstanding mental ability, would be almost impossible to prove and seems much more doubtful. But there is ample opportunity for taking in more of the 'slack' at the bottom end.

It is as much due to the work of Piaget† as of any other single psychologist that we no longer think of intelligence as a definite entity or power, an autonomous mental faculty, which simply matures as children grow up. It has to be conceived rather in terms of a cumulative building up of more complex and flexible 'schemata' (Piaget's term) or what Miller, Galanter and Pribram call 'plans', through the impact of the growing organism and the environment on one another. These schemata depend on active exploration and experiment by the former, and on arousal and reinforcement by the latter, and they are formed and organised by use. Piaget has studied the kinds of mental processes characteristic of children of various ages, ranging from the sensory-motor responses or reflexes of the newborn, through the illogical notions and limited reasoning of the preschool and young school child, the more realistic conceptions and flexible thinking of older children (concrete operations), up to the fully rational and scientific kind of problem solving (formal operations) of which the clever adolescent and well-educated adult are capable. Each percept or concept, each motor or

---

* The effects of current programmes for the 'disadvantaged' are discussed in Chapter XI.

† Cf. Piaget; Hunt; Lovell 1961; Flavell.

thinking skill, has a long history and passes through a succession of stages. (Other investigators, working in many different ethnic groups, tend to find much the same sequence of stages, although it is generally agreed that they may be attained at earlier, or at much later, ages than was suggested by Piaget's original, rather rigid, formulation.) For example the baby does not initially perceive a world of objects outside himself which stay the same regardless of the angle or distance from which they are viewed, and regardless of his own wants and feelings. This is not an innate understanding but a complex acquirement, which he builds up during the first year or two of life by viewing, touching, exploring and experimenting with objects and people, and correlating his experiences. Likewise many of the conceptions that we take as self-evident or 'given', such as our notions of space, time and number, or of cause and effect, are remarkably primitive even among western children up to six–eight years, and much later – as we shall see – in less advanced societies. They are acquired and gradually corrected and extended through communications from adults and other children, but chiefly through the lessons provided by practical experience.

Bruner (1966) diverges from Piaget on a number of points, but likewise suggests that children's mental functions and learning progress through qualitatively different stages. He distinguishes three main levels of schemata, or modes of processing information, which he calls the enactive, the iconic and the symbolic. Enactive functioning implies adaptation at the motor level, as when a child acquires the capacity to move around, to reach and grasp, and thereby shows a practical understanding of space though lacking an organised mental conception. We ourselves can learn to ride a bicycle at the enactive level. At the iconic stage he conceives of the world in terms of percepts and images of a concrete kind, but fails to relate these. One aspect of a situation tends to dominate, as in the familiar experiment with two balls of plasticine, where he insists that the one rolled out into a sausage is larger because he cannot take account of length and thickness simultaneously. At the symbolic stage he has developed more general and abstract ideas which can be expressed in words or numbers, such as the notion that the amount stays constant regardless of perceptual changes.

A significant feature of Bruner's scheme is that it helps to describe not only the mental processes of western children and of more backward people, but also the predominant system of education or transmission of 'techniques' to children. It is characteristic of backward societies that children learn more through doing than through words; they imitate older children and adults and thus acquire their skills and concepts of the world in a concrete context. There is very little telling-out-of-context, or explicit teaching, except for a few rituals and legends. This was equally true, of course, of western nations up to the nineteenth century. It is only recently that education in a separate system of schools and colleges has become available to more than a minority, and has been conducted at a predominantly symbolic level.

In Piaget's view also, most of our basic concepts of the world and our thinking skills are acquired more through prolonged and varied practical experience of how things behave, and through discovery, rather than through what we are told at school. Take number for example: children of four or so are readily taught to count by rote, and when they go to school they can be drilled to do the four rules and learn multiplication tables, etc. But they do not fully understand what they are doing or make real progress until they achieve the concepts of class, ordering or seriation, and conservation of quantities, usually around seven–eight. Indeed our schools have realised the value of play with concrete objects, sand-pouring and manipulations of blocks in providing a firm basis for more formal teaching of number.

Similarly in the verbal field, we can reason far more freely and widely with abstract concepts than with concrete images, but there is always the danger that they are too much divorced from reality.* The danger appears to be even more marked in less advanced countries, where education has to be conducted in a second (or third) language. In the western world children progress naturally through Bruner's and Piaget's stages and achieve a fair degree of integration; their abstract ideas and verbal concepts develop out of and fairly easily connect back to practical activities and concrete operations. But for the African, academic education in English or French tends to be more segregated from real life – an activity all on its own. Many pupils and students, being strongly motivated, acquire the language and use it to learn western mathematics, science, etc. But because these do not arise out of their earlier enactive and iconic learning, also because of the poor quality of much of the teaching, their education is far too formal and mechanical. This theme recurs constantly when we come later to look at the schooling and attainments of non-western groups.

A caution must be raised here since we seem to be falling into the trap of equating the mentality of non-western people with that of younger western children. Lévy-Bruhl has been heavily criticised for talking of the 'prelogical' mentality of the African; and other writers such as

---

* It was pointed out in Chapter 1 that differences in the use of abstract words are largely responsible for the controversies over 'intelligence'.

Carothers have claimed that these peoples are incapable of 'abstract' thought, that they function only at a concrete level. That such statements can be misleading is illustrated by McConnell's study of Mexican Indians, and Jahoda's (1956) work with schoolboys in Ghana, using the Kohs Block test. Though the scores of these groups were lower than those of whites, few of them failed to perform at the abstract rather than the concrete level as described by Goldstein and Scheerer.

On the other hand, a convinced exponent of the common developmental principle is H. Werner, whose *Comparative Psychology of Mental Development* is largely concerned with the resemblances of the cognitive processes of primitive peoples to those of immature children. Both are characterised by diffuse, undifferentiated thinking as contrasted with articulated, organised; both show animism, syncretism and magical features; both are concrete rather than abstract. For example, movement and action in space are well developed, but geometric conceptions of space are lacking; and time is a continuum of concrete events rather than an objective framework. Werner provides a wealth of evidence from many parts of the world, admittedly more anecdotal than experimental, and it might well be objected that he generalises too broadly. Nevertheless there are many common features in the stages of mental development of different ethnic groups, and there are 'modal tendencies', as Doob argues,* which can reasonably be abstracted and even measured. This does not mean that differences between more 'primitive' and more civilised mentalities are due to genetic limitations; rather we should look for their origins in the upbringing of the children and the nature of the society. We must not forget also that there are wide individual differences at all ages in all societies. Just as *more* middle-class than lower working-class children in England are good at abstract reasoning, so are *more* western than non-western children.

At the same time one cannot say that there are merely differences of degree, not of kind. In a sense every society is unique, and there are certainly differences between them in modes of perception or conception arising from their different languages, physical circumstances, traditions and values. Even in western society the adult imbecile differs in many ways from the average five-year-old who obtains the same Mental Age on the Binet scale, and the middle class differ (modally) from the working class not only in average IQ or scholastic attainment but in many cognitive and linguistic characteristics, as well as in attitudes. The level of reasoning depends too on the context in which it is

---

* L. W. Doob provides a balanced discussion of the rationale and the pitfalls in generalising about more and less civilised groups.

applied: Africans who appear unable to abstract or deduce in school obviously do so in many of their games, and in their legal systems. Price Williams (1962) stresses the familiarity of the materials that the person is asked to think about. He found that Nigerian children of six to eleven did well in classifying and abstracting the common features of indigenous plants, though they were less successful with animals which played a less important role in their lives. Intelligence, then, is complex, and while useful generalisations can be made about its growth, there is also a need for more studies of particular cognitive developments in particular groups.

IV

Factorial Conceptions of Intelligence

Current notions of intelligence have changed tremendously in yet another respect over the past half-century or so. We realise that mental abilities are much too varied to be adequately described in terms of a monolithic general intelligence or Spearman's g-factor. There are many more specialised types of ability – verbal, numerical, spatial and perceptual, memorising, reasoning, mechanical, imaginative and so on, and the same individual may well be quite high in one, low in another, although on the whole they tend to correlate positively. However there is some divergence of views between British and American factor psychologists regarding the number of these ability factors and their distinctiveness (cf. Vernon, 1965b). Thurstone, Guilford and their followers in the USA tend to break down the mind into a very large number of independent primary abilities or faculties, while admitting that these sometimes overlap, i.e. that there are also more general or 'second-order' factors. This is a legitimate model when dealing with highly selected or homogeneous groups such as university students. But British writers have been more concerned with representative samples of adults or with whole age groups of children, and when these are tested the correlations between quite different tests tend to be so high that it seems more logical to recognise a common underlying component or g, and to regard the more specialised abilities as subsidiary group factors. In other words we can picture the mind as a kind of hierarchy or genealogical tree, where the g-factor is the most prominent component in the sense that it accounts for the greatest proportion of differences in abilities (Fig. 1).

Over and above this, abilities tend to fall into two major types – the verbal-educational ($v : ed$ factor) and the spatial-perceptual-practical ($k : m$ factor). Children, or adults, may differ appreciably in their performance in these two areas, although at the same time most people who are good at verbal tests will also score above average on spatial or mechanical tests, since both types of ability involve g. With more

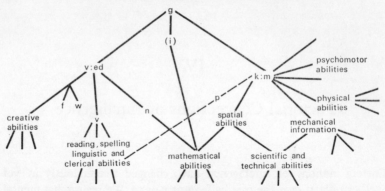

Fig. 1. Diagram of the main general and group factors underlying tests
relevant to educational and vocational achievements.

detailed testing these major ability types can readily be broken down
into more specialised ones such as f (fluency), n number, i (induction),
p (perceptual speed), or further subdivided into numerous minor group
factors indicated in the Figure. However, when considering the whole
spectrum of abilities, these are relatively much less influential. We do
not gain a great deal of additional information about most people by
going to the trouble of measuring them accurately, though they may be
particularly important in some cases (e.g. a person may be highly musical though below average in most other areas). At the bottom of the
hierarchy are the specific (Spearman's s) factors, which underlie high
or low performance on a particular test, but tell us nothing about
ability at anything else.

The role of factor analysis in the study of individual or group differences should not be exaggerated. Primarily it is a formal scheme for
classifying and interpreting test performances, and should not be considered as a means to identifying the basic abilities of human beings.
Also, as we have seen, alternative classifications are possible depending
on the predilections of the factorist and the kind of group, and the tests,
he is investigating. (In other words, we are talking about Intelligence C
rather than Intelligence B). Nevertheless the hierarchical scheme has
considerable advantages in cross-cultural investigations, since it would
be extraordinarily difficult to test a large number of Thurstone's or
Guilford's factors in different groups and to explore the agencies (environmental or other influences) responsible for any group differences.
It is more feasible to study the agencies contributing to the general
ability factor and those particularly relevant to verbal-educational and
to spatial-practical factors, i.e. the factors which are most predictive of

achievement in daily life, at school or at work. We could then proceed, given sufficient resources, to find out more about contributory influences to such main factors as creativity, number, art, music, athletic ability and so on, over and above intelligence or g-factor.

Let us now try to bring together the developmental and the statistical approaches to intelligence. In British researches, the tests showing the greatest dependence on g, or the largest g-loadings, are tests like Progressive Matrices, Shipley Abstraction and Arithmetical Reasoning, which essentially involve high-level symbolic skills – comprehension, grasping relations, problem solving and logical reasoning. Each of these tests usually shows some group factor content in addition, e.g. a small amount of verbal or spatial ability. And the more conventional intelligence tests based on vocabulary, analogies, similarities and other verbal problems involve both high g and high verbal factor. To a lesser extent g enters into any other cognitive performances, depending on how far they entail symbolic processes as contrasted with the more enactive and iconic skills.

Psychologically, Intelligence B is the cumulative total of the schemata or mental plans built up through the individual's interaction with his environment, insofar as his constitutional equipment allows. It includes the fullness and discriminativeness of his perceptions, and the adequacy and range of his practical techniques. Most important, though, are the thinking skills which, as G. A. Ferguson points out, have been distilled from experience in a variety of contexts, and are transferable to a variety of new situations. Harlow found that apes do not merely learn the solutions to particular problems; they learn how to learn to deal more quickly and effectively with further problems. Similarly our capacities for grasping relations between, and manipulating, concepts open up fresh worlds to conquer.

Coming back to the problem of Intelligence B in other cultures: on the one hand we should expect people like the Eskimos or Australian aboriginals to be handicapped in using the symbols, or acquiring the mental skills, which western culture has evolved. On the other hand we should not claim that they are intelligent in a different way just because they are better than us at survival in the snows or in the desert. These are traditional, lower-level skills, built up over generations and possessing little transferability. But they are intelligent if they can cope with new problems that arise within their own realm of experience by means of their own symbols, problems maybe differing in content but similar in complexity to those the western mind can handle. In other words, one can conceive of some common scale based on the adaptability of a cultural group and the complexity of its symbols and reasoning, though it is unlikely that such a scale could be implemented in practice because these qualities have such different manifestations in different cultures. Inevitably, therefore, this book is mainly concerned with a more limited and more ethnocentric aim, namely the extent to which groups differ in their facility at the various abilities comprised under western-type Intelligence B, and why they differ.

APPENDIX A

CATTELL'S FLUID AND CRYSTALLISED INTELLIGENCE

An important alternative formulation of the basic factors underlying cognitive abilities has been proposed by R. B. Cattell.* He considers that the general factor which emerges from the correlations between batteries of varied tests to be an amalgam of two components, which he calls fluid and crystallised intelligence, or Gf and Gc. Gf represents the influence of biological factors on intellectual development (i.e. what we called constitutional equipment), whereas Gc is the result of the skills and concepts which have become established through cultural pressures, education and experience. However this differs from our conception of Intelligence A and B in that he regards both components as measurable, the former by tests such as his Culture-Fair battery, where the testee has to reason with or manipulate abstract shapes, etc., the latter by the more conventional intelligence tests based on comprehension and manipulations of learned materials, especially verbal. Another difference between fluid and crystallised abilities is that measures of Gf tend to show much greater variance or spread, the standard deviation of IQs being 25 or over as contrasted with the figure of 15 typically found for verbal tests. The reason is that cultural pressures produce greater uniformity in the latter; to a much greater extent children acquire each successive set of skills and understandings at the same age. A further important feature of Cattell's hypothesis is that crystallised abilities will be much more affected by personality traits, for example by his Conscientiousness and Excitability factors.

In practice, however, these two aspects of intelligence cooperate and are difficult to separate. Cattell regards them as second order factors which are oblique (i.e. themselves intercorrelated), and which underlie

* R. B. Cattell 1963; Horn and Cattell 1966.

in varying degrees the more specialised factors such as Thurstone's primaries. In his more recent publication he has suggested additional second-order factors or generalised aspects of performance in many tests; these include *Gv* – general visualisation, similar to our own major spatial group factor; *F* – general fluency or quickness and richness of associations; *Gs* – cognitive speed, and possibly *Carefulness*. Two large-scale experiments have been reported, using his Culture-Fair and Thurstone's factor tests among others, together with personality tests. One was based on seventh to eighth grade students, the other on a heterogeneous adult sample, and both largely confirmed the hypothesised grouping of factors.

Now the same kind of distinction has often been made by psychologists in the clinical field. For example, Babcock, Wechsler and Shipley use tests such as vocabulary to indicate the maximum level of conceptualisation which a mental patient has achieved in the past, and a variety of tests of new reasoning (Matrices, Abstraction, Similarities, etc., i.e. 'Don't Hold' tests) to indicate the level of mental efficiency to which the patient has now deteriorated. Cattell's scheme has the advantages of integrating a clear theory of mental development (and decline) with the extremely complex and hitherto somewhat chaotic results of factorial research. His empirical findings could indeed be subsumed under the hierarchical group factor theory if one regards his fluid ability as g with a slight admixture of spatial ability,* and crystallised ability as g with a considerable proportion of $v : ed$ factor. But one would agree that his oblique second-order factors are more psychologically intelligible than g and group factors. The main weakness in his theory is the claim that fluid ability tests are largely immune to cultural influences. The skills required for reasoning with these abstract materials would appear to be built up in just the same way as those involved in verbal reasoning; and the evidence presented later demonstrates at least as great variations attributable to cultural differences. In other words, all the majority of contemporary psychologists have concluded, there is no such thing as a culture-fair test.

* Cattell misstates the present writer's views by saying that these identify fluid ability with $k : m$ (spatial-mechanical) factor.

V

What is Potentiality?

The potential achievement of an individual, or a group, raises difficult problems which cannot be dismissed merely by pointing out the nature of Intelligence A and B. Neither genetic potential (innate mental power) nor constitutional potential are any use to us for predicting likely achievement, since we cannot measure them. Nor is Intelligence B (as measured by C) any longer appropriate if we admit that it is itself a form of achievement and affected by much the same factors that affect educational or vocational achievements. Nevertheless teachers and parents will not be dissuaded from believing that Johnny is not 'working up to capacity', nor psychologists and others from claiming that the underprivileged classes or the peoples of underdeveloped nations could achieve much more under better conditions.

In the first place what is the distinction, if any, between Intelligence B and scholastic or other achievements? Both, admittedly, require adequate genetic endowment and adequate environmental stimulation. Thus many psychologists have largely given up using the term intelligence, on the grounds that it is likely to continue to lead to misunderstandings. Mental testers in the United States often speak rather of 'developed abilities'; and they apply to their students tests of 'verbal and quantitative abilities' which do not attempt to differentiate between skills or ideas which have been taught and those which have matured internally. In the UK also the chief purveyors of mental tests – Moray House and the National Foundation for Educational Research – no longer issue 'intelligence' tests, but tests of 'Verbal Reasoning', or 'Verbal' and 'Non-verbal' tests. Nevertheless a relative distinction seems possible and useful, namely: attainments or achievements refer to the more specialised skills which are taught in schools or elsewhere, and which depend greatly both on the effectiveness of instruction and practice, and on the child's interest in the topic, his motivation and his adjustment to school and teacher. Whereas intelligence, as shown above, refers to the more generalised thinking capacities which can be applied in any kind of new learning; and these are developed as much by home and out-of-school as by school experiences. For example it is likely that boys will develop their Intelligence B better by planning how to rob a farmer's orchard, or by puzzling out how to make model aeroplanes on their own, than by being drilled at school in formal arithmetic and English. There is considerable justification for this view in that educational achievement usually correlates more highly than intelligence scores with favourable home conditions and (especially in underdeveloped countries) with quality of schooling. Also it has been found that identical twins brought up apart tend to differ more from one another in achievement than intelligence.

To this extent, therefore, an intelligence test gives a somewhat better index of potentiality than other measures of achievement to date. But mainly it is useful in predicting educability or trainability because of its greater generality, and because it samples the reasoning capacities developed outside school which the child should be able to apply in school, e.g. to new subjects. This does not mean that the Intelligence B which we observe in a child's behaviour or sample with our tests can be regarded as a cause of, or limiting factor to, attainment.

The so-called Achievement or Accomplishment Quotient was a statistical absurdity, and fortunately it has been generally abandoned. Yet psychologists continue to use discrepancy between intelligence scores and scholastic performance to show 'underachievement'. Many British school psychologists do not think it worth giving much remedial help to the child with low EQ *and* low IQ on the grounds that he is dull and is already doing the best of which he is capable; whereas the one with low EQ and average or superior IQ is more likely to be emotionally maladjusted or to have been badly taught, and therefore should be treated. There is some sense in this policy, though not for the reasons usually given. As has often been pointed out,* there are just about as many children whose EQ exceeds their IQ, i.e. children who are achieving above their intelligence level as those achieving below. This illogicality disappears if we simply admit that any child can differ in his achievements along different lines. Just as he can be better in English than arithmetic or vice versa, so he can be better in general reasoning than school performance or vice versa. Note that it is particularly inappropriate to use non-verbal tests as measures of educational potential, since non-verbal and verbal abilities naturally tend to show quite wide discrepancies. We are likely to get much better predictions of the school achievement of which a child should be capable by applying oral

* See, for example, Vernon 1958; and Crane.

vocabulary and verbal reasoning tests (e.g. Terman-Merrill or WISC Verbal).

In America also we still meet innumerable investigations of 'under-achievement', which explore the family background, attitudes, etc. of children with low achievement but normal or superior IQ (cf. Kornrich). Their results are highly inconsistent since the discrepancy between intelligence and achievement scores is, by its very nature, highly un-reliable. More sensible are straight comparisons between good and poor achievers, without reference to intelligence. But as some critics are beginning to realise, the whole conception of underachievement is pretty shaky. Does it not arise more from unrealistic expectations among teachers and parents than from personal shortcomings in the pupil or student ? Some children do not satisfy their parents because the parents are projecting their own aspirations rather than considering the child's interests; and many do not satisfy their teachers because the school has failed to stimulate them or has taught them badly; or they prefer the peer culture to adult values.

As Burt (1935) pointed out more than 30 years ago, the causation of backwardness or low achievement is multiple – usually a combination of genetic, physiological, social, educational and personality factors. We would hesitate to accept his view that the clinical psychologist can usually diagnose the main causes in the individual case, especially by the use of intelligence or other tests; since the intelligence score needs ex-plaining almost as much as the educational achievement. But we would agree that the psychologist can often make a better informed guess than the teacher or the parent, and suggest useful lines of treatment. From this point of view we might hazard a definition of underachievement and potentiality: an individual is underachieving when a psychologist or other knowledgable person can indicate a likely causal factor or factors *and can produce improvement fairly readily by counteracting these factors*. If the state of health, the already developed abilities, the home attitudes, the motivation, etc. are too unfavourable to be remedied by means at the disposal of the expert or the community, that individual has not got potentiality.

Though such a definition seems vague and unscientific, it also helps to clarify our notions of the potentialities of groups. For example, many would say that Eskimos have considerable potential, not merely because they show resourcefulness in survival and talent at carving (these would be more traditional, enactive skills), but because when given the chance they become adept mechanics. And the correlation between mechanical ability and *g* is generally sufficiently high to make it likely that they could learn in other directions. (Also, as we shall see,* they do perform quite well on a wide range of tests.) They don't however usually do well at school or vocational training, nor adapt to the modern world; they are low achievers. The Canadian Government, with its teachers, administrators, etc. has improved their health and education and is trying many measures aimed at habilitation, though with only limited success. Certainly it should search for, and press, any measures at its disposal; but it is baulked, partly by the geographical difficulties, partly by the social and personality qualities and the traditional values of the people. From this point of view, their potential cannot be rated very high, at least for the time being.

* Cf. Chapter xxvii; also MacArthur 1967.

PART II
Factors Influencing the Mental Development of Children

VI

Nutritional and Health Conditions

It is all too easy to demonstrate that people brought up in poor environments tend to achieve poorly in school and to score below average on intelligence tests, but practically impossible to disentangle the precise effects of any one factor. More often than not there is a syndrome of mutually interacting adverse factors, for example poverty, poor nutrition and health, overcrowded home, lack of intellectual stimulation, inferior language background, lack of parental interest in education, poor schooling, and insecure economic future all cooperating. In addition we have seen that the possibility of genetic differences cannot be neglected. We cannot, as with rats, study the effects of a single factor while holding other relevant conditions constant. Sometimes indeed the opportunity does occur to observe and measure the consequences of some fairly clearcut change, such as rehousing of slum families in a new area, or a change in methods of school teaching. But even here the results are equivocal – are they due to better health and less overcrowding, or to the development of greater self-respect and ambition among the rehoused families? Is there at the same time greater social discord or delinquency because the families have lost their familiar roots? How far does the 'Hawthorne effect' operate, i.e. do the experimental groups tend to show improved attitudes or achievements largely because they know they are being studied and this helps to motivate them, usually to produce the results the investigator wanted? And is any rise in achievement consequent on changes in teaching due more to the personalities and keenness of the teachers concerned than to the methods as such? Thus the classical experimental approach does not often provide the most convincing answers in the social sciences as it normally does in the biological.

Alternatively there is the longitudinal study where a large sample of individuals is picked out and followed up, and tested or interviewed periodically in the course of their natural lives. No arbitrary changes are introduced, but a wealth of data becomes available on the later differences between those who were brought up in different circumstances or underwent different experiences. Though many worthwhile studies have appeared, or are still proceeding, they are apt to be disappointing, partly because of attrition or loss of cases and the costliness of tracing and assessing the surviving members of the sample, and partly because the sheer mass of material seems to create difficulties in disentangling major trends.

To a large extent then we have to make do with cross-sectional surveys (either correlational or analyses of variance), where a complex of interacting factors can be shown to be associated with good or poor achievement. As everyone knows this does not tell us which factors are the crucial causative ones. Nevertheless progress is being made; different investigations, carried out from various viewpoints, or with different samples, tend to complement and reinforce, or to correct one another, and to suggest further hypotheses which can be tested. Moreover there has been tremendous growth in recent years both in the resources put into research, and in the methodology of assessing relevant variables and analysing their inter-relations.

With so much to draw on, the following survey is inevitably highly selective. Its aim is chiefly to highlight the major factors which constantly recur in studies of abilities, and to discuss some of the more recent and pertinent investigations. Chapters VI to IX are concerned with those factors that are thought to operate from the early years of childhood – nutrition and health, sensory-motor stimulation, language and patterns of child-rearing; while Chapters X to XIII will deal with more general studies of social class and ethnic group differences.

At first sight it might seem comparatively straightforward to determine the effects of diet or disease on human mental growth. The topic is of immense importance and is being studied from many different angles in many parts of the world (cf. N. S. Scrimshaw). But at once we run up against the difficulty that nutritional defects are mixed up with economic, cultural and other physiological handicaps.

This is well brought out in the attached chart by Cravioto *et al.*, which shows how technological backwardness and its accompanying features are related to low Weight Gain. Now weight or height of babies or older children are commonly used as indices of physical growth, but they have obvious defects, particularly if we are more interested in mental growth. First, we do not know what are the standards of normal growth under adequate nutritional conditions. It is absurd to compare African or Asian children, for example, with Americans who are racially different in physique, and pampered in feeding and medical care; yet this is often done. More justifiable are comparisons with the relatively well-fed and well-cared for children of upper class families in the same community, though these are still difficult to interpret since such children may also be genetically superior.

Secondly it is usually impossible to identify the true ages of children in backward countries or to follow them up from birth for any considerable period. Thirdly, physical indices beg the question of the relation

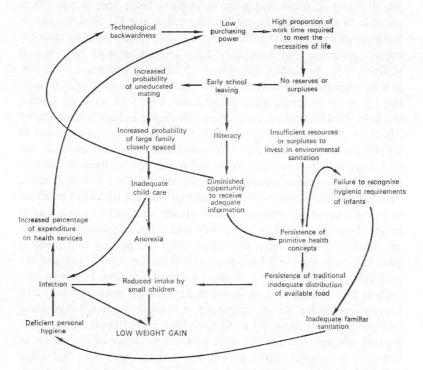

Chart of interrelations among biosocial factors and low weight gain (by J. Cravioto *et al.*).

between physical and mental capacities. It is well known that the correlations between height, weight or brain-size and intelligence among adults or children of a particular age are so small as to be of scarcely any predictive value. And it has been argued (e.g. by D. G. Paterson) that the human brain is so well insulated that mental capacities develop largely regardless of bodily health and physique, except in the case of diseases like meningitis which attack the actual brain membranes. Here also we cannot, as with rats, carry out microscopic examinations of brain cells at different ages among children who have undergone malnutrition or are affected by the common diseases of underdeveloped countries.

Fourthly, mental capacities cannot, like height and weight, be measured on absolute or ratio scales. We cannot say whether a mental test result is high or low except by referring it to the distribution of results in a population of comparable people, and this greatly increases the difficulty of measuring gains in abilities from year to year. It is possible to apply developmental tests such as the Gesell schedules to babies in different ethnic groups,* but as these chiefly measure sensory-motor capacities, they have very little correlation with later mental abilities. The intellectual abilities of children in backward countries, in which we are really interested, can hardly be measured reliably until the age of about seven, when performance tests such as Kohs Blocks, the individual Progressive Matrices, or Birch and Lefford's Intersensory Modality test begin to register. If these or other tests are applied to children with kwashiorkor or other deficiency diseases, certainly the scores are low, but how are we to tell if this results from the disease itself or from other circumstances in the children's background? Similarly within western cultures, children who are backward at school or below average IQ commonly show greater susceptibility to a host of minor diseases, as well as to sensory and other physiological defects (cf. Burt 1935). But again the upbringing, the poverty and possibly genetic factors may well have produced both the poor health and the poor achievement. A few controlled experiments have been reported such as that of Harrell *et al*, in which low-income mothers were given supplementary diet during pregnancy, and their children scored some five points higher mean IQ at three to four years than the children of control mothers. But for the most part our evidence of the effects of nutrition is indirect, derived from experiments with rats and other mammals, from general medical examinations of mothers and infants and from observations of nutritional habits.

Now in most low-income countries there is a fairly abundant staple diet such as maize, rice, banana or breadfruit, which supplies carbohydrates, but which is particularly deficient in proteins. Even when the protein could be made up from other sources, e.g. fish, the people are generally unaware of the connection between diet and health, or they

* Cf. M. Geber. Reference may also be made here to recent press reports on the work of O.S. Heyns at Witwatersrand. It is claimed that his technique of assisting childbirth by decompression of the mother's abdomen results in developmental quotients among the infants (both white and African) averaging more than 20 points higher than those of matched control groups. This may or may not show itself in their intelligence quotients several years later.

may have superstitions and taboos about eating unusual, but more valuable, foods. Then again it is common for the men to get most of the better food that is going, and for the women to do much of the heavy agricultural labour even during pregnancy, so that the nourishment available for the foetus or infant is quite inadequate. Thus malnutrition is an almost universal problem in developing countries, and there seems little hope of solving it for many generations. Naturally too it renders the children less resistant to other infectious diseases (cf. Cravioto's chart).

The position, so far as we know it, may be summarised as follows. Apparently the infant brain is particularly vulnerable to dietary deficiencies during later pregnancy and early feeding, say from three months before to six months after birth. The damage occurring then to the brain cells from lack of protein, proper vitamins and other crucial elements may be irreversible; it cannot be made up even if the older infant or child is relatively well fed. The extent of the deficit is indicated by a research in S. Africa by M. Stoch, who followed up coloured children severely malnourished in the first two years of life for over five years, comparing them with a group of adequately nourished children of similar socioeconomic level. The experimental group scored 15·7 IQ points lower on a S. African version of WISC Full Scale. Both their Verbal and Non-verbal and their subscale score patterns are claimed to resemble those of brain-damaged children.

It is much more difficult, however, to demonstrate the effects of nutritional deficiencies after weaning when the basic structure of nervous tissue has been laid down. Weaning itself is apt to be traumatic in many societies, and the retardation of physical and mental development sometimes observed at this period may be psychological rather than the result of the change from mother's milk to staple foods. At later ages marasmus and kwashiorkor, and the endemic tropical diseases such as malaria, hookworm and bilharzia certainly appear to lower the work-efficiency of adults and the school-efficiency of children. But it is usually the more extreme cases who come to the attention of the doctors, and the evidence that they generally affect mental abilities is inconsistent. S. Galal, for example, found no differences on attainment and intelligence tests among nine to twelve year Egyptian children between those afflicted with or free from bilharzia. We might guess, perhaps, that after the crucial stage around birth, malnutrition and disease may not directly retard intellectual growth, but are more likely to reduce the amount of energy which the growing child, in more favoured communities, puts into learning about the world and concentrating on school learning.

School medical services are seldom available in underdeveloped countries, and a large proportion of children may have to contend with the dietary deficiencies and diseases just mentioned, or with defects of vision, throughout their school days. Travelling distances in hot climates may be long, and most children are expected to undertake heavy chores at home in the mornings and evenings. We simply do not know the effects of these on their learning, but they may well be considerable. Similar problems occur among 'disadvantaged' subgroups in western societies, even if to a lesser degree.

We will not attempt to survey here the effects of brain damage or anoxia and other prenatal or perinatal conditions, since little is known of their relative incidence in different ethnic groups. Though they severely affect psychomotor functions and social adjustment, their influence on cognitive development is highly complex and often indirect. As S. A. Richardson points out, the brain-damaged child may be backward because he cannot explore his physical and social environment normally and play with other children, or because he is either overprotected or rejected at home.

VII

Sensory-Motor and Perceptual Factors

Piaget's observations of infants and his theories of development imply that young children require a rich variety of sensory stimulation and kinaesthetic experience if they are to establish the schemata underlying perception of a world of objects; also that later conceptual development rests on this prior perceptual stage. Similarly Hebb considers that phase sequences are built up through appropriate experience at the appropriate age; and he has supplied experimental support by his work on dogs and rats brought up either in the meagre environment of a cage, or as pets with the free run of a more stimulating and varied environment. The latter animals showed greater learning and problem-solving capacities as adults than the former, i.e. they had developed better Intelligence B. The mere handling of baby rats is found to increase their later responsiveness, according to S. Levine. The studies described by Spitz, Goldfarb and Wayne Dennis appear to show that Hebb's findings apply at the human level. Babies who were reared in institutions with minimal human contacts or sensory stimulation were grossly retarded, or they even regressed in perceptual and motor development. These, however, were extreme conditions and it seems improbable that, even in quite primitive ethnic groups, infants do not normally see plenty of shapes, objects and people on which to try out their maturing skills. They may have no toys, bricks, blocks or pictures, few utensils and no furniture, but nature surely supplies plenty of sticks, stones, water, light and shade, noises and human contacts, through which the basic schemata can be laid down.

There is much stronger evidence that prolonged institutionalisation of children during the preschool period, involving diminished adult attention and linguistic stimulation, poverty of play materials or opportunities for activity, result in retarded intellectual and linguistic growth. This was shown, for example, by the classic studies of the Iowa school. Though these have been severely criticised on methodological grounds,*

* See Q. McNemar.

much of the opposition, according to J. McV. Hunt, probably arose from the vested interests of psychologists in the 1930s in preserving the innateness of intelligence. H. M. Skeels has recently traced two groups of orphans (24 in all) who were originally tested in a highly unstimulating environment around one-and-a-half years of age. One group was transferred to an institution where they received much greater attention and care. Twenty-five years later this group appear to be normal adults who are self-supporting in a wide range of jobs, whereas almost all the control group are still institutionalised or in low-grade jobs. The Iowa psychologists also made spectacular claims for the effects of nursery school attendance on subsequent development, whereas other investigators have obtained more inconsistent and inconclusive results. However it now seems clear that the stimulation provided by such schooling does benefit children who come from the poorest homes, where there is a real lack of interesting experiences and conversation suited to the children's level. In this country, J. Tizard has shown that the traditional segregation of the mentally subnormal in institutions and hospitals tends to retard still further their intellectual development. If they can be found jobs in the community which motivate them, their work capacity and even their IQs improve. The effects are most noticeable among those coming from the most unfavourable homes. Later we will comment on the effectiveness of preschool programmes for underprivileged children.

However such environmental deficiencies which particularly affect children (or older defectives) during Piaget's preoperational stage should surely be termed conceptual rather than perceptual deprivation, and we will supply plenty of further evidence of its importance below. Most psychologists seem convinced that early learnings, before the onset of effective speech, are the most crucial. Bloom (1964), for example, points out that they are more 'over-learned' than anything acquired later, and are all the more lasting because they are not accessible to memory. Actually it is particularly difficult to prove the effects of early stimulation or lack of it on the subsequent intelligence of babies, except in such gross instances as total deafness or cerebral palsy. The present writer is inclined to lay at least as much stress on the circumstances operating over the period when children are actually learning to think as on the first year or two of life. However a very interesting case has been made for certain effects of the physical (ecological) environment on spatial perception and conception, and this presumably operates from as soon as children start using their eyes.

One of the first cross-cultural psychological studies was that of

Rivers in 1901 in the Torres Straits. He found that the natives were less prone than Europeans to the Müller-Lyer illusions, but more susceptible to the Horizontal-Vertical illusion. Subsequent studies, too numerous to mention, have reported ethnic group differences in perceptual phenomena; and in particular Segall, Campbell and Herskovits have extended the work on illusions to many parts of the world. According to these writers the crucial feature in the Müller-Lyer illusion is whether or not children are reared in a man-made or 'carpentered' environment, where they see many rectangular houses, windows, objects and corners, or in a more curving, rural environment. The former learn to interpret obtuse or acute angles as cues to the third dimension and this affects the way urban dwellers perceive the illusion. A rather different feature affects the Horizontal illusion: it is said that groups living on flat plains with wide vistas will be more likely to exaggerate the horizontal than those dwelling among tree-trunks. Several independent investigations tend to confirm these theories. For example Gregor and McPherson found two tribes of Australian aborigines, accustomed to desert living, high on the Horizontal-Vertical illusion, while the tribe which had more contact with whites and their buildings were much more susceptible to the Müller-Lyer. Again Allport and Pettigrew report that unacculturated Zulus (living in round huts) are less liable to the Rotating Trapezoid illusion than urbanised Africans or whites. However the results do not always fit in with expectation. Jahoda (1966), for example, found no difference on the Müller-Lyer between Ghanian tribes which differed in type of dwelling and furnishing, though he confirmed the greater susceptibility of Europeans. And the Horizontal–Vertical results for forest vs. open parkland groups were inconsistent. While the discrepancy might be attributable to differences in the apparatus used for testing, Jahoda suggests that access to education is an important factor in helping to familiarise Africans with western-type 3-dimensional interpretation.*

In a particularly well-designed study, J. W. Berry applied perceptual and other tests to three groups of 120: members of the Temne tribe in Sierra Leone, living in rounded houses, in an environment of bush and trees; Eskimos living in carpentered shacks, but depending for survival on fine perceptual discrimination and localisation in an environment of snow and ice; and Scottish people, who represented a western control group. Each group included males and females ranging in age from 10+ to 40+, and each was further subdivided into more traditional land-dwellers and more acculturated urban dwellers. Though all the

* Cf. also discussion by Biesheuvel 1966.

subjects had been screened for adequate visual acuity, the Eskimos were best in a closure test of discriminating small details, Scots in the middle and Temne the poorest. Four perceptual or non-verbal intelligence tests – Kohs Blocks, Embedded Figures, Coloured Progressive Matrices and Morrisby Shapes, put the Scots and urbanised Eskimos rather uniformly at the top, traditional Temne at the bottom. The Müller-Lyer and Sander illusions tended to go with carpentered environment, but the Horizontal–Vertical illusion failed to yield the expected differences. Other tests indicated the Eskimos as more "active, analytic, independent' in their perceptions, and generally not much behind the Scots, while the Temne were more 'passive, global, dependent'. Berry points out that the groups differ culturally in social organisation and child upbringing, the Eskimos emphasising individual resourcefulness, the Africans conformity; and as the ecological and sociocultural factors interact, one cannot say which is the primary influence. However he rejects an explanation in terms of racial or genetic determination, since the more acculturated Eskimos and Africans differ from the traditional and generally come closer to the whites.

A later study of Nigerian Ibos by Wober (1967b) indicated that they are 'field-dependent' only in visual perception of space, not in proprioceptive or kinaesthetic abilities.* Their scores were low on Embedded Figures and on Witkin's Rod and Frame test; but when they themselves were tilted and had to adjust a rod to the upright position, scores were superior to those of American whites. Wober suggests that proprioceptive and auditory sense modalities are better developed in Africans, the visual sense in western peoples.

Another perceptual characteristic which has been reported from many parts of Africa is a particular difficulty in understanding pictures. Even clever pupils in secondary schools are often puzzled by pictures in geography and science textbooks, and several studies have shown that posters designed to provide information on health, safety precautions and the like, fail to get across, particularly to unacculturated and illiterate Africans.† Partly this is a matter of unfamiliarity with western representational conventions; many cues to meaning which we take for granted arouse different associations. Further, while Africans can handle replicative designs, e.g. on pottery, they are less able to break down analytically and grasp the relations of parts. Ombredane suggests

---

* The concept of 'field-dependence', and Witkin's work, are explained in Chapter 9.

† See Winter; and Hudson 1967. P. A. Schwarz points out that similar findings have been reported from Latin American cultures.

that this may help to explain low scores on tests like Matrices and Embedded Figures. But in particular Africans do not readily interpret two-dimensional cues such as superimposition, perspective and fore-shortening as indicating the third dimension. Biesheuvel (1949) des-cribes the inability of Bantu subjects to connect a drawing of a mech-anical object with the solid object itself. Thus they are consistently handicapped in constructional tasks.

Fig. 2. Picture 2 from W. Hudson's Pictorial Depth Perception Test (National Institute for Personnel Research).

The most extensive work on 3-D perception is that of W. Hudson, who has developed a series of pictures which are differently interpreted according as the viewer takes account, or fails to take account, of depth cues. Fig. 2 shows one of these, in which the 3-D viewer says that the man is aiming at the buck, the 2-D viewer that he is aiming at the elephant. Illiterate mine-workers saw every picture two-dimensionally, and even among graduate teachers one third of the responses were wrong, showing little improvement over those of Standard VI children. Another of Hudson's tests presented two pictures of an elephant from above, one with legs splayed out (as on a 2-D rug), the other correct. Here illiterate Bantus most often preferred the first, saying that the second elephant was dead because it hadn't any legs. School children did better but were a long way behind whites. Hudson's work has been criticised because of the ambiguity of the materials and pictures (e.g. subjects might say the hunter is aiming at the elephant since it is more dangerous than the buck, rather than from lack of 3-D perception). He claims, though, to have tightened this up without any effect on the results. It seems also that performance is considerably influenced by the presence or absence of texture clues.

At least we can admit, from this and other work to be cited later, that there is a deficit in certain perceptual-spatial abilities among a wide range of African subjects. What is the most likely explanation? Might it be merely that Africans have so little experience of pictorial representation, either in their own art forms, or in books, at least until a fairly advanced educational level? This seems to be contradicted by the writer's finding, below, that land Eskimos, who equally lack books, do well on the Hudson pictures, and show considerable pictorial and mechanical aptitudes. Later we will follow up Berry's suggestion that social training and family relationships may be involved. But perhaps the major factor is the relative lack, in the upbringing of most Africans, of visual-kinaesthetic experience from infancy and throughout childhood. The infant is normally carried on its mother's back, where it has little opportunity to grasp and manipulate; (one might add that this is a rounded visual environment). The parents do not play much with their children nor encourage them to achieve a progression of psycho-motor skills, whereas western mothers, even those of poor cultural and economic level, tend to set goals and to provide a good deal of feedback,* which reinforces their efforts to master their world. African children sit a great deal of the time doing nothing, and, according to E. T. Abiola, adults are insensitive to their natural interest and curiosity, and frustrate their attempts to explore, or to play with plants, water and so forth. In addition there is a far greater lack than in western homes of manipulative objects – cutlery, doorknobs, scissors, buttons, as well as toys. So that although the children engage in imitative play – cooking, brushing, digging, etc. – they have less opportunity for developing fine psychomotor skills, for coordinating these with vision and therefore, one might suppose, for interpreting visual perceptions three-dimensionally.

Now though these difficulties of manual learning and visual interpretation are so widely observed in Africa, one important experiment suggests that they are less deeply engrained than would be expected if perceptual experience in early childhood were all-important. McFie (1961b) applied six of the WISC tests, including Kohs Blocks, together with a Memory for Designs and Weigl Sorting test, to boys in a technical training school, and retested them two years later. The largest increases in scores occurred on Kohs Blocks and Memory for Designs, and these were due, in McFie's view, to the experience they had had in studying

* Experiments on cats by Held and Hein (1963) showed the need for kinaesthetic feedback in addition to visual experience in the development of the capacity to make spatial responses, e.g. to the 'visual cliff' test.

physical objects, in accurate spatial orientation and working at speed. If this were confirmed and extended it would indicate that the deficit arises less from sensory-motor experience in infancy than from meagre experience of, and opportunity for, constructional tasks in later childhood. Thus McFie and others have strongly stressed the need for more practical activities in the primary and secondary school curricula, less emphasis on purely verbal learning.

VIII

Language

The well known study of Viki, the chimpanzee, by the Hayes indicated that she was fully the equal, or in advance of, the human child at Bruner's enactive level. The crucial factor which inhibited her further cognitive development was her lack of speech, that is a genetic difference between the ape and human species in the capacity to use and organise words as signs and symbols of experience. Psychologists nowadays generally realise that speech and the use of language cannot be explained in terms of ordinary learning theories, though at the same time they are obviously culturally conditioned. The child's genetic endowment makes it possible for him to acquire speech more or less readily, but the verbal concepts and ways of inter-relating them are laid down by his cultural group just as are the correct noises. Moreover, while language gives him extraordinary flexibility in the formulation of new utterances for describing and analysing his world, at the same time it restricts his thoughts very largely to those conceptualisations recognised by his particular group.

The relations of language and thought are too complex and controversial to be brought out here. Clearly there are many important cognitive schemata which are not primarily linguistic, nor based on other symbols such as numbers. Even highly intelligent adults carry out much of their thinking enactively or iconically, in terms of images, feelings, action tendencies, etc. Indeed Piaget warns against confusing verbalism with conceptual development and considers thinking to derive basically from prelinguistic processes. But although he insists that concepts such as conservation and causality arise out of practical experience and internal maturation, one suspects that they depend at least as much on children learning to interpret words like 'bigger', 'same', 'alive' and so on correctly. Thus Bruner and his colleagues lay more stress on children's internalisation of 'techniques' such as language from their culture, if they are to progress to symbolic thinking.

Some important evidence on this point is provided by studies of deaf

children. H. G. Furth cites the work of Oléron who found that the deaf
are not handicapped in comparison with normals at such tests as
Progressive Matrices, or at Piaget's conservation tasks. Perhaps Furth
does not recognise the extent to which most deaf persons can, through
various channels, build up verbal concepts which are functionally
equivalent to those of normals. But admittedly their handicaps must
result in some reduction of linguistic stimulation, feedback and reinforcement. Hence much of their reasoning is presumably independent
of the verbal 'technique'.

M. M. Lewis provides an admirable survey of the development of
speech, and its cognitive, social and moral functions. He shows how the
initial instinctive vocalisations become shaped by reinforcement from
adults or older children, and how their meanings progressively come
to approximate to adult usage. During the first two years speech is used
mainly as a means of emotional expression, of making social contacts
and influencing people; but during the third year (given normal
development) it is playing an increasingly important part in perceptual
development, as the child comes to realise that each thing or action has
a permanent name. This enables him to sort out and classify the world,
and through his innumerable 'What' and 'Why' questions to test the
correctness of what he is absorbing. It facilitates his recall of the past
and his anticipations of the future. The role of adult and peer group
communications in expanding the child's universe, in telling him what
things are and what to do about them, is obvious. In addition, attention
has been drawn by the work of Russian psychologists such as Vigotsky
and Luria to the importance of inner speech in self-direction and the
planning of actions at quite an early age. By verbalising the situation,
the child can greatly abbreviate lengthy trial and error learning and
thus cope more effectively with life's problems. Again when, for example,
he says 'No' to himself he is representing anticipated adult disapproval,
and in this way is beginning to internalise the norms of his culture.
Another particularly significant function is that the child learns about
himself through what others say to him as well as from their behaviour
to him, and his self-concept, e.g. that he is clever or stupid, greatly
influences his motivation to learn.

Now the main point of this brief outline is to bring out how totally
dependent children's thinking must be on the speech models and communications they receive – chiefly from the parents, but also from older
children and contemporaries, from teachers, from television or cinema
where available, and later from comics, books and newspapers.
Inadequate linguistic stimulation by illiterate parents is a theme which

continually recurs in discussions of social class differences in ability and achievement. Moreover, probably to a greater extent than the other factors so far considered, it acts continuously on children's mental growth from about six months to adulthood.

In underdeveloped societies, linguistic handicaps are well-nigh universal. Few such groups possess a comprehensive and uniform language. Instead we find a wide range of dialects in neighbouring tribes; and frequently the lingua franca or even the mother tongue is a debased and simplified pidgin or Creole. None of these provide adequate media for advanced concepts or abstract thought. Thus the main medium of instruction virtually has to be one of the western languages, usually English, French or Spanish, and unless the child can acquire complete facility in this second language, he is inevitably retarded in reasoning as well as in attainment. Often he can learn to speak it and even to write it fairly accurately, but does not naturally think in it; instead he tends to revert to the less efficient but more deeply rooted mother tongue.

As might be expected, linguistic handicap is more closely associated with scores on educational attainment and verbal intelligence tests than with non-verbal tests, i.e. with $v:ed$ rather than with g and $k:m$ factors. But the latter tend to be affected too, if only because the solution of difficult problems often involves logical analysis in terms of words or numbers, whatever the nature of the material. J. D. Nisbet makes a plausible case for attributing the negative correlation of around $-\cdot30$ between family size and verbal intelligence, commonly found in western societies, to the sheer reduction of adult-child communications in larger families. However in a study of ten thousand Army recruits, Vernon (1951) found as high a correlation for number of sibs with his g factor as with more verbally-loaded tests.

B. S. Bloom reports an interesting Ph.D. study by Wolf in which ratings on 13 home variables were compared with IQs of the children on the Henmon-Nelson test. The following variables were found to give a multiple correlation of $\cdot76$ with child intelligence, as against $\cdot40$ for parental socioeconomic status with intelligence.

Parents' intellectual expectations of child
Intellectual aspirations for child
Information about child's intellectual development
Rewards for intellectual development
Emphasis on the use of language
Opportunities for enlarging vocabulary

Emphasis on correct usage
Quality of language models available
Opportunities for learning in the home
Opportunities for learning outside the home
Availability of learning supplies
Availability of books and periodicals
Assistance in facilitating learning

Note the considerable stress on linguistic factors, though these are mixed up with other kinds of intellectual stimulation and with parental attitudes. In a similar study by Dave of general educational achievement, much the same factors emerged, together with parental interest in the school and the value they placed on education.

A major contribution to the understanding both of social class and of ability differences has been made by B. Bernstein's (1961) studies of language. While admitting the difficulty of singling out the most significant factor in a complex syndrome, he argues that the predominant language codes of the middle- and lower-working classes underly their whole systems of relations to objects and people, and the patterns of learning which their children bring with them when they start school.

In outline, he distinguishes the 'formal' or 'elaborate' language code from the 'public' or 'restricted' code. The former emphasises precise description of experiences and feelings, allows for subtle discriminations by appropriate adjectives and adverbs, and makes possible the analysis of relationships and sustained concentration on significant themes. In contrast, public language is much simpler, disconnected, 'bitty'; thoughts are strung together ungrammatically and much of the meaning is carried by gestures, pitch and stress or by uninformative but emotionally reinforcing phrases ('You see, Just fancy, Wouldn't it'). Its main function is still similar to that of infant speech, namely to express feeling and enhance social solidarity with the listener; it emphasises the present rather than the past or the future. It is inefficient for tracing causal relations, and incapable of providing a medium for Piaget's formal operational type of thinking. Hence, although lower working-class pupils can accomplish a fair amount of mechanical learning, they are much more handicapped in attempting academic secondary school work. The middle-class child is familiar with both codes, and indeed uses 'public' language quite largely in interpersonal contacts. But the working class is relatively incapable of 'formal' speech. Again the middle-class child becomes accustomed to attending to long speech sequences, whereas the lower working-class child, in a noisy, incoherent environment, if anything learns *not* to attend (cf. M. Deutsch, 1963).

Closely bound up with verbalisation of experience, feeling and intention in middle-class families is the tendency to orient the child, from the earliest years of conversation, to future goals. His life is planned and he lives in a stable framework of rewards and punishments; his behaviour is commented on so that he gets to know that he is a responsible, self-regulating, individual. The working class child lives much more in the present; rewards and punishments tend to be inconsistent and arbitrary, and he has no clear status or planned future. For example at mealtimes the middle-class family discusses a child's experiences at school or play and helps him to sort them out and organise them rationally, whereas working class conversation tends to consist more of abuse for misdemeanours or assigning chores (cf. Deutsch, 1965). Middle-class parents encourage their children to ask questions, and even if they cannot always answer them, they usually convey the view that it is possible to find out, e.g. through books, that the world is rational and can be mastered, whereas working-class parents often do not know the answers or cannot be bothered, thus prolonging the period of irrational beliefs that Piaget has described. Moreover the working-class child does not so readily turn to adults as sources of information.

The effects of such differences on children's reactions to education are particularly serious, since schooling is conducted almost wholly in the formal code, largely by teachers who – if not middle-class initially – have absorbed middle-class speech and values. Hence for the middle-class child, school is a continuation of home training and he settles down easily, whereas for the lower-working class it is a completely new world. The teacher doesn't understand him nor he the teacher. He is bewildered and his self-respect is damaged by the rejection of his natural speech. Particularly in large classes there is little opportunity for the personal approach, through the public code, to which he is accustomed.

Now any theory formulated in terms of contrasted types tends to exaggerate, to give the impression that there is an unbridgeable gulf rather than a continuum. If Bernstein's analysis was taken too literally, social mobility would hardly be possible; whereas the fact is that the greatest number of grammar school pupils are drawn from the working classes (not so often, of course, from the lower working class), and that many of them themselves become teachers. However as a description of the extremes it is illuminating, and much of it has received experimental confirmation from recording and analysing the speech of boys in different socioeconomic groups. Bernstein has shown too that working-class boys are much less handicapped on non-verbal tests such as Matrices than on verbal ones. This is a common finding, and Jahoda's results (1964) are particularly striking. He selected groups of middle-class and unskilled working class boys aged 10 and 16 and matched them on Matrices scores. The vocabulary of the middle-class group was clearly superior at ten years, and the discrepancy increased still further during adolescence. More recently (1966) Bernstein has investigated patterns of mother-child interactions at five to eight years in middle- and working-class families. There was a greater amount of verbal communication and answering children's questions in the former, and the mothers were more apt to regard play and toys as means whereby children find out about things. Such characteristics not only differentiated the classes but also correlated positively with intelligence tests *within* social classes.

The linguistic differences observed within British culture have close parallels among the more and less advanced ethnic groups. Thus Bruner (1966) reports a series of studies of Wolof children in Senegal, of Mexicans and Alaskan Eskimos, using categorisation tests, some of Piaget's or other conservation tasks, and tests designed to reveal strategies of thinking and the role of language. Although mostly tested in their own tongue they were greatly handicapped in symbolic thinking, especially those who had not attended school. Doubtless the difficulty is enhanced when the formal language has to be learnt in middle childhood, without any reinforcement from the home.

A final point to consider is whether the categories of thought implicit in the mother tongue of such people do not adversely affect their capacity to acquire new concepts and skills, much as the western working-class child's public code unfits him for formal learning. This is the well-known hypothesis of Whorf – that the language of a society not only reflects but determines its ideas. Or as Sapir puts it: 'We see and hear and otherwise experience very largely as we do because the language habits of our community predispose certain choices of interpretation.' Now obviously this is true in so far as each society differs in the sort of things it notices and has names for. For example some African languages have no word for snow, whereas Eskimos are said to have 16 words for different varieties of snow, and are correspondingly more discriminative in a snowbound environment. In Berry's research, referred to above, Eskimos were found to have more geometrical-spatial and 'localiser' words in their vocabulary than the Temne. Thus each people evolves a language which is adequate for handling its own range of problems. But it seems more doubtful whether conceptual categories or types of thinking are so specifically culture-bound, and experimental tests of the Whorfean hypothesis have provided only rather weak confirmation. We can recognise that some languages are more 'public' and suited to social and concrete purposes, others more 'formal' and suited to abstract thinking, but so far there is not much evidence of other qualitative differences.

IX

Child-Rearing Practices and Parental Attitudes

Particular importance has been attached by Freudian-oriented psychologists and anthropologists to the infant's feelings of emotional security, the warmth of mother-child relationships, to the earliness or abruptness of weaning, severity of toilet-training, and to such practices as binding, in children's psychological development. While Whiting and Child have had some success in relating rearing practices to the beliefs and values of different ethnic groups, any generalisations as to their effects on personality or intellectual development are dubious. As Whiting points out elsewhere (1961), a far greater variety of conditions may be found in non-western groups than in our own culture, and it is difficult for the psychologist from outside to tell what are the most significant parameters in child-rearing.

Even within western culture, follow-up studies seldom give any confirmation for apparently plausible hypotheses regarding the long-term effects of treatment of infants.* Some years ago, much was heard of the dangers of maternal deprivation, resulting for example from hospitalisation of either child or mother during the early months of life; and J. Bowlby suggested that intellectual impairment, as well as permanent emotional damage might ensue. However in 1956 he published a careful follow-up, after five to ten years, of children who had experienced various amounts of separation, and this gave little evidence of any persisting effects. It is generally agreed (cf. L. J. Yarrow) that hospitalisation without provision of an adequate mother substitute may lead to a temporary trauma, often followed by rejection of the mother and difficulties of readjustment. H. R. Schaffer gave the Cattell Pre-school Scale to a group of infants who were hospitalised for a considerable period around the age of 12 weeks and found Developmental Quotients averaging 13 points lower than those of a control group shortly after admission and just before discharge. Note though that there was no cumulative deterioration. After 10–18 days at home and

* Cf. H. Orlansky; and W. H. Sewell.

again after three months they had completely caught up with the controls. Schaffer concludes that the main effect of such deprivation is one of apathy, and that cognitive development is actually proceeding throughout the period of relative inactivity and emotional shock.

One study of the apparent effects of sudden weaning is often quoted, that of Geber and Dean in Uganda, and elsewhere in Africa. They applied the Gesell Developmental Schedule to African babies and found them somewhat more advanced in liveliness, motor control, etc. than the American norms during the first years of life. But soon after there seemed to be a regression or period of stagnation, and this they attributed to the often abrupt cessation of breast feeding around 12–15 months. The change to a less nutritive diet may be one factor but more importance was attached to the change in the mother's attitude from warm affection to complete rejection; the infant might even be sent away to live with children in another family. However there are some doubts about these data, and both Falmagne and Biesheuvel (1966) find no general superiority in Bantu babies to European ones on the Gesell tests; they do better in some, worse in others. A further study of Zulu children abruptly weaned at about 19 months was conducted by Albino and Thompson, and only a rather temporary disturbance was found in most cases. They reacted by negativism to the mother, and aggressive or attention-seeking behaviour, but over a longer period showed improved independence and social adjustment. The picture seems quite similar to that of western infants after hospitalisation.

Probably it is best to confess our ignorance and our inability to conduct watertight investigations of the long-term effects on cognitive development of treatment in the first year or so of life. There can be little doubt that severe and prolonged deprivation of human contacts has catastrophic effects, and that it is largely as a result of interaction with people that the infant learns to perceive and cope with his world, as well as to talk and later to think. But he seems to be remarkably plastic and resilient to variations, within wide limits, in emotional, as in physical, conditions, especially during Piaget's sensory-motor stage. It is at rather later stages that differences in the attitudes, values and socialisation practices of parents become more clearly influential.

Bernstein's analysis of speech differences between social classes brings out two other major contrasts in character development. First it shows that the working-class child is relatively uninhibited in the direct expression of aggression and other feelings; he reacts overtly to frustration and hits out, not merely because he has not been taught to repress instinctive tendencies, but because he imitates the way adults react to him when he annoys them. His parents are much more likely to use corporal punishment and physical coercion. In contrast the middle-class child's verbalisation is bound up with the process of Superego formation, whereby he internalises the moral values and prohibitions of his culture, and is controlled in his conduct by his own guilt feelings. His parents tend to discipline more by psychological methods, by talking out misdemeanours, arousing guilt and anxiety by pointing out consequences, or at most by withdrawing privileges. Thus, according to Miller and Swanson, the middle-class child turns aggression in on himself and reacts to conflict situations by repression, whereas working-class boys resort to denial and displacement and are more apt to blame the environment than themselves. Miller and Swanson refer to the 'motoric' and 'conceptual' styles, which have obvious links with Bernstein's 'public' and 'formal' codes and with Bruner's 'enactive' and 'symbolic' processes.

Secondly the middle-class culture emphasises delayed gratification – the Reality principle as against the Pleasure principle. The whole of western economy is based on planning for the future, and this attitude, together with the notion that education is necessary for later success, is implanted in the middle class from early years. Quite apart from psychoanalytic explanations, it is obvious that life for the lower-class family is less purposive, since future economic circumstances, housing, etc. are largely outside their control. True there has been an extraordinary upsurge in valuation of education at all socioeconomic levels of western society over recent decades, but we still find greater encouragement of intellectual progress and interest in schooling as we ascend the socioeconomic scale.

Now while there is certainly some truth in these generalisations, they may also be dangerously oversimplified. Patterns of family upbringing, socialisation and character training, are extremely varied within any one western nation, and there is little scientific evidence of their effects on the development of abilities. There are fairly consistent differences between the social classes in the handling of infants even in the first year of life. For example the data collected by the Newsoms from a representative sample of mothers in Nottingham showed more planned consistency and controlled permissiveness in middle-class families. The classic study by Sears, Maccoby and Levin, however, brought out the complexity of rearing practices even in a rather homogeneous American surburban sample. It did demonstrate some relation between the development of a conscience in five-year-olds and psychological as contrasted with physical methods of control, but emphasised that cause-effect relations are seldom straightforward. Miller and Swanson's investigations were more penetrating, but they relied almost wholly on projective materials for eliciting the moral attitudes of boys and their types of reaction to frustration; and we have good reason to doubt whether projective responses bear much relation to real-life behaviour (cf. Vernon, 1964). Nevertheless several other more objective, yet relevant enquiries may be cited.

Schaefer and Bayley assessed the behaviour of mothers towards their children on a large number of variables, and showed that these could be classified under two major dimensions: Love vs. Hostility and Autonomy vs. Strict control. Follow-up observations of the children revealed considerable correlations with their social and emotional characteristics, even into adolescence, and particularly among boys. Though the results of ability tests are not quoted, it was clear that the children's behaviour in taking tests – the amount of interest, effort, cooperativeness, shyness, etc. were related to maternal attitudes.

An earlier study by Baldwin *et al.* did provide some evidence that the intelligence of young children develops better in a 'democratic' home atmosphere than when the parents are either too autocratic or rejecting, or too indulgent and over-protective. Further work at the Fels Institute by Sontag *et al.* confirms that children's IQs are likely to rise when mothers encourage independence at an early age and use democratic methods of disciplining. Chance, on the other hand, claims that first-grade children whose mothers favour independence training make poorer progress at school in reading and arithmetic. But she was concerned with differences between achievement and intelligence test scores and, as noted earlier, this Achievement Quotient approach generally yields inconsistent results.

Especially pertinent is Kent and Davis's study of 118 eight-year-old children, which showed that the type of disciplining practiced by the mother is associated with test performance, independently of social class. Children in 'demanding' homes, where rewards are conditional on achievements, scored highest all round, and especially on the verbal side, as shown in Table 1.

Children of 'over-anxious' and protective mothers did better on verbal Binet than non-verbal WISC, whereas those from 'normal' homes, where discipline was tolerant but firm, were equal on these tests. Children of 'unconcerned' parents showed the opposite pattern, and scored particularly badly in reading. The numbers are small, of course, and we do not know the intelligence level of the parents. Thus it might be that more intelligent parents are more often demanding, less often unconcerned.

TABLE I. *Intelligence quotients of children from different types of home* (*Kent and Davis*)

Home	Normal	Demanding	Over-anxious	Unconcerned
No. of children	41	38	30	9
Mean Binet IQ	109·9	124·2	107·3	97·0
WISC Performance IQ	110·4	113·4	100·7	103·0

E. Bing reports a very detailed study of mothers' attitudes and statements about upbringing in relation to the abilities of 60 5th-grade boys and girls. These were chosen to be relatively high *either* on verbal ability, *or* on spatial or number ability, as measured by the Thurstone Primary Mental Ability tests. She claims that most of her hypotheses were confirmed – that a strong degree of mother-child interaction favours verbal ability; that spatial ability is promoted more by interaction with the physical than the interpersonal environment; while number ability depends on independence training and encouraging concentration to carry out tasks on one's own. In fact rather few of the obtained differences appear to support these generalisations, and scarcely ever are they consistent in the two sexes. (Once again, though, long-term trends seemed to be more clearcut in boys than in girls.) No doubt the small numbers of cases and the rather poor validity of the PMA tests for measuring the desired abilities are partly responsible.

Much more substantial are the investigations of Witkin and his associates, and these will be considered in some detail since they have important implications for the present writer's researches.

Witkin starts out from certain perceptual tests such as the Rod and Frame and the Gottschaldt Embedded Figures tests which are claimed to measure the ability to see the world objectively, analytically or 'independently', and to differentiate figures from the surrounding 'field'. This is much the same as Werner's distinction between articulate and global modes of perception (cf. Chapter III). Performance at these tests of 'field independence' correlates more highly with Kohs Blocks and other tests of spatial ability and flexibility of closure than with verbal tests, and the field independent person shows characteristic responses in a wide variety of tests including Rorschach, TAT, Draw-a-Man, and in interests and attitudes. Indeed independence of perception is linked with independence of personality and style of life generally, and its origins can be traced in the child's home upbringing, though genetic influences may also be involved. The independent person is more active, resourceful, self-directing, less affected by social norms, more realistic in self-appraisal, and he displays greater clarity in his concepts, e.g. about time, space, occupations, etc. (Incidentally, one of the few kinds of tests Witkin has not explored is the Piaget-type task of operational thinking.) The major underlying influence is the extent to which the mother encourages the child to develop an identity of his own, and to master the world, or how far she thinks more of her own convenience and of conformity to social norms. This in turn depends on her own confidence and stability, or on whether she communicates fear and distrust of the world. Discipline in the independent home is permissive rather than authoritarian; it sets definite, consistent standards and is neither over-protective and indulgent, nor coercive and arbitrary. Comparatively little is said about the father, but it appears that the presence of a strong father-figure with whom the son can identify is important, also that father and son should share in masculine-type activities; whereas maternal over-dominance and an ineffectual father foster dependence. (One might note that the latter situation is more likely to occur in modern society, where the mother and female school teachers undertake most of the child-rearing, than in the days when fathers mostly worked near the home, and brought up their sons to follow in their footsteps).*

Now the evidence for these ramifications of field-independence which Witkin and his collegues have published is very extensive and, for the most part, convincing. Independently, J. A. Seder has confirmed many of his findings with ten-year-old American boys and girls. Again Berry's cross-cultural study of Eskimos and the Temne tribe (Chapter VII) fits in very neatly with Witkin's main theories. Temne children are reared for conformity and are harshly disciplined. Eskimos are reared for self-reliance and are always kindly treated by their parents. Berry also applied a test of acquiesence, based on Asch's group-norms experiments, and this confirmed that the former are much more dependent on group opinion than the latter. Correspondingly, as we have seen they score much lower on spatial-perceptual tests, though closely comparable in amount of schooling. Moreover Berry found that Temne subjects who stated that their mothers had been 'very strict' did particularly badly on the Kohs Blocks test (though those whose mothers were 'not so strict' did not perform any better than those with 'fairly strict' mothers). The same result is reported by J. L. Dawson, who also worked in Sierra Leone. On the other hand Berry was unable to find any connection

* Cf. E. S. Ostrovsky.

between father-dominance or father-identification and good performance on spatial tests.

Clearly Witkin's theories and results are of considerable help in interpreting certain differences both within and between cultures. The main trouble is that he seems to prove too much: there are so many cross-currents and so many possible underlying factors that it is hard to tell whether the measured ability differences should be attributed to general intelligence, to social-class attitudes, to sex, to temperament and personality or to neurological characteristics, rather than primarily to mother-child relationships. The following Appendix tries to sort out some of these strands.

APPENDIX B

UNDERLYING PARAMETERS IN WITKIN'S FINDINGS

Table 2 summarises the main features of Witkin's 'syndrome' and suggests, in the last column, the relevant parameters that may be involved. In the first place, some clarification is needed as to what is being measured by perceptual field-independence tests. What is the factorial composition of the ability that Witkin is talking about? Embedded Figures and the Kohs Block test are good measures of the k factor of British psychologists (or rather of $g + k$); and this is much the same as Thurstone's original S (spatial) factor or Guilford's Vz (visualisation). I. McF. Smith's thorough survey, *Spatial Ability*, defines it as the capacity to hold in mind the structure and properties of a figure grasped as a whole. But we do not know whether Witkin's Rod and Frame test covers a rather different, though related. aspect of spatial ability which might give different correlations with other tests or with background factors.

Next there is the problem of sex differences. Witkin finds females, on average, more field-dependent than males, but does not make clear whether the same dynamic factors are supposed to operate in both sexes. Usually the correlations among females are lower and more inconsistent. At the same time his description of independent and dependent personalities (in western cultures) are strongly reminiscent of sex differences. Now it is well-known that girls and women score lower on k-tests, and are less apt at mathematics, scientific and technical subjects, than boys or men, while superior in most verbal abilities. Moreover Smith finds some correlation between k vs. v tests and the Terman-Miles masculinity-femininity scale; and this scale yielded the highest masculine scores

TABLE 2. *Main findings of Witkin* et al. *Studies of Field Independence*

Datum	Characteristics of Field Independent Persons	Resemblance to Other Parameters
Cognitive Tests	Rod and Frame, Embedded Figures, Kohs Blocks, WISC Performance vs. Verbal	Flexibility of Closure and Spatial Ability or k factor
Achievements	Mathematics, Technical, Scientific vs. Linguistic	Spatial Ability Male vs. Female
Personality	Self-sufficient, active coping vs. passive, conforming	Masculine vs. Feminine
Posture	Active-assertive vs. slouching	Mesomorph vs. Endomorph
Concept Development	Mature, realistic appraisal of Self and Others; sophisticated vs. primitive human drawings	⎫
Interests	Sophisticated, self-chosen interests	⎬ General Intelligence ⎭
Clinical	Intellectualisation vs. denial or repression	Introvert vs. Extravert Obsessional (anal) vs. Hysterical (oral)
Mother Interviews	Permissive, encouraging independence vs. over-protective, conformist	⎫ Democratic vs. Authoritarian: Middle vs. Lower Working Class ⎭
Disciplining	Reasoning, deprivation vs. threats, physical, inconsistent. Internalised controls.	
	Father participation and identification vs. maternal dominance	Spatial vs. Verbal ability

among engineers and architects, the most feminine scores (for males) among writers, ministers and artists. Does this suggest then that a genetic or a culturally-induced masculinity-femininity dimension is a crucial component of field independence-dependence?

Another possible constituional determinant of field independence or k is the somatotype. Several bits of evidence indicate that mesomorphs are higher in spatial than verbal abilities, and are apt to show active, aggressive, often delinquent, traits.* Witkin does not comment on body types,† but does say that independent boys maintain better muscular postures.

* Cf. Glueck; and Davidson *et al.*

† J. L. Dawson found higher Kohs Block scores in more muscular than more linear African males.

Alternately one can make a case for cortical representation of spatial abilities. McFie (1961a) claims that there is strong evidence of the effects of right-sided cerebral lesions on non-verbal, spatial and arithmetical test performance, of left-sided lesions on verbal functions (regardless of handedness). The side of the lesion can be determined in 75 per cent of cases by the Wechsler Verbal vs. Performance score pattern.

Next consider Witkin's view that field-independent children possess greater objectivity and maturity of concepts and interests. Surely these are characteristics of the generally intelligent child, and Terman's studies of very high IQ children would tend to link these qualities more closely with verbal intelligence. A serious weakness of Witkin's findings is that many of them could have derived from the g rather than the k component of his tests.

Socioeconomic class differences are obviously involved also, since the pattern of child-rearing and disciplining said to favour field independence is very similar to that attributed, above, to middle-class families. But here there is a conflict in so far as higher social class is known to be associated with better performance on verbal than spatial tests. Thus we might have expected the middle-class child to be less field independent than the working class, except in so far as he has higher g. Again, while the middle-class home does more to encourage psychological autonomy, it also provides more physical protection; the working-class child has more independence in the sense of having to look after himself at an earlier age.

Finally, there is the question of personality factors. Witkin finds that field-independent neurotics are more liable to obsessional or dysthymic disorders, dependents to hysterical disorders, and according to Eysenck this would mean that they are introverts and extraverts, respectively. In confirmation Smith finds small but consistent correlations between k and introversion, while Cattell uses verbal fluency – an aspect of the $v:ed$ factor – as a measure of 'surgency'. In addition there are links with authoritarian vs. democratic personalities, since Witkin's account of the parental handling of dependent boys in many ways resembles Adorno's, and Allport and Kramer's, descriptions of upbringing associated with authoritarian prejudice. Eysenck indeed claims that the 'tough-minded' are more extraverted than the 'tender-minded', but the correlation is certainly not high. Here again, then, we find that numerous overlapping dimensions may be involved.

In conclusion, a great deal more research is needed to map out a clearer taxonomy of field independence. Probably the effects of social class, general intelligence and sex should be held constant, and thereafter it would be profitable to explore what aspects of personality and of family upbringing are associated with what particular group-factors of spatial ability.

X

Studies of Intelligence, Achievement and Environment in Britain

Our object here is to review a few investigations carried out in the UK which are: (a) fairly recent; (b) large-scale; (c) very thoroughly conducted, and which (d) attempt to bring out the influence of several contributory factors, not merely to report overall correlations between parental job level, or family size, etc. and abilities. A valuable study was made by E. Fraser of a representative sample of 408 12-year-olds in Aberdeen secondary schools, where a large amount of home data was collected by interview and correlated with IQ and a measure of school progress. The main figures are shown in Table 3.

TABLE 3. *Correlations of background factors with intelligence and achievement of school children (E. Fraser)*

	IQ	Achievement
Parents' education rating	·423	·490
General book reading in home	·280	·329
Newspaper and magazine reading	·381	·398
Income	·350	·444
(Small) Family Size	·404	·458
Living Space	·363	·447
Occupation (not correlated but significant at ·001 level)		
Abnormal or broken home environment (not correlated but significant at ·01 level)		
Parents' educational and vocational aspirations	·297	·391
Parental encouragement	·604	·660
General family atmosphere	·393	·460
Mother at work	N.S.	N.S.
r_m	·687	·752

'Parental Encouragement' gives the highest correlations; but as it was based on school teachers' assessments, not on interviewer observations, it is obviously contaminated. Apart from this it is clear that several indices of socioeconomic status, of parental educational level and attitudes, and of an emotionally secure home, are substantially related to general intellectual level at this age, and even more strongly to actual attainment. However little attempt was made to analyse the interactions among these factors.

Wiseman's book, *Education and Environment*, is noteworthy especially for a series of ecological investigations in the Manchester and Salford conurbation.* Instead of studying the background of individual pupils, districts of a city or whole schools were taken as units. For example the illegitimacy rate or the infant mortality figures for a number of districts were correlated with the proportions of 14 year pupils in the secondary modern schools in those districts who were backward in intelligence, reading or arithmetic.† The same approach had been used by Burt around 1920 in studying the demographic and educational characteristics of 29 London boroughs, and he had obtained extremely high correlations of ·8 to ·9 between backwardness and infant mortality, mental defectiveness, overcrowding and death rates. Forty odd years later the coefficients are considerably lower, suggesting that, with improvements in social conditions, the various areas of Manchester are no longer so uniformly good or poor in health, housing, crime and educational standards. Nevertheless there are still very significant correlations in the ·3 to ·7 range between backwardness and such variables as birth and death rates, mental deficiency, illegitimacy, infant mortality and juror index. In the same book Warburton found rather small coefficients, though in the expected direction, between backwardness in a sample of schools and both school and neighbourhood characteristics.

Much the same factors correlated with intelligence as with attainment quotients and, rather surprisingly, most of the IQ coefficients were higher. This contradicts Fraser's finding, but it can probably be explained by the use of ecological rather than individual measures. It is

* S. Wiseman, 1964 and 1966. Cf. the similar study by L. H. E. Reid of schools in Jamaica, summarised in Chapter XXI. Another investigation of 50 London primary schools, carried out under the present writer's supervision, by L. C. D. Kemp, yielded correlations around ·52 between a composite index of social class level of the school and mean intelligence and attainment scores.

† Correlations were also obtained with proportions of bright children, i.e. those with IQ, RQ or Ar.Q of 115+. But these yielded lower and more variable results, probably because selective schools were excluded, hence the score distributions were truncated at the top end.

very likely that the schools serving the worst areas would concentrate more on improving their pupils' reading and arithmetic than would schools in the better areas. This of course would distort, and tend to reduce, the normal correlations with attainment, but would have relatively less effect on correlations with intelligence tests.

By applying factor analysis to the correlations between the environmental indices, Wiseman and Warburton find that the major conditions influencing children's abilities at the present day are not so much economic as: (a) the morale vs. social disorganisation of the neighbourhood; (b) the standards of maternal care, and (c) school characteristics, e.g. progressiveness. However on the basis of their own results and of an extensive survey of the literature, they conclude that the most crucial factors in intelligence test scores are the parents' own intellectual level, and their attitudes to education and aspirations. While in relation to scholastic achievement, school characteristics and the 'peer group climate' are also particularly vital.

The work of J. W. B. Douglas (1964) is important, not merely because it involves the long-term follow-up of an almost complete cross-section of the child population, but because it proved for the first time that environmental handicaps continue to operate cumulatively in middle childhood. They do not merely affect test performance at eight years but produce still more marked differences at 11 years; or in other words they correlate with actual increases or decreases in ability between 8 and 11. For example there is a ten per cent increase in the differential between upper-middle and lower-working class children in Britain over this period.

The sample consisted of some 5,000 children born in one week of 1946. Their home conditions and maternal care were studied in infancy; then at 8, and 11 they took short batteries of intelligence, English and arithmetic tests. The homes were recontacted, and teachers' ratings on school behaviour were collected. Most of the analyses are concerned with the effects of environmental differences on combined test scores, or on the concurrent 11+ selection examination results, since it is claimed that the results for intelligence and attainments tests were usually too similar to be worth separating. Social class was decided on a basis of parental job and education, and it was found that the influence of mother's and father's education was much the same. Better-class children were more often found in the higher streams of streamed schools than would be expected from their test scores alone, showing the influence of other factors that generally go with 'the good home' on school adjustment and achievement. A very striking feature was that changes in level of parental employment over the 8–11 year period, or changes in housing, were associated with slight improvements or decreases of test score (though obviously this might mean that the more ambitious parents have children who are 'improvers', rather than that economic or housing conditions as such directly influence achievement).

Naturally it is difficult to sort out the relative importance of the contributory factors when they generally tend to work together. However by skilful use of analysis of variance Douglas was able to show their influence even when social class is held constant, or else that they operate differently at different social class levels. For example, poor attendance records do not pull down the scores of the upper-middle class and have less effect in the best primary schools; but frequent absences are associated with poorer performance in lower-middle and working-class children (Douglas and Ross 1965). Certainly one of the most important influences in raising scores is the child's attitudes, i.e. whether he is assessed as hardworking or lazy. But we know from many other researches* that teachers' personality judgments are mainly based on school achievement, hence this cannot be taken at its face value. More lower-class children tend to be rated as 'lazy', also as 'lacking concentration' or 'poor discipline' or 'having difficulties with other children'. The most important factor in achievement (over and above social class) would appear to be parental interest and aspirations, as evidenced by school visits, intention to continue schooling beyond 15, and desire for a grammar school place. When this factor is held constant, other factors often cease to show any significant effects.

Overcrowding, unsatisfactory home conditions, and family size are clearly unfavourable, but difficult to disentangle from poor maternal care and lack of parental interest. Though birth order as such has no consistent effects, eldest children do tend to improve more from 8 to 11 and to get more grammar school places. Plausible explanations might be that parents have higher aspirations for the first-born, or that they can talk to him (or her) and give him more attention than to later-born.

It is generally found that girls adjust better to primary schooling and are more docile than boys. Thus they achieve better by 11 years, particularly at English and verbal intelligence tests. But in view of our discussion of middle-class upbringing and speech, it is interesting that Douglas finds very little sex difference in abilities in the middle-class children, much more in the lower-working class. His data further indi-

* E.g. A. S. Walker.

cate that the earlier physical maturation of girls than of boys is probably not responsible for the sex differences in achievements; for his earliest maturing girls did not achieve appreciably better than later maturing. Finally Douglas has demonstrated that good schools, namely those that obtained most successes in previous 11+ examinations, affect ability, and this is not due merely to the more intelligent and better class parents choosing them, since all the children attending them tended to improve more from 8 to 11.

This summary represents but a small selection of the findings that seem most significant to our purpose. But a comment is in order regarding the conclusions drawn from this or other evidence of the association between social class and achievement. Not only do many educationists and public speakers, but also social scientists who ought to think more rationally, frequently state that the superior scholastic achievement or Intelligence C of the upper and middle class is in some way unjust, or attributable to class privilege. Thus Douglas claims that there is 'no justification for social class inequalities in the distribution of selective secondary school places', although his data, as much as anyone's, have shown that lower-class families are not only less able but also less interested, and less likely to make good use of the costly facilities provided in these schools. Naturally we are moved by the squalor under which far too many children are reared, their poor health, sheer lack of food, let alone of enjoyment; and we recognise that the State, through redistribution of incomes, should spend more on them, and do all that is possible to improve their housing, health and education. We can agree further that through such improvements and through the extension of high-quality education to larger proportions of the population, abilities will tend to rise, and that many children who were previously unable to reach the necessary standards will add to our resources of educated and intelligent manpower. The western nations are already vastly more advanced in this process of social uplift than the non-western countries which cannot afford so much; the conditions of the lower classes in the latter are far poorer still. Yet much more could, and should, be done within our own countries as well. None of this, however, alters the fact that our lower-class children are, on average, lower in effective intelligence and educability mainly for the following reasons:

(a) because there are certainly some genetic differences between the classes;

(b) because they have usually received poorer pre- and post-natal care;

(c) because their parents have not brought them up to be as intelligent or as motivated to intellectual achievement.

In other words, the 'unfair' economic or educational conditions are not the sole or the most important explanation. It is the people and not only their material conditions that we must strive to change.

XI

American Studies, Particularly of Negroes

Naturally there is even more documentation and empirical evidence for the effects of social class and associated environmental conditions on intelligence and achievement in the USA. If anything the correlations are higher because of the greater heterogeneity of the population. Historically the lowest socioeconomic classes have been largely composed of negroes or of recent immigrants – Italians, Irish, S.E. Europeans and now Puerto Ricans and Cubans, and they have produced the greatest problems of school adjustment and achievement. A similar situation is emerging in Britain today with immigrant West Indians, Indians, Pakistanis and Cypriots. But all the researches cited in Chapter X were based on almost wholly white populations, whereas to a much greater extent in the USA socioeconomic class is intermixed with ethnic group* and linguistic, or with racial, differences. In the larger cities, the poorest housing areas are peopled more and more by negroes, and by still incompletely acculturated immigrants, while the whites move out to better areas with higher standards of schooling. Again over the country as a whole there is greater heterogeneity, with pockets of extreme economic and educational backwardness, so that rural vs. suburban (rather than urban) differences in ability are often much greater than any recorded in Britain. Likewise differences in quality between schools in the best and worst areas are exaggerated.

It is curious that American researchers seldom seem to have asked directly whether white middle and working classes, backward rural communities, unacculturated whites, negroes, Indians and Puerto Ricans all lie on the same continuum, as it were, or if not, what differences in ability and personality patterns arise from their different ethnic backgrounds. This may be due partly to the desire to play down ethnic and racial differences, and partly to the prevailing neglect of any genetic factors.

* It may well be that some of the contrasts measured by Wiseman arise from the large Irish element in the Manchester conurbation.

Thus current discussions of the 'disadvantaged' or 'underprivileged' child, including many of the powerful writings of the Chicago school – Havighurst, Davis and others – tend to reflect negro-white as much as social class differences. However the major study of 'cultural bias' by Eells, Davis *et al.* in 1951 was carried out with some 5,000 white pupils in a midwestern city. The authors agree that ability differences can be explained either genetically, or developmentally, or in terms of test bias, but they concentrate on the latter. They demonstrated large differences between high and low status groups, over the 9–14 year range, on intelligence test items, particularly vocabulary and verbal items, though less marked with geometrical and picture items. And they attribute this mainly to the social-class bias of the schools, in which the reading books and other materials, and the systems of rewards and punishments are all geared to the middle-class child. In particular the tests reflect middle-class thinking and values rather than ability in relation to real-life problems. Such tests, they admit, are good predictors of future educational and vocational success, but this involves a circular argument. Children's motivations and abilities have been pretty well fixed by their home and school environment by the age of 10 or so, hence naturally their future performance remains similar. But we do not know whether the less educable pupils would stay the same if conditions were different. The authors also reject the view that a middle-class upbringing stimulates the intellect generally, claiming that a lower-class one is as stimulating in relation to its own needs.

While one would agree that western middle-class culture should not be regarded as the ideal for everybody (cf. Chapter XIV), this argument is surely rather an illogical one in view of what we know about the efficacy of symbolic thinking. The authors' criticisms of tests for reflecting class differences is rather like blaming the weighing machine when it shows an undernourished child to be below normal weight.* Indeed the weakness of their position is illustrated by the fate of the Davis-Eells Games test, which they devised specifically to emphasise lower- rather than middle-class content. This test still continued to correlate with social class, and has never been shown to have useful validity for any purpose.

Jensen (1966) further criticises Eells and Davis's analysis of class differences in ability since it stresses too much the *content* of ideas and the kind of information which the middle class, or alternatively the lower class, are more likely to have acquired. The really important differences lie in transferable *skills*, such as the middle-class child's

* Cf. Doppelt & Bennett.

capacity to pay attention to communications, to notice similarities and differences, gradations and relations between things and to label them, to talk to himself, and so on.

A valuable survey of a large amount of experimental literature is given in Bloom, Davis and Hess's *Compensatory Education for Cultural Deprivation*. The authors draw attention to much the same factors that we have discussed – inadequate motivation, health and sleep, linguistic handicap, lack of intellectual stimulation in the home or concern for achievement, conditions not conducive for study, clash of values between lower-class parents and the school. But it further emphasises the effects of school experiences on the deprived child's self-concept. There is experimental evidence that teachers tend to expect lower-class children to be ineducable, and even if this is not communicated, they naturally tend to reward the high-achieving middle-class child and to depress the self-esteem of the slower learners. As a result the deficit in achievement gets progressively worse, and unsuccessful pupils become more defeatist and either apathetic with regard to schooling or rebellious. Even in non-intellectual, extracurricular activities they take less part than higher-status pupils. Particularly during adolescence the peer group or gang offers greater rewards such as enjoyable company and freedom from adult controls. Thus drop-out rates from High School are large, and if attendance is enforced, Blackboard Jungles may be created.

Bloom and his colleagues believe that the situation is best tackled at the time of initial introduction to schooling. Only too frequently the schools attended by lower-class children are themselves inferior. But even if they were all as good as the typical suburban school, this equality of opportunity would not be enough. There should be 'compensatory education' before, or at, entry to try to make up for the handicaps imposed by home upbringing. To get into the homes and re-educate the parents would be a practical impossibility (though in the the present writer's view the ultimate solution must involve changes in the home). Hence there are a number of schemes in the USA like Operation Headstart, which attempt to give preparatory education to deprived preschool children, and others which introduce special remedial programmes at later ages. These preparatory schemes, it is claimed, should be quite different from the ordinary nursery schools patronised mainly by the middle class: they should aim to train children to perceive and attend, to link perceptions to language, and generally to improve speech. They should develop a sense of mastery over environment, interest in, and enjoyment of, learning.

Considerable claims have been made for the success of these ventures in improving achievement when children start normal schooling, though they have not yet been followed up sufficiently to prove that their effects are lasting. A great deal more research will be required to prove that there is not merely some improvement in initial adjustment, or a Hawthorne effect which soon wears off. Too often the follow-up tests contain items which have been specifically trained by the programme, and therefore do not prove that thinking and motivation generally have been stimulated. Stricter controls are needed, too, to isolate the effects of particular changes, since otherwise we cannot tell which features of a remedial scheme are valuable, which not. The need for caution is indicated by the many studies of remedial reading which have produced striking initial effects, that have not been maintained some years later.*

Concurrently in the US there is the widespread trend towards integration of schools hitherto segregated either because of racial discrimination, or simply because negroes and whites generally live in different areas of a city. It is only natural that white parents and teachers should fear that this will result in a lowering of standards, though there have been some studies which indicate that the attainment of negro pupils are raised through working alongside whites under better conditions, without pulling down those of the white children (e.g. in Washington, D.C.). But the problem is not merely one of modifying the attitudes of white parents, pupils and teachers; the negroes themselves, particularly in the Southern States, have such engrained feelings of deference and inferiority, and tend to be so much behind the whites in abilities, that a lot of stress and frustration is engendered which interferes with learning (cf. I. Katz). Obviously it would be improper for a British writer to comment on American policies, though we have sufficiently similar difficulties to make us realise that there is no simple, quick solution.

As a psychologist, though, one is still entitled to criticise the emotional illogicalities of much educational and sociological writing – for example the contradiction between the frequent claim that negroes, immigrants and other lower-class children have the same intellectual potential as normal whites on the one hand, and on the other hand the view that the curriculum and teaching must be modified to suit such children (cf. Passow *et al.*). It is admitted that there is no longer any widespread assumption of genetic inferiority, but a writer such as K. B. Clark complains at: 'the pervasive and archaic belief that children from culturally deprived backgrounds are by virtue of their deprivation . . . inherently ineducable'; also at: 'the appalling, anachronistic . . . educational snobbery' of Conant's argument that what a school can and should do must

* Cf. for example, J. E. Collins.

be guided by the status and ambition of the families it serves. One can only repeat that children are what their parents and background have made them, and that while every effort should be devoted to improving their background, and offering more adaptive, better quality, schooling, people cannot be changed overnight, even in a rich society.

There is room for much more fruitful discussion and experiment on the proposition that deprived pupils will adjust better to school and make more useful progress if, in any way, the curriculum could be better related to the lives they have lived and will be living. Could it not take more account of their developmental state, their preference for concrete activity over verbalism, and their need for immediate rather than long-term satisfactions? This should not necessarily mean that they could not proceed to symbolic thinking with verbal concepts later, but it does seem to imply segregation in the sense that different forms of schooling would have to be provided for different kinds and levels of mentality. Inevitably, therefore, it is politically controversial. Much the same problem recurs later when we consider the development of abilities and of schooling in the far more seriously handicapped non-western nations.

A few examples of recent negro test results will be relevant at this point, and interesting for comparison with the writer's results later. A. M. Shuey's exhaustive survey of negro intelligence indicates an average quotient in the low 80s, though there are of course considerable variations for different samples and different tests; and the deficit is far less marked among preschool children than with older adolescents and adults. She has been rightly criticised* for her assumption that the sheer number of concordant investigations favours a genetic rather than a primarily environmental explanation, but justified – as we have seen – in refusing to ignore possible genetic influences.

Passow's book quotes the following mean IQ figures for New York schools:

	Negro	Puerto Rican	All Others
3rd Grade	90·8	86·7	104·0
6th Grade	89·0	81·2	108·4

Here the negro results are distinctly higher, and there is little age decline, which accords with Klineberg's finding that economic and educational conditions for negroes in New York are rather better than in many other areas, particularly the southern States. Puerto Ricans are considerably more handicapped, especially at later ages. Many investigators have

*E.g. Dreger & Miller.

tried to arrive at fairer estimates of ethnic group differences by holding socioeconomic class constant. But this is an illogical strategy since obviously the parents' job distribution is determined in part by their own ability or lack of it, though in part also by discriminatory customs or by caste.

Kennedy *et al.* collected a normative sample of some 1,800 southern negroes and applied the Terman-Merrill Form L-M, California Achievement tests and the Goodenough Draw-a-Man test. The overall mean IQ was 80·7, but in five-year-olds it was 86 and by 13 years had dropped to 65. Similarly in achievement, the second-graders were two months behind white norms, sixth-graders 14 months behind. Generally the negroes performed better on arithmetic fundamentals, worse on arithmetic reasoning and reading comprehension; and in the Binet they did worse on the abstract verbal, vocabulary and comprehension items than on rote memory and everyday information items. The Goodenough scores were much superior, averaging 101 at 6 and 7+ but dropping again with age to around 80 by 12–13. An interesting study of white and negro seven to nine-plus children in a poor socioeconomic area of a North-eastern city gave the following results (Higgins & Sivers):

	White	Negro
Terman-Merrill	90·6	90·3
Raven Progressive Matrices	90·8	80·5

The lower-class whites score as badly on Terman-Merrill as the negroes, but the latter fall much further behind on the non-verbal reasoning test. The authors conclude that the Matrices is not a test of 'intelligence' but of some rather specific skill which discriminates against negroes. Our own findings in Jamaica (Chapter XXII) suggest on the contrary that negroes score most poorly in symbolic thinking with non-verbal materials, though they have enough verbal facility to do relatively better at verbal intelligence tests. Teahan & Drews report no difference between the mean WISC verbal and performance IQs in a small group of northern negro children, but an 11½ point lower performance quotient among southern negroes.

	Verbal	Performance
Northern	87·4	88·4
Southern	80·3	68·8

L. E. Tyler's survey of race differences likewise indicates that the greater deficit of negroes, especially from the southern states, on non-verbal materials is a frequent finding. She suggests that there may be greater 'perceptual deprivation' among these negro children. Equally one might say that northern families have to a greater extent absorbed white culture and methods of child upbringing which help performance on such tests. Other studies of differential abilities tend to be inconsistent, probably because negroes in different parts of the US are heterogeneous. Thus Anastasi indicates that they perform poorly on tests of Thurstone's Perceptual Speed and Spatial factors; but R. E. Stake obtained relatively good scores on these factors in Atlanta, Georgia. It is generally agreed, however, that they do well on rote learning tests (e.g. Semler and Iscoe).

If it is asked what might differentiate the intellectual development and school performance of American negroes from that of equally depressed whites, we would naturally look for an answer in terms of colour prejudice. But since their scores are fairly similar to those obtained in the West Indies, where no similar prejudice operates (but where schooling tends to be even more inadequate), we might consider another factor which is frequently mentioned in the literature.* This is the factor of broken homes and absence of the father. In slave times, the family was deliberately broken up, and since then the constant underemployment of negro males has undermined their role as the strong head of the household, as well as discouraging any planning for the future. Loose marital relations and promiscuity have further strengthened maternal dominance and the lack of male models for identification in a large proportion of families. Disciplining of boys is severe, and an additional reason for their dislike of school is thought to be their resentment against continued restraint by predominantly female teachers. Negro girls however do have identification figures and generally tend to perform better in school. There are obvious resemblances between this situation and some aspects of Witkin's picture of field-dependence.

It should hardly be necessary, in conclusion, to warn against generalisations about an ethnic group as a whole: the wide range of individual differences has already been mentioned. Obviously the negroes produce large numbers (even if a smaller proportion) of well-educated men and leaders in every sphere. Although some of these vehemently oppose white domination or paternalism, more commonly they absorb white middle-class speech, aspirations and values; and the teachers among them are apt to despise the lower-class negro culture which they have outgrown.

* E.g. Ausubel; and Deutsch 1963.

XII

Some Effects of Schooling and Age

While there are clear indications that schooling helps mental development in general, and that – on the whole – the more the better, it is much more difficult to prove that any particular type of schooling is more favourable than another. Most educators have strong beliefs, e.g. that a liberal education does more to develop the mind than say a technical one; and psychologists such as Susan Isaacs, Bruner and Cronbach clearly advocate approaches to teaching which will promote transfer, stimulate curiosity and active problem-solving rather than the implanting of information or drilling of specific skills. But in fact there is extremely little experimental evidence that the study of some subjects is preferable to others, or that some methods are mentally stimulating, others not.

As regards amount of schooling, we have seen that preschool experience appears to help children from poorer homes to make a better start. Many cross-cultural researches point to the handicap of groups who have had no schooling of any kind. Thus Bruner and Greenfield applied a Piaget conservation task to three groups of Wolof children in Senegal – urban-educated, bush partly-educated, and bush without any education. There was little difference between the younger children (6 to 9 years) in the three groups, but the unschooled children made no further progress from 9 to 12. Lack of schooling was clearly more important than rural vs. urban locale.

On the other hand, Price Williams's (1962) study of classifying and abstracting familiar objects showed no difference between Nigerian six to eleven year children who were or were not attending school. L. Doob suggests that, whether or not schooling actually stimulates mental growth generally, there are many experiences relevant to test performance which can be transferred from the school situation, for example following instructions given by a relatively strange adult, concentrating on tasks that fall outside normal life experience, and taking an interest in novel problems.

Ombredane, in Central Africa, found a rise in performance on the

Coloured Progressive Matrices with age, but among Africans receiving no schooling there was no rise beyond 12 years, and those aged 17 scored no better than six-year-olds. P. Weil has used a test similar to Matrices with large numbers of Brazilians and claims again that the completely unschooled make no progress beyond the normal six-year level. These results are open to criticism since, as will be shown later, performance at the Matrices depends considerably on how successfully the tester 'gets across' what the subject is supposed to do. However another research by C. Ramphal with Indian schoolchildren in S. Africa yielded comparable results both with Matrices, verbal intelligence tests and school attainments. The shortage of school places for this racial group is so severe that many are unable to gain entry at seven years. Even children from better social classes may have to wait till eight, nine or ten. Ramphal was able to show that lack of schooling from seven to ten retarded intellectual development and school progress by an amount roughly equivalent to five IQ points per year of delay.

Similar problems occur in many African countries where children enter primary schooling late, or miss a year or so, usually because their parents need them at home, or cannot manage the fees, or because the nearest school is too distant for younger ones to attend. Thus when they reach the top standard and take the secondary school entrance examination, they may be 18, 19, even 20 instead of the more usual 13 to 15. Secondary school Heads tend to suspect these older candidates of having shot their bolt, and believe that they are unfitted for secondary work. As their true ages are often unknown, the Heads may reject them on the (highly untrustworthy) grounds of apparent physical maturity. Not all, of course, are unsatisfactory students, and those who are may be unamenable to school discipline rather than intellectually incapable. Also they naturally tend to come from poorer, more remote families and schools, i.e. to be of poorer intelligence for other reasons. Hence they provide less convincing evidence of the effects of delayed schooling than does Ramphal's investigation, where economic class and area were controlled. Nevertheless they tend to confirm our supposition.

Within western cultures there was the early study by Gordon in 1923 of canal boat and gipsy children, whose Binet IQ deteriorated after six when they failed to attend school, but whose scores on performance tests were less affected. Then there was the finding in 1917–18 that American Army recruits averaged no better than 13 year-olds on intelligence tests. For many years most psychologists were content to explain this in terms of mental growth tailing off and reaching a constant level by about 14. Other researches however demonstrated increases even into the 20s among students still at school or college. This apparent contradiction becomes quite intelligible if it is admitted that growth, at least at the kinds of reasoning measured by intelligence tests, ceases when people leave school and enter jobs, or engage in leisure pursuits, which provide little further intellectual stimulation. This hypothesis was confirmed by the writer's analysis of Matrices scores of some 90,000 recruits by age and civilian occupation. It showed a general tendency for scores to decline with age from 17 or 18 years; but among men in more highly skilled jobs, requiring most 'use of their brains', the scores stayed up longer and declined more slowly than among unskilled workers and labourers.*

All the work mentioned so far was cross-sectional, i.e. based on differences between testees in different age, or schooling, groups. But I. Lorge in America and T. Husén in Sweden followed up the same individuals who were tested as children and retested them as adults, thereby proving that those who had received the greatest amount of education in the intervening period ended up with higher scores. Vernon (1957a) retested 865 boys at 14 years who had been tested three years earlier before entering various types of secondary schools. After allowing for differences in initial ability of those entering different schools, it was found that mean IQ changes ranged from +6·9 in the 'best' school to −5·5 in the 'poorest'. Now to a large extent pupils admitted to the better schools would come from better-class homes where there would be more stimulation and more favourable attitudes to schooling. Thus these effects could not be attributed to quality of schooling alone. However there was a correlation of ·79 between the local Education Officer's ranking of 14 schools in order of 'stimulating-ness' and the mean rise or fall of the boys in each school. In another research by Lovell (1955), comparisons were made between boys in relatively 'good' and 'poor' schools, also between youths who had continued with Further Education after leaving and a group of prisoners who had had little or no education beyond 14. A wide range of tests was used and much the biggest positive differences between 'stimulated' and 'less stimulated' was found on tests of mental flexibility – speed of switching from one cognitive task to another, tests of concept formation and of verbal and non-verbal classification; whereas the smallest differences occurred on vocabulary, reading comprehension and standard tests of non-verbal intelligence and Abstraction.†

* Cf. Vernon & Parry.
† The researches surveyed in this paragraph cast some doubt on Bloom's (1964) claims for 'stability' in human growth. He argues that the main bases of

More research is needed on the mental faculties or factors which are most affected by education or lack of it, and by age. Lovell's findings are not unlike those obtained in studies of deterioration among older adults, where tests of Similarities, Kohs Blocks, Matrices, Cattell's Culture-Fair, and other tests involving flexibility and speed of response tend to show earlier and more rapid deterioration than vocabulary and most verbal and informational tests. A. T. Welford's work on ageing in relation to industrial jobs is illuminating also in showing that older workers are not greatly handicapped by declining visual or auditory acuity, speed of movement or reaction time. They can compensate for these and, because of their experience and responsibility, they tend to do better than young ones at familiar tasks or those requiring accuracy which can be performed at their own rate. But they are less able to work under speed stress, and they show their greatest difficulties in coping with many stimuli simultaneously, in breaking down habitual skills and rebuilding new ones, and more generally in tasks requiring the interpretation and organisation of unfamiliar material. Likewise in the educational field, adults have advantages over young school children in learning to read and write a foreign language, but not in pronouncing it.

There have been some longitudinal studies in which adults were retested over long periods. These have not yielded any clear picture of how abilities deteriorate with age,* partly because they have been based very largely on adults of superior ability, and partly because it is difficult to control the effects of practice or test sophistication. Apparently the scores of educated adults on verbal intelligence tests tend to go on increasing much longer than was previously supposed, even into the 40s and 50s. H. C. Lehmann has shown that the peak of productivity of major contributions among creative scientists tends to come quite early,

---

mental, as well as of physical, growth are built in during the very early years, and that there is progressively less changeability in later years. For example his careful analysis of follow-up studies with intelligence tests indicates that 50 per cent of the 17 year-old intelligence level is already determined by 4 years, and over 90 per cent by 13 years. These figures support the 'overlap hypothesis', i.e. that the correlation of IQs from one age group to another is a direct function of the percentage of development at the later age which has been achieved at the earlier age. But his empirical data were derived from populations growing up in a rather standardised environment, and though marked changes of circumstances doubtless occurred in many individuals during later childhood or adolescence, these would tend to be randomly distributed. If systematic differences between more or less educated, or otherwise stimulated, groups are examined, it seems that current and recent environment may have more influence than Bloom's conclusions would indicate.

* J. P. Guilford brings together a large amount of evidence showing how complex are age declines in different mental factors.

around 30. But the period of high productivity has a wide spread, and in some other fields such as literature and music it may extend into the 60s and 70s.

What may we conclude about mental development and decline from these varied observations? It would seem that every mental schema or 'plan' that we acquire carries within it the seeds both of further progress and of inhibition – of positive and negative transfer. A mental skill built up in one context can be applied in other situations and integrated with other schemata, and thus opens up the way to a higher order of thinking. Often, though, it is overpractised in one context and tends to become fixed and rigid, and resistant to extension or reintegration. The child's understanding of number and conservation provide a necessary basis for later growth of formal operations or scientific reasoning; but if he is merely drilled in the manipulation of number combinations, and is not stimulated to see their wider implications, he may become less fitted to advance to more complex understandings. In particular the child who is not exposed to any schooling builds up skills largely at the enactive level which are adequate for everyday living. But the longer he operates with these, the more difficult it is for him to acquire fresh concepts or move on to symbolic thought. He has learnt to be unintelligent.

Not only is varied stimulation from the environment of the utmost importance, but also the curiosity that the child brings with him to expand his universe is essential; and this, as we have seen, may be reduced by lack of physical energy due to malnutrition, or by repression or frustration which lead to apathy. It is often reported of North American Indian tribes that their children show fairly normal intellectual progress and educational achievement till adolescence, but then, when they realise the depressed status of their minority culture and the absence of opportunity for progress and advancement, they lose all interest and drop back in their work. Whether test scores actually come to a halt, or decline, does not seem to have been proved. Similar views have often been voiced about the incapacity of Africans to progress intellectually beyond the stage of elementary schooling, but again what incentive has there been for the great majority? In the newly independent African countries, much larger numbers of boys and girls than in the past are entering secondary schools, with good economic prospects ahead; and they are showing plenty of enthusiasm and capacity for further growth. One might go further and suggest that, in western society, adults continue to grow intellectually to 20, 30, 50 or more so long as they retain curiosity and aspire to conquer new worlds; but once they accept a mode of life and 'settle down', deterioration begins. This too would be difficult to prove, since we are far from consistent in our various spheres of activity. Conceivably cultural interests and insights might go on growing after job skills have passed their peak, but the available intelligence and other tests would not provide a good measure of either.

Many of the phenomena of mental growth and decline can, then, be explained in terms of cognitive transfer and motivation. But physiological as well as psychological changes are obviously involved in the reduced plasticity of the mind in old age, and we must not ignore physiological conditions underlying development. We know that new pathways and neural connections are cumulatively laid down from the undifferentiated brain tissue as the organism acquires its successively more complex schemata. But it is also widely believed that particular kinds of connections must be established at particular stages. The phenomena of imprinting in animals, and observations on primates brought up in the dark, indicate that there are critical periods for the acquisition of many sensory-motor responses. Senden's work on cataract patients likewise suggests that individuals who receive vision when fully grown have far greater difficulty in building up perceptual schemata than do normally stimulated infants. Does this imply then that intellectual impairment through early rearing in an unstimulating environment or through defective schooling is also irremediable? It is not possible to give a definite answer, but the indications are that there is rather more give and take in conceptual development than there is in the building of the sensory and motor foundations of mental activity.

Some pointers have already been mentioned – the apparent trainability of African youths in spatial discrimination, and the changeability of western IQs even in later childhood. Gesell's and other studies of infant maturation showed that it is no use trying to train psychomotor skills, such as climbing up stairs, too early; and it is likely that western education often tends to introduce children to reading, number, grammar and mathematics before they are ready for them. Much quicker progress occurs when these are postponed for a year or so, and the later starters do catch up with the earlier. Such findings prove that the sequence of development is pretty invariable, and that – depending both on genetic equipment and previous stimulation – some children progress through the sequence more rapidly than others. But they do not support the notion that successive steps must be accomplished by particular ages.

On the other hand this give and take may well be limited, and the impairment due to delay more serious in more extreme cases. The evidence from so-called wolf children is unreliable, and we can never tell that they were not basically imbecile. But there are some fairly well authenticated cases of children who have suffered almost complete deprivation of human company for the first 5 years or more of life (cf. L. J. Stone). Apparently they have the utmost difficulty in learning to speak and are largely ineducable. Probably though the more moderate types of impairment which we find in such studies as Ramphal's can be explained in terms of environmental and motivational inadequacies and maladaptive schemata, without resort to biologically delimited critical periods.

XIII

Types of Social Structure and Values

If the values and aspirations of the different classes in western society are so intimately bound up with children's intellectual development, how much greater must be their effects in non-western ethnic groups ? The trouble is, of course, that societies and their values are tremendously varied, and there is no generally accepted taxonomy, though several attempts have been made to distinguish contrasted types. L. Doob, while admitting the uniqueness of each culture, makes a good case for classifying as it were on a unidimensional scale from 'more' to 'less civilised'. From anthropological evidence and from his own testing and interviewing in African countries, in Jamaica and in American Indian reservations, he arrives at a generalised picture of the 'less civilised', which includes the following characteristics:

They tend to live in small communities, each of which is economically self-supporting. There is little trading or competition, and few contacts, between communities.

All members of the community have face-to-face contacts with all others, and tend to have common understandings of status and of the world in which they live. Social structure is rigidly prescribed, and there are strong pressures to conformity.

The society is essentially static and conservative, yielding only slowly to change when influenced by other cultures. (Most of Doob's book is concerned with the conditions under which such changes occur.) Their beliefs are characterised by absolutism: the order of the world was fixed from the beginning, their customs are hallowed by the experience of generations.

Life is relatively simple, since there are well-tried methods for coping with daily needs or emergencies. Though there may be specialisation and an elaborate social structure, there is little compartmentalisation of spheres of life: work, religion, the family, bringing up children, are all of one piece.

Since their activities are mainly centred around satisfying the biological needs, they live primarily in the present. And they are more concerned about continuity with the past, i.e. with the spirits of their ancestors, than with planning for the future. (However it would not be true to say that the principle of postponed gratification is lacking; clearly it operates when a nomadic people changes to an agricultural, though still uncivilised, mode of life.)

Note that there is not much resemblance between these attributes and the attributes of the lower working classes in a western society. However when the 'uncivilised' become 'more civilised' they do tend to take on western ideas and attitudes. Doob's data show that the better educated and more acculturated members of his samples scored more highly on most of his tests. In the course of his extensive studies of mine-workers in Sierra Leone, J. L. Dawson developed a questionnaire on traditional vs. western beliefs, with questions on the place of women in society, superstitions about illness, etc. Not only did this correlate highly with scores on several aptitude tests but also gave, if anything, better predictions of work efficiency than did the tests.

In contrast, the American 'core culture', according to F. R. Kluckhohn, is:

Active rather than passive. The environment does not have to be accepted, it can be manipulated.

Individualistic rather than collective. Man is responsible for what happens to himself and is judged by his own character and abilities.

Future rather than present oriented.

This epitomises the western middle-class culture that we have already described, though it is much less characteristic of poorer-class western groups. It is also almost identical with Max Weber's analysis of the Puritan ethic, to which he attributed the rise of capitalism in western Europe. Calvinistic Protestantism taught that man is his own saviour, and that evil resides in him, though it can be overcome by the building up of internal moral controls. Consonant with this asceticism is the view that work is a duty, a way to grace, and that man should strive to save for the future rather than enjoy the present. In Riesman's terminology, western man is 'inner-directed', not 'tradition-directed' like less civilised peoples, and he is competitive rather than cooperative.

Weber's portrayal of western middle-class values is extremely far-reaching: it contrasts not only Protestant with Catholic, and more with less civilised people, but also the higher with the lower social classes, and even industrial with rural. Zentner (1964) helps to clarify this by his threefold classification into the Pre-Neolithic ethic, the Feudalist-Agrarian and the Post-Industrial ethic, the latter being identical with Weber's Puritanism.

The Pre-Neolithic refers to the hunting economies of the American Indians, and is essentially individualistic, based on providing subsistence for the family or the small group. The world is there to be exploited and is regarded as fundamentally hostile. (A fuller description appears in Chapter XXV).

The Feudalist-Agrarian or Catholic ethic derives from the Judaistic conception of a patriarchal supreme being, and is typical of the agricultural economies of the middle ages. It denies worldly values and accepts poverty and pain in the present life for the sake of salvation hereafter. It is collectivist, stressing dependence on the family, and is organised hierarchically (e.g. the village under the lord of the manor). Status is hereditarily determined rather than dependent on man's own efforts.

Other writers have drawn attention to the contrast between hunting and rural economies within less civilised groups. Particularly relevant is the attempt by Barry, Child and Bacon to delineate the 'modal personalities' and child-rearing practises of cultures which do or do not accumulate food. The latter, i.e. the hunting, fishing, food-gathering and nomadic peoples (like Zenter's Pre-Neolithics) stress more aggressive or resourceful traits, while the agricultural peoples favour conformity with the group and docility. Berry's experimental study of Eskimos and Temne people provides further confirmation. Although Zentner's Catholic agrarians are obviously very different from, say, African agrarians, they do show some similar traits which are opposed both to those of hunting peoples and to the Puritan, middle class, industrialised, civilisation.

We must stress again that not only do these types overlap in a confusing way, but that each one conceals a wide range of ethnic group differences. However the discussion suggests an interesting link-up with ability differences, which is crudely represented in Fig. 3. It shows the western middle class as high in intellectual ability or g-factor and 'formal' language, and contrasted with the less civilised and with the western working classes. Cutting across this dimension is the spatial-verbal which tends to differentiate hunting from agricultural peoples. Note that this does not imply that agriculturalists are necessarily high in verbal ability (unless they also have sufficient g), only that they are relatively better on this than on the spatial side. Witkin's dependence dimension is shown as oblique, since it combines elements of g and k, of middle classness and of resourcefulness.

The use of factorial concepts in classifying cultures is not new. R. B. Cattell, in 1949, collected measures of 72 demographic and other

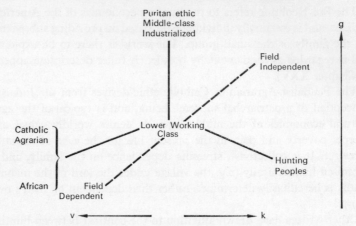

Fig. 3. Diagram of Dimensions of Cultural Groups.

variables on 69 nations, and showed that they could be resolved into some 10 meaningful dimensions. Much the largest general factor (before rotation) clearly corresponds to standards of living. Subsequent factors show no resemblance, however, to those which we have hypothesised, probably because the great majority of his nations were 'civilised'. The second largest factor appeared to represent the amount of educational and political activity, and the third the size of the country. But Cattell's notion of the 'syntality', i.e. the factor-pattern or syndrome of traits displayed by a nation or other ethnic group, would be well worth following up.

PART III
The Application of Tests in Non-Western Cultures

XIV

General Principles

In 1949 Anastasi and Foley wrote: 'Intelligence tests measure certain abilities required for success in the particular culture in which they were developed. Cultures differ in the specific activities which they encourage, stimulate and value. The "higher mental processes" of one culture may be the relatively worthless "stunts" of another.' Though somewhat exaggerated, perhaps, this represents the general view of most contemporary psychologists. It has even, in effect, received legal endorsement in the USA by a ruling that the application of western tests to negroes for vocational selection purposes constitutes racial discrimination and contravenes the Civil Rights Act of 1964, since the tests are unfairly weighted against them. More humorously, L. C. Bernadoni makes the same point by his parable of the Ugh, the No and the Oo-La-La cultures. If these cultures value different behaviours, then a test which is designed to suit one of them is likely to be the more valid the more it discriminates against members of other cultures.

Two cogent reasons for accepting this view of intelligence testing have emerged from the preceding Chapters – first the mass of accumulated evidence showing the dependence of test scores on nutritional, linguistic, home and educational conditions. We should remember, though, that the interpretation of this evidence is often open to doubt; some of it could conceivably be explained in terms of the genetically less intelligent creating their own bad environment. And secondly the whole of the discussion of the growth of Intelligence B implies that our cognitive skills – perceptual, linguistic and conceptual – are culturally conditioned. The group of skills which we refer to as intelligence is a European and American middle-class invention – something which seems to be intimately bound up with puritanical values, with repression of instinctual responses and emphasis on responsibility, initiative, persistence and efficient workmanship. It is a kind of intelligence which is specially well adapted for scientific analysis, for control and exploitation of the physical world, for large-scale and long-term planning and carrying out of materialistic objectives. It has also led to the growth of complex social institutions such as nations, armies, industrial firms, school systems and universities. But it has been notably less successful than have the intelligences of some more primitive cultures in promoting harmonious personal adjustment or reducing group rivalries. Other groups have evolved intelligences which are better adapted than ours for coping with problems of agricultural and tribal living.

However it is not quite so meaningless as Anastasi's statement suggests to apply the western yardstick to non-western groups; no more so indeed than to use it in assessing lower-class children in a western society. Doob sticks his neck out by claiming that all ethnic groups must become civilised in time, or perish; and he denies that this is mere ethnocentric prejudice. For contacts between cultures cannot be avoided altogether, and whenever a less civilised comes into contact with a more civilised people, it sees advantages in, and absorbs, some of their attributes. Often, as Doob points out, it absorbs only some of the segmental trappings of civilisation, and it always modifies its acquisitions to make them more acceptable to its own traditions and needs. Nevertheless, once the process gets started, it is irreversible. True, the civilised countries have an irresistible urge to civilise others too rapidly whether for religious, commercial, political or humanitarian reasons; but equally the greater prosperity, efficiency and physical health of the civilised have an irresistible attraction. All groups nowadays are in a state of transition: characteristically in the underdeveloped countries, the urban centres are expanding, the poorest rural dwellers crowding in and trying to adapt to a cash instead of a subsistence economy, and the new ways that they learn are percolating gradually to more remote areas. One would certainly not claim that that this is always to their advantage – that would indeed be ethnocentrism. The old is breaking down before they are ready for the new; detribalisation and the loss of the security provided by the traditional social organisation lead to drunkenness, crime, promiscuity, and other forms of instability. Nor of course does this process mean that all societies are rapidly going to become all alike, or that anyone would wish them to do so. Every social group derives much of its cohesion and strength by emphasising its unique features – its differences from outsiders. So that while all groups are tending to follow the same path, they are not necessarily converging to uniformity. Scotland and England have both improved their social welfare and education during the twentieth century, and culture-contacts between them are abundant, but there is little sign that their distinctness is disappearing. The more farseeing leaders of developing countries are already aware of the tremendous problems of grafting onto their peoples those aspects of western technology and civilisation that will help them, without consequentially destroying their own basic values.

As hinted above, western middle-classness has its defects as well as its virtues, and is far from being the ideal for all societies. Freud has shown that it is based on repressions which erupt in neurosis, large-scale warfare and other discontents. The civilised as well as the less civilised cultures are in a state of flux; and new values and social norms, perhaps more adaptive, perhaps more self-destructive, are emerging. The English middle-class ideal appears to be declining, and it may be that the Russian, the Israeli, the Japanese or other versions will be more successful. Bronfenbrenner has attempted to compare American and Russian methods of character education. While the former relies on family socialisation and the internalisation of moral controls to produce individual responsibility, the latter lays more emphasis on socialisation by the peer group (under impersonal adult guidance) and group competition, to produce the collectively-oriented person.

Thus although there are, and are always likely to be, innumerable variations in cultural values, which are reflected in ability differences, it is reasonable to recognise a general dimension of civilisation, which tends to be associated with complexity of intellectual processes. Despite their varying needs and ways of life, all peoples have problems to solve, new situations to meet, and it is likely that they can cope with these more effectively through logical thinking of the same kind of complexity as that built up in the western world. Enactive and iconic processes will generally suffice for a static society, but for change and progress some members at least must develop an intelligence based on seminal and flexible linguistic and numerical symbols. There is some justification, then, for applying western-type tests to non-western peoples – tests which attempt to sample such thinking, though we must admit at least two major limitations. First the tests will fail to sample many skills which are more valued by the peoples themselves, for example effectiveness in hunting or agriculture. These may be of a lower order of complexity, but generally play a larger part in daily life than does more symbolic thinking. (But equally, of course, our tests give quite poor samples of vocational effectiveness within western society; they become relevant chiefly when vocations depend on advanced education and logical reasoning.) Secondly it is always possible that the particular concepts and samples of thinking embodied in the tests are culture-bound, and that non-western or non-middle-class groups could display equally complex reasoning if the materials were more familiar to them. In this sense our tests may merit Anastasi's phrase – 'useless stunts'. However this is a matter for investigation rather than speculation, and it is now time to ask how valid and useful the tests have actually proved to be within groups other than those for which they were devised.

SOME VALIDITY FINDINGS

Immediately we are faced with the problems of setting up appropriate criteria. What sort of intelligence or effectiveness of thinking in non-western peoples might we hope to measure? Even if we narrow the question down to the effectiveness of Africans, for example, in particular employments, any kind of output assessments or ratings of their abilities tend to be even less trustworthy than at home.* Supervisors will have little knowledge of the performance of particular workers, especially when the work is done in gangs rather than individually, and will seldom know whether inefficiency is due mainly to lack of ability, to mal-nourishment, to resentful attitudes or other causes. When Biesheuvel (1949) developed his General Adaptability Battery for S. African mine-workers, the only usable criterion appeared to be differences in scores between more and less skilled groups of workers. The battery consists of five tests given in group form – a version of Kohs Blocks, two tests of sorting objects, Cube Construction, and assembling pieces to make a tripod. Sufficiently good differentiation was obtained to justify its continued use by the mining industry, but clearly the validation was rather crude. Moreover Hudson *et al.* found that differentiation between different levels of semi-skilled employment was even less effective. These authors suggest that the battery is chiefly measuring group acculturation differences: i.e. African workers who score relatively well on the white man's tests tend to adapt better to working in industries run by whites.

However P. A. Schwarz has undertaken extensive development of paper-and-pencil tests of non-verbal reasoning, mechanical, spatial and clerical abilities, working mainly in West African countries. He has been able to show that appropriate batteries of these sub-tests can pick out good trade trainees with some success. Special precautions (cf. Chapter XVI) were taken to make the tests intelligible to the candidates. Though exact figures are not published, the correlations with instructors' assessments would be of the order of ·40 upwards, which is probably as high as might be obtained in similar job-selection situations in a western

* Cf. Hudson, Roberts *et al.*

country.* MacArthur, Irvine and Brimble claim similar results in N. Rhodesia (Zambia), though less consistent, since they were baulked by the criterion problem. It should be realised that in almost any validity study carried out on small groups, if one gives a sufficient number of tests, some of them are sure to correlate positively with measures of success, and a sizeable multiple correlation can be achieved. But this would not necessarily apply to other similar groups unless, as in Schwarz's work, repeated confirmation is obtained.

During the Second World War, when there was little opportunity to do more than adapt western tests, considerable use was made of performance tests with illiterate recruits in Africa and India.† Positive correlations with efficiency ratings were obtained, though among the relatively unacculturated Gurkha recruits, the highest coefficient was only ·33.

J. L. Dawson gave a battery including Kohs Blocks, Passalong, Three-dimensional Perception, Morrisby's Compound Series, Minnesota Paper Formboard, and a Verbal and Clerical test, to several groups of mine employees in Sierra Leone ranging from labourers and trainees to clerks and nurses. He was fortunate in collecting good work assessments and obtained correlations of ·3 to ·5 for manual workers. Kohs Blocks and 3-D Perception were generally most successful, Morrisby, Minnesota and Passalong much less so. Among clerks, several validities were in the ·70s to ·80s. However, as mentioned earlier, his questionnaire on western vs. traditional beliefs achieved at least as high correlations, suggesting again that the tests are predictive partly because they are measuring co-operativeness with Europeans. Dawson agrees that American and British tests can be useful in selection for European forms of employment, but believes that better tests should be constructed in terms of the indigenous culture.

In a still more unusual setting, namely Papua and New Guinea, where literally hundreds of different dialects are spoken, I. G. Ord has adapted a battery of performance tests which can be given through mime, or more usually by an interpreter. This includes Cube Imitation, Bead-Threading (from Terman-Merrill), simplified Passalong, Form Assembly (based on Minnesota), Recalling objects (Kim's game), and Design Construction (a two-dimensional version of Kohs Blocks). This has proved useful in vocational selection of adults, e.g. for the army and public service, and for educational selection of children. Here too the Kohs is the best single test.

MacArthur‡ has urged that Canadian Metis and Eskimos possess

---

* Cf. Vernon & Parry. † See A. MacDonald; and F. W. Warburton.
‡ MacArthur 1964; MacArthur & Elley 1963.

considerable educational and vocational potential which could be realised through more 'adaptive treatment', i.e. through education and training better geared to their needs and traditional skills. Though rejecting the notion that innate potentiality can be measured by culture-free tests, he argues that non-verbal tests like Progressive Matrices, which contain fewer culturally-biased elements, can give useful indications of educability and trainability. Obviously no direct criterion of these people's ability under 'adaptive' conditions is available, but he suggests several indirect indications of the construct validity of the tests he has used: first, that the tests should be highly loaded with the general factor underlying all forms of cognitive activity. In this respect his non-verbal tests do well. Second, that they should yield smaller deficits in performance among culturally deprived groups than more culturally loaded tests. This too he has demonstrated, though other reasons will be suggested later (Chapter XXVI) to explain why Eskimos do relatively well on tests like Matrices. Third, they should give moderate correlations with educational and other achievements under current conditions, though these could hardly be as high as those obtained among western testees for whom the tests were constructed. In two follow-up researches with Meti and Eskimo pupils, correlations ranging from ·4 to over ·6 were obtained between Matrices or other non-language tests and school achievement three or four years later, and the correlations for verbal tests were only slightly higher. Normally verbal (and number) tests are far better predictors of educational achievement than non-verbal or performance tests, not only in western countries but in studies of African pupils. Presumably, though, these Canadian indigenes on entry to school are at very varying levels of fluency in English, hence the non-linguistic predictors work as well.

The most widespread use of western-type tests has been in connection with selection for secondary schools in almost all anglophone African countries, in the West Indies, and elsewhere. Verhaegen and Laroche favour the use of achievement tests for this purpose on the grounds that pupils will at least be assessed on the basis of skills that they have had an opportunity to acquire. On the other hand Vernon (1967a), Silvey (1963) and others have pointed out that there is an even stronger case for applying intelligence tests than in western countries, since underdeveloped countries can afford secondary schooling only for a small proportion of the population which is most likely to benefit (usually around two per cent), and the candidates come from such heterogeneous linguistic and cultural backgrounds and have received primary schooling of such variable quality, that their performance on achievement tests or examinations at the end of primary school gives a rather poor indication of their further educability. H. C. A. Somerset followed up 881 elementary school leavers in Uganda till School Certificate in 1964 and obtained an overall correlation of only ·374 between the Leaving Examination in English and arithmetic and the Certificate aggregate. Moreover the regression was nonlinear, that is the Leaving Examination picked out the high performers fairly accurately, to an extent represented by a correlation of around ·7; but it was far less discriminative near the borderline, where the equivalent correlation was about ·2.

Vernon (1961b) found that the three Moray House tests of Verbal Reasoning, English and arithmetic, which were used for selection in Jamaica, all gave correlations of around ·55 with secondary school marks one and three years later. Note that the intelligence test was not superior to the attainment tests. In Rhodesia, Irvine (1965) correlated Leaving Examination marks and experimental tests with performance in Form 1 of the secondary school. Some of his figures were:

Total Standard VI examination	·56
Primary Heads' estimates	·56
Grading of primary school quality	·26
NIPR Spiral Nines test total	·48
NIPR English Attainment battery	·35
Progressive Matrices	·23

Similar results have been reported by Silvey in Uganda and Vernon in Tanzania. In no case do the intelligence tests predict better than the conventional primary attainment tests or examinations though, as Irvine shows, they could add appreciably to the accuracy of prediction.*

It is not easy to tell whether such figures mean that the tests are working better or worse than they do in their country of origin. For the absolute size of follow-up coefficients like these depends more on the range of ability, or the selectivity, in the group that is studied than on the worth of the tests (cf. Vernon, 1957b). Hence test predictions in American secondary schools, where the populations are more heterogeneous than in England, are quite non-comparable. But taking this factor into account, it would appear that the figures are little, if any, lower than those obtained in the UK. We would naturally expect that tests based entirely on concepts and methods of teaching current in the UK would be somewhat less reliable and valid when applied to Jamaicans

* In fact these figures overestimate the value of the objective tests since they were not actually used in the selection process, as was the Standard VI Examination.

or Africans. But on the other hand these non-western pupils all start with a severe language handicap and have to carry out their secondary school studies in English; hence it is not surprising that tests requiring a knowledge of English should give fair predictions of future attainment.

In conclusion: objective tests of aptitudes or achievements constructed in a Cultural Group X can be applied in Group Y, although they might appear inappropriate in form and content to Y, for assessing abilities similar to those valued in X. Thus they can validly measure the educational capabilities of the lower social classes in a western country, or those of African or other students who are pursuing a western-based education, or recruits for the Army, for industrial training or employment. Probably the greater the cultural overlapping, the more justifiable is this practice. We would hardly expect similar tests to be applicable, say, to Kalahari Bushmen, but then few bushmen would want, or be capable of, western education or employment. Rather surprisingly, suitably adapted tests work with illiterate adults as well as with the partly acculturated and educated, though perhaps not very well. But then tests for manual workers within western countries tend to show quite low validities also.

CROSS-CULTURAL COMPARISONS

The fact that culturally-loaded tests can sometimes be used *within* another cultural group does not justify making comparisons *between* groups. For inevitably the members of these groups will have had different opportunities for building up the cognitive schemata sampled by the tests. G. A. Ferguson points out that, in testing intelligence, or more specialised aptitudes, we are assuming that all testees have overlearned certain skills, e.g. methods of reasoning, and are applying these to the solution of new problems; they have reached their peak for their age. But if they are still at different stages of learning due to environmental handicaps, this assumption breaks down. Another way of putting it is that testees have to display their abilities through a common medium of expression if we are to measure them, and if they are not equally at home with this medium, we cannot compare them. American lower-class negroes are retarded in acquiring this medium below American whites. Africans in underdeveloped countries are still more retarded.

However this does not imply a blanket condemnation of all cross-cultural studies, or of comparisons between subgroups (such as social classes) within a community. It all depends on the kind of comparison. Maybe the low-scoring group is as retarded on the criterion we want to predict as it is on the tests, but this has to be proved. H. P. Langenhoven has pointed out that the more distant the inferences made from a test score, the more doubtful they become. We must be cautious in inferring that low scorers would perform the same test equally badly if they took it under somewhat different conditions, still more so in inferring their performance on other apparently similar tasks. (For example two groups might differ on a test of mechanical aptitude, but not necessarily in ultimate skill at a mechanical job.) Especially dubious are inferences to general mental faculties which are supposed to underlie performance in a variety of situations; and this, of course, is what we do when we apply intelligence tests.

Langenhoven is particularly concerned with the problems of norming tests which are to be used in multi-lingual or other heterogeneous groups, as among English-speaking and Afrikaan whites in S. Africa, or French and English Canadians, or Welsh and English in the UK, not to speak of negroes and whites in the USA. In Canada, during the Second World War, the Army sometimes applied different cut-offs on their aptitude tests for the allocation of English and French speakers to the same job. It is known in S. Africa that Afrikaaners score lower on translated verbal, or on non-verbal, intelligence tests than whites of British descent (cf. Biesheuvel and Liddicoat), yet there seems to be little or no corresponding difference in their business efficiency or in the educational standards of their children. Dreger and Miller hazard the guess that American negroes operate in daily life at an average (white) IQ level of about 90, though the mean scores of school leavers on intelligence or educational achievement tests are considerably lower.

Now theoretically one can get round this problem, whenever there is a definite criterion to predict, by finding the actual regression lines of criterion on test scores in the two groups separately. Thus it is defensible to use the same non-verbal intelligence test with English and Afrikaan speaking children and require the former to score more points in order to achieve a certain IQ, since it has been shown that these unequal scores predict equal educational or other performances later. In other instances, for example among N. Africans undergoing technical training in France, it has been found that the same regression lines do apply (cf. Faverge and Falmagne), and probably this is the more common situation. Often, though, it may be technically impossible, or too politically controversial, to set up a satisfactory criterion. Another difficulty is that the criterion may be best predicted by one set of tests in one group, and by a different set, or with different weightings, in another group. This has seldom been investigated, but a study of white and negro pilots in the US Army Air Force by W. B. Michael indicated that the regression equation which applied to the former was inappropriate for the latter. The alternative, as Langenhoven shows, is to develop separate tests for different subgroups, with their own norms. But then this rules out the possibility of making comparisons when the subgroups are competing for the same jobs, or the same secondary school or university places.

Apart from predictive studies, tests can also be used cross-culturally in the manner stated by Doob (p. 3 supra), that is for comparing variations of scores with variations in antecedent conditions, in order to throw light on the effects of such conditions. Here too, clearly, the type of inference made is important. Malnutrition, lack of education, etc. might affect scores on intelligence tests differently from their effects on intelligence in other situations.

It would seem to follow from Langenhoven's analysis that the main problem in testing groups with diverse backgrounds is, not to find a culturally unbiased test, which is impossible, but to find tests from which safer inferences can be drawn. The question is, do these tests constitute good samples of the abilities we are interested in, or are the results distorted by irrelevant factors such as failure to understand instructions, or factors of motivation. Biesheuvel (1952) distinguishes these 'extrinsic' factors which particularly handicap the test performance of unsophisticated peoples from 'intrinsic' factors which affect the underlying ability; and in Chapter II we drew much the same distinction between Intelligence C and Intelligence B.

We turn now to the discussion of such factors.

XV

Extrinsic Factors in Test Performance

The following are some of the main irrelevances which the tester should seek to avoid:

1. Inability of the testee to understand the instructions, whether given in printed form or orally. Particular words or phrases may mislead or convey the wrong 'set' towards what he is supposed to do. Such misunderstandings arise not only from lack of facility in the language, or from differences in pronunciation between tester and testee, but also from insufficient attention or interest, or from anxiety.

2. With rare exceptions (notably most of the Stanford–Binet) western tests are couched in a somewhat artificial form, mainly for ease and reliability of scoring. Group tests largely employ multiple-choice, odd-man-out or even more complex item-forms, which certainly don't resemble the way we usually think, nor even how we are required to work in schools (outside the USA). Performance tests often have to be started at a signal, or other restraints are imposed. The sophisticated testee has become used to this artificiality. In printed tests he can cast his thinking into the appropriate mould, e.g. he will often read the answers before the question, and will be aware that the longest or most qualified answer is often the correct one. He develops a know-how which helps him to tackle more difficult items than when he first met this type. In much the same way the crossword addict becomes familiar with the style of clues set by the crossword author in his daily newspaper, but finds greater difficulty in tackling the puzzles in another paper. Moreover such sophistication is certainly not confined to verbal tests. The practice effects on retesting or taking parallel forms of Kohs Blocks, Formboards, Matrices and other non-verbal tests tend to be larger than with conventional intelligence or attainment tests.*

3. In timed tests particularly, the sophisticated testee does not waste time on items to which he sees no immediate solution. He knows that

* Cf. Vernon & Parry; Vernon 1962.

he can probably score more by going on and returning to them if there is time at the end. He is aware of the importance of spending time on reading the instructions carefully, so as to avoid errors of Type 1. He knows that he will probably gain by guessing. But in other cultural groups there may be no stress on doing things in a set time, and the giving of answers of which one is not sure may be discouraged.

4. The western school-child has had plenty of experience of doing written work on his own, and keeping his attention on the job for quite long periods; also of competing against his fellows, or of trying hard to answer just because the teacher says so, even if the questions seem pointless. He wants to do his best to please, or to avoid criticism from teachers and parents, and he readily transfers these motivations and attitudes to the psychological test situation. In other ethnic groups, particularly when testees have not been exposed to schooling, the culture pattern may be entirely different, and the whole test situation meaningless. Competition for personal gain may be frowned upon. Important problems are discussed cooperatively with the elders of the tribe, not left to individual initiative. Even the habit (or possibly instinct) of paying attention to unfamiliar stimuli may be undeveloped.

5. The testing situation, whether individual or group, is a social situation, and often the tester is a stranger – sometimes, in western schools, a psychologist from outside with an unfamiliar accent – sometimes, in other countries, a person of different nationality or colour. Even if he is working through an interpreter or native supervisors, he is obviously the person in charge. All of us are wary of strangers and need convincing of their friendliness and trustworthiness before committing ourselves to doing what they ask. Africans, Arabs, Asians and Australian aboriginals are particularly likely to have engrained attitudes of distrust for whites, which must interfere with their cooperation and understanding of his instructions. Also the foreign tester is naturally handicapped in understanding their attitudes and reactions, or in knowing how to appeal, or explain, to them.

6. Elements in the test materials can easily stimulate different associations in different cultures. A word or phrase, diagram or picture, may carry unintentional meanings. For example pictorial representation as such is discouraged among Moslems, so that even apart from the unfamiliarity of most Arab children with pictures, there may be inhibitions against recognising the objects portrayed.

When testing abilities, we normally assume that the testee is producing his maximal performance, uninterfered with by partial learnings, distractions or emotional inhibitions. The more unsophisticated the testee, the less is this likely to be true; and as Irvine (1966) points out, this means that different sources of variance enter into test performance. In other words the test is not measuring the same thing as it measures in test-wise subjects. In their investigations of psychomotor abilities, Fleishman and Hempel have shown that the factorial content of tasks alters as the learner progresses from complete unfamiliarity to advanced stages of practice. Just the same is true of tests of mental abilities, though in western societies we can usually afford to ignore the alterations since our testees usually start well up the learning curve, having had sufficient previous experience of answering questions orally or in writing, of attending, and working at speed.

Now it would be a mistake to draw too sharp a line between such extrinsic influences and intrinsic ones. All the factors just mentioned, No. 6 in particular, shade off into the linguistic, perceptual, motivational and other conditions discussed in Part II. When a lower working-class British child, or an African, does badly on a verbal test, we would usually attribute this to the intrinsic effect of inadequate English. But if the test is non-verbal or spatial, and if his performance improves when the instructions are expanded or simplified, or even given by gestures, his deficiency in English comprehension might be termed extrinsic. Perhaps the distinction can best be formulated by calling extrinsic all those determinants which can fairly readily be reduced or eliminated by changes in the instructions or administration, or minor changes in the form or content of items; or else by giving a limited amount of practice through which the testee becomes familiar with what he has to do, and willing to do it. Whereas intrinsic refers to influences which can be modified, if at all, only by education or training over a lengthy period designed to develop the underlying ability. Clearly this is a matter of degree rather than of kind.

Another useful indication of the operation of extrinsic factors occurs when a sizeable proportion of the testees turn out to be 'non-starters'. This has been observed by testers who have tried to give the Progressive Matrices both to poorer-class children in Venezuela, and to young immigrant children in London. They are willing to try, and we have reason to believe that the test discriminates down to their level of ability, yet they just don't get the hang of what they are supposed to do. The Kohs Blocks test is even more striking (cf. Wober 1967a). Even with repeated demonstration, some English boys and many more West Indians and Africans completely fail to break down the printed designs and reproduce them with the painted blocks; they can only copy the block models. They may produce roughly the same Gestalt, as though working from memory, and even be quite satisfied that their pattern:

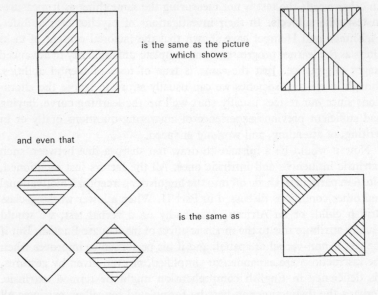

is the same as the picture which shows

and even that

is the same as

M. B. Shapiro also found a marked tendency among Africans to rotate the reproduction. In a test based on drawing Kohs-like designs, illiterate workers from Nyasaland rotated much more than English mentally defective children, brain-damaged patients, or educated African teachers; and they in turn were significantly poorer than normal white controls.

It seemed to Ord that these difficulties with Kohs Blocks arise partly because of the confusion of having to attend to the tops of the blocks and to disregard the sides. He therefore substituted flat pieces, and showed pictures of the same size as these squares. This version of the test 'got across' much more readily, and Heron* found that it discriminates quite well even among seven-year-old Zambian children; whereas scores on the standard version pile up seriously at the bottom end. More generally, bimodality in a distribution is an index of the presence of extrinsic difficulties. A test that yields a unimodal curve is probably getting across fairly uniformly to a group of subjects, even though their scores may all be lowered by intrinsic factors.

Yet another technique for studying the problem is to compare the order of item difficulties in different cultures. If there are sources of

* Private communication from A. Heron, University of Zambia.

variance peculiar to a non-western group (as suggested in No. 6 above), then this group will find some items relatively more difficult, others relatively easier, than will a western group. Irvine (1967) obtained high correlations between item-difficulties for the Matrices test in English and African groups, but also small, consistent differences. Vernon (1967a) obtained similar results with other non-verbal tests, but indicated that the underlying cultural factors are not readily identifiable. For example it could not be claimed that Africans did better on more holistic, English on more analytic, items.

INVESTIGATIONS OF PRACTICE EFFECTS IN NON-WESTERN GROUPS

A. Ombredane, working in the Congo, discovered large score increases when the Progressive Matrices was given a second or third time, and concluded that the results of an initial test are quite unreliable with un-sophisticated subjects. He suggests either that scores should not be accepted until the subjects have had practice on the test itself or on similar materials (he used the Coloured Progressive Matrices for this purpose), and reached their maximum level; or that the test should be treated as a learning situation, and the subjects be assessed on the trend of their scores with practice. Similarly Ortar (1960), who used the Arthur Stencil (non-verbal) test to assess multilingual Israeli immigrant children, found the initial performance too chancy. Arguing that no test problem can be equally familiar or unfamiliar to all testees, she advocates giving a parallel test first and then accepting the score on a second test. The second proposal – for treating tests as learning situa-tions – is also put forward by Silvey (1963) and has many apparent attractions. However for various technical reasons, which are discussed in Appendix C, it just does not work.

More detailed information on practice effects is supplied by Jahoda (1956), who retested 317 W. African schoolboys at the end of elementary education with Progressive Matrices in three successive weeks, and obtained a mean overall rise of 6·5 points. Perhaps this is an under-estimate, since many boys obviously became bored and scored lower on the third than the second test. However the interesting point, not noticed by Ombredane or Jahoda, is that this figure is very much the same as that obtained on retesting British recruits, namely 4·7 points.* Again Silvey, working with secondary pupils in Uganda, obtained a rise

* Cf. Vernon & Parry. The African and English figures would be much closer if allowance could be made for the skewedness of score distributions on the Matrices.

of 4·84 (from a mean of 35) on retesting. But when he supplied additional explanations and demonstrations there was an additional gain of 2·43 points.

The similarity in improvement between Africans and British recruits (who were, early in the War, pretty unsophisticated to tests) does not mean that unfamiliarity or cultural bias of materials and instructions can be ignored, but does suggest that it is not abnormally large when the group concerned has been exposed to some schooling.

A more extensive study was carried out in S. Africa by Lloyd and Pidgeon, using the National Foundation for Educational Research Nonverbal Tests 1 and 2. These contain several different subtests, instead of a single item-form like the Matrices, and therefore might be expected to cause difficulties to African, Indian and white children of 10½ to 12½ years, none of whom had taken any objective tests before. Two groups of each race, numbering about 140 each, took two tests a fortnight apart. One of each pair of groups benefited on the second occasion from practice alone, while the other groups received two additional half-hour periods of coaching during the interval, in their own tongue. The main results, given in Table 4, show the low IQs of African and Indian

TABLE 4. *Practice and Coaching Effects in South African Schools* (*Lloyd & Pidgeon*)

	European	African	Indian
Mean Initial IQs	103·2	86·8	86·8
Practice Gains	7·39	6·95	5·65
Additional Coaching Gains	3·21	7·60	0·45

children and the considerable practice gains of 5·6 to 7·4 IQ points in all three races. The additional gain from coaching is indeed very large in the Africans – a total rise of over 14 points – but negligible in the Indians. This surprising finding is difficult to explain though the authors suggest that it may be due to the considerable anxiety among the Indians to do well at first, and their later lack of interest in nonverbal materials.

Vernon (1967a) gave two parallel forms of three subtests in 14 top elementary school classes in Dar es Salaam. These were a Number Series test, a Figure Classification or odd-man-out, and a Matrices test in creative-response form (i.e. the pupils drew in their own responses). At the first testing the instructions were printed in English or Swahili, or read to them by an English or an African tester. The second test was given under the same or different conditions, various kinds of coaching being applied to the various classes. All scores were expressed in terms of Deviation Quotients, comparable to IQs. The main findings were:

(a) At the initial test, both the use of Swahili instead of English, and of oral as against printed instructions, improved scores on Number Series and Figure Classification by about four points, but made no difference to creative-response Matrices which is almost self-explanatory from its sample items.

(b) The effects of coaching and practice on the second test were quite variable from one class to another. It was observed that the gains were particularly high in two classes which were given a special 'pep talk' by a Swahili-speaking tester. This suggests that motivational and attitude factors are more important with unsophisticated Africans than with English top primary pupils.

(c) Overall, however, the practice effect on printed or oral tests in English averaged 3·4 points, in Swahili 4·3 points. Additional explanations or various forms of coaching by English testers produced a total rise of 5·7, and by the Swahili tester 7·0 points (i.e. including the practice effect).

(d) These effects differed somewhat in different subtests and at different levels of ability. Thus coaching was more effective than practice in Number Series especially for high scorers, whereas coaching did not specially help in the Matrices test except among low scorers. There were no consistent differences between coaching at the blackboard versus coaching individually.

(e) When compared with school gradings, the second test was not found to be more valid than the first, as Ombredane and Ortar allege. However the correlations varied with the type of coaching, and they showed a slight improvement when the second test was given in Swahili, instead of English.

(f) The overall effects of practice or additional explanations are no larger than those commonly found in experiments in the UK, and certainly smaller than those obtained by Lloyd and Pidgeon. Though the Tanzanian pupils had not taken intelligence tests previously, they had become accustomed to objective attainment tests in their secondary school selection examinations. Thus it is probable that they were able to transfer their familiarity with printed tests to new intelligence test materials.

The effects of test-unfamiliarity on different social classes in a western country have seldom been investigated, though Haggard claims to have shown that higher and lower-class American children react differently to different testing and motivating conditions He did not find, as expected, that lower-class pupils benefit more from previous practice on a group intelligence test; but they do seem to have been helped more by simplification of test materials and by oral presentation. However the issue is a complicated one since changes on retesting are always liable to be distorted by regression effects; i.e. initially low scorers tend to move up, and high scorers to move down, nearer the mean. Despite this statistical trend it is commonly found that duller children learn least from previous experience of a test, and that up to about IQ 120 the amount of improvement increases (cf. Wiseman and Wrigley). The very bright cannot usually gain so much as the moderately bright because they are too near the test ceiling.

APPENDIX C

TESTS OF LEARNING

A strong case can be made for assessing unsophisticated persons on the basis of how well they learn to do an unfamiliar problem, rather than on how well they do it before or even after instruction and practice. This should overcome the difficulty that different groups or individuals within a group will always be at different stages of familiarisation. In theory we should, as it were, be able to plot their positions on a learning curve and discount the accident of where they happened to start. Moreover we frequently want to predict how well they will learn in future. It is surely illogical to give Kohs Blocks or other performance tests to an immigrant child in a London school who speaks little or no English, and to predict how well he will learn English. Might it not be more revealing to give some task with which he is partly familiar and observe and measure the progress he makes over a period of time, i.e. to institute a teaching situation in miniature ? This should also give the tester better opportunities than does a conventional test to observe the child's methods of tackling difficulties, his attention and perseverance. It is indeed curious that we use intelligence tests mainly to predict capacity for learning and yet none of our tests involve any learning; instead they give us a cross-section of what has been learned.

There have been a number of relevant investigations, but their results are not very promising. It is quite possible to give short tests of rote memory, based on learning of paired associates, words, pictures, digits, etc. Anastasi (1930, 1932) and Thurstone have shown that these measure one or more distinctive memorising factors, and Guilford claims to have isolated 15 of such factors. However these tend to be fairly specific to the type of material and the conditions of presentation and recall. There is no evidence that they correlate with school learning, except in so far as they involve *g* or verbal ability. H. Woodrow practised two groups of subjects repeatedly on a number of simple tasks such as cancellation, anagrams, mental arithmetic and length estimation, and found that the factor content of the final scores differed considerably from that of the initial scores (much as Fleishman Hempel found in the psychomotor field). However measures of the actual gains achieved on the various tasks gave little correlation with one another, or with tests of general intelligence.

One reason for these negative results may have been that the tasks were too simple, too unlike the logical or meaningful learning involved in most school work. J. W. Tilton measured achievement in eight school subjects among fourth-grade pupils and retested them 20 months later. He was able to demonstrate considerable positive correlations, averaging ·30 (·51 when corrected for attenuation) between the gain scores, thus demonstrating a prominent general factor in school progress. Gains also correlated positively with initial achievement; i.e. those who were more able in any subject tended to progress better than those who were initially weak.

Allison (1954, 1956) and Mollenkopf, as part of a programme for selecting US Navy personnel, designed performance tests involving the learning of mechanical tasks. The subjects were instructed in assembling certain models and tested after each period of instruction. It was found that the scores predicted achievement at the end of technical training at least as well as the Navy's Basic Battery of aptitude tests, and that they were capable of adding appreciably to the predictive efficiency of the battery. Note, however, that the authors did not use actual gain or progress scores as predictors, but rather the overall scores at both early and later stages of learning.

Two large-scale investigations have been reported from the Educational Testing Service, Princeton. R. E. Stake applied a dozen learning tasks, each involving several trials, to 240 seventh-grade pupils. Both verbal and non-verbal, rote and meaningful, tasks were included, and an extensive battery of reference tests was added. Each learning task was scored for total errors or overall success, for slope of learning curve (i.e. speed of progress), and regularity of progress. The regularity measures gave mostly negligible correlations, but the success ones correlated positively both with intelligence and with scholastic achievement. On factorising his complete battery, Stake concluded that there is no general learning ability, but a number of factors for different kinds of tests, also that there is little relation between slope or rate of learning and other abilities.

Allison's study (1960) was similar, but it included a greater variety of learning tasks – psychomotor, mechanical, rote learning and concept formation – which were given to 315 adult recruits. These were scored for average rate of progress and for faster or slower progress in the second than in the first half of trials. Fairly clear learning factors were obtained among: (a) the conceptual tasks, (b) the mechanical and motor tasks and (c) rote learning; and these related to general verbal intelligence, spatial-mechanical ability and to rote memory factors respectively. However there was no evidence that they would help to predict future scholastic or occupational achievement.

In general then these results confirm Guilford's contention that learning ability is certainly not identical with intelligence, and indeed that there is no general learning ability common to all types of tasks. Rather there seem to be a number of poorly defined factors in learning progress or gain scores, and there is little indication that these possess any useful diagnostic validity. However the findings tend to be more positive when complex tasks are learned.

Mackay and Vernon carried out a study of learning tests under classroom conditions, in which nine tasks involving various kinds of meaningful learning were applied six times each to groups of eight to nine and 10–11 year pupils in an English primary school. (Two of these tasks were later abbreviated as the Word Learning and Information Learning tests in the writer's battery for cross-cultural testing.) The main findings were that the progress or gain scores were low in reliability and largely specific to the particular task. It would have taken some 20 hours of class learning tasks to achieve a measure of improvement with an overall reliability of ·80. Some of the correlations for 10–11-year-olds with achievement at the end of the school year were as follows:

Previous achievement	·830
Intelligence tests	·774
Initial performance on learning (combined) tests	·528
Final performance	·705
Gain scores	·298

These show that the gain scores yield small positive correlations with the children's later achievement, but that they were less valid than either achievement at the beginning of the year, or standard intelligence tests. More promising as predictors were the final scores, after pupils had worked at these new tasks for some time and become thoroughly familiar with them.

Now these disappointing results could probably have been anticipated on statistical grounds. First – progress scores are necessarily measures of the differences between early and late achievement, and all difference scores are weak in reliability, the more so the higher the correlation between the initial and final measures.* Secondly, it was pointed out by J. E. Anderson in 1940, and elaborated by Bloom in 1964, that because mental growth is essentially cumulative, the actual progress made in a short space of time may have little or no correlation with ability or achievement. What children can do in, say, a year's time, depends far more on what they can do now than on differences in their progress during the year. Hence the likelihood of obtaining meaningful information from short-term measures of learning, lasting an hour or so, is extremely thin. In addition it is far from easy to devise cognitive tasks covering a sufficiently wide range of difficulty for both the younger or duller, and the older or brighter, children to make measurable progress. On the other hand these results, like those of Fleishman and others, confirm the view that, when a task is unfamiliar and scores improve with practice, later scores tend to be more valid than earlier ones.

* Cf. Vernon 1960, p. 119.

XVI

Practical Conclusions

TESTING NON-WESTERN SCHOOL PUPILS

It would appear that in testing children in non-western societies who have been exposed to several years of schooling, or schooled adults, the problems of unfamiliarity of test materials and instructions are very similar to those at home. Naturally 14-year-old Africans, say, will need simpler explanations and more demonstrations than English children, because their mean performance may be equivalent to that of average English nine or ten-year-olds, and the most backward ones may score at five to six year level. The difficulties will obviously be greater if instructions have to be given in a second language such as English. But if these points are borne in mind, the same policy as is commonly adopted in the UK at the 11+ stage should generally be effective, namely to allow the pupils to take a parallel test beforehand and to spend half-an-hour or so giving additional explanations or coaching. This produces average rises in Verbal Reasoning or intelligence quotients of some five to ten points, though the figure varies considerably, depending mainly on the extent to which the pupils have become accustomed to other tests in their ordinary school work. Verhaegen & Laroche comment that there is less difficulty in getting Africans to respond to competition than there is among N. American Indians.

Wiseman and Wrigley, and others, have criticised this policy of previous coaching with some justification, on the grounds that the amount of improvement will depend on the particular teacher who does the coaching; and no doubt this would be true in preparing African or other pupils for selection tests. However studies in the UK show that practice in taking parallel tests under identical conditions is the major factor in improvement; what the tester or teacher adds to this is appreciable, but less important. Moreover it is only when testing has to be carried out on a large scale that numerous teachers, who vary greatly in efficiency, need be involved. The testing of smaller groups, for experimental research or, say, for selecting technical school apprentices, can be better controlled and the testers trained to use a uniform procedure.

When such practice is not feasible, the type and amount of explanation are important. Irvine (1966) gave the Matrices to three groups of African boys (13–16 years), (a) with ordinary instructions and a 30-minute time limit, (b) with demonstrations of sample items by flannel-graph, (c) with separate timing of the five sections so that testees did not spend too long on any one section. The mean scores were 24·8, 30·0 and 26·9 respectively; (but it is not known how closely matched the groups were in ability). Actually the scores obtained under condition (a) showed the best spread and reliability, suggesting that differences between boys in learning how to do the test are wider than differences in reasoning ability.* The tester should therefore aim to follow Schwarz's methods (described below) of teaching the testees what kind of responses to make, though his extreme elaboration may be unnecessary. Indeed, in the present writer's view, the difficulties of testing partially educated non-westerners are not so much cognitive as motivational. And Irvine agrees that the main requisite is to allay fear and suspicion by kindness, personal attention, humour and face-saving for the duller testees. Also it is particularly desirable to avoid speed stress. Provided the test is constructed at a suitable level and range of difficulty, it is less of a problem than some writers have supposed to get across what the task is through the usual techniques of explicit directions and sample items. It is true of course that we seldom know whether most or all of the testees have reached their maximum: with further practice or coaching there might be further rises. But this too applies to testing in western schools, and there is no evidence to justify the supposition that tests achieve greater validity when the testees are still more highly sophisti-cated.

TESTING THE UNEDUCATED

Much more radical modifications are needed when testing children or adults with little or no education, nor experience of written work. Among the more primitive people such as Australian aboriginees or Kalahari bushmen, the investigator cannot hope to set up a formal

---

* Elsewhere, Irvine (1967) criticizes the Matrices test as culture-biased on the grounds that different African testees were found to use varying 'strategies', i.e. some were relatively more successful on some types of items, others on others; also because the test is factorially complex. But this is equally true when it is used in the country of its origin, and indeed would apply to any other test composed of rather heterogeneous items.

testing situation. Cooperation must be won, perhaps through the influence of an administrator whom the people have learned to trust, or through long residence in the community, or by persuading the elders, giving presents, etc. (cf. Wober, 1967a). And endless time may be needed in getting across to each individual, through an interpreter, what is wanted.

Many studies are on record of the application of western performance tests such as the Pintner-Paterson battery to remote tribes. Nissen *et al.* were fairly successful in 1935 with Sousou children in French Guinea, probably because the subjects had had a little schooling. Median IQs were very low on American norms (53½ for their older group of 10–13 years), but at least they did score on all tests except Digit-Symbol. Whereas M. Fahmy, who gave a similar battery to primitive Nilotic Skillak children in Southern Sudan was unable to get scoreable responses to half the tests. Such studies nowadays seem to have gone out of fashion, since there is no satisfactory way of determining what intrinsic or extrinsic factors are responsible for failure. Current investigations are more concerned with choosing tasks relevant to an explicit hypothesis; and care is taken to prepare materials that are comprehensible and meaningful to the particular group.*

There is a large middle range in between the primitive and the literate, and here particular attention has been paid to the problems of administration by Biesheuvel and by Schwarz. The former's General Adaptability Battery (p. 78) is given to quite large groups of men, of varying language backgrounds, at a time. Apart from a simple introduction by an African tester in the local pidgin (Fanakolo) all instructions and demonstrations are given by a silent motion picture of an African miming the actions. Trays containing the materials for the first test are taken round by assistants, and afterwards removed for scoring; then the pieces for the next test are given out. In this way, conditions are standardised for all testees, and the possible anxieties or resistances aroused by white testers are avoided.

American psychologists tend to prefer group paper-and-pencil tests to performance tests, even with testees who may have had little experience of writing or drawing. (Admittedly the evidence, in western countries, suggests that the former are more reliable and can be as valid for vocational predictions as the latter.) Schwarz, of the American Institute for Research, has mainly been concerned in selecting elementary school leavers for occupational training, and has extended his testing to nonliterate adult Africans. The latter could cope with some of the

* See, for example, J. W. Berry's investigation.

tests, but schoolchildren below the age of 12 were found to be almost untestable. He soon concluded that elaborate steps were needed to get across his tests of general and specialised abilities, and that as much time, or more, should be spent on teaching the testees how to do the test as on the test itself. We will quote the main principles of administration that he has formulated, with some additional comments.

1. *The testing procedure should not pre-suppose any response as being automatic on the part of the examinee. It should include explicit provision for teaching him every response that he will be expected to make.* This includes the handling of pencils, test booklets and answer sheets, and the recording of answers.

2. *The design of the test booklet should minimise the number of constraints imposed on the examinee's performance in working from the first page to the last. Insofar as possible, instructions and cautions irrelevant to the solution of the problems should be eliminated.* Thus each test should be in a separate booklet, and testees should not need to decide for themselves when to turn over, etc. If there is more than one part or subtest, the instructions should be given separately and the part completed before proceeding to the next. This means that 'omnibus' tests are undesirable, where several types of items are mixed up and the instructions for all of them presented at the outset. Nevertheless the Spiral Nines test of general ability, devised by the National Institute for Personnel Research, is an omnibus test which has worked well in top elementary classes of African schools.*

3. *The test should not rely on any printed instructions for teaching or controlling the responses to be made. The test booklet should include no such instructions* (e.g. turn over, stop, etc.) Africans are not accustomed to receiving directions in printed form. While agreeing that oral instruction is preferable, we should recognise that this increases the dependence of the test on the clarity, intelligibility, efficiency and manner of the particular tester.

4. *The most effective means of teaching the test is through the use of visual aids, supplemented by active demonstration. These aids should explicate as closely as possible the exact operation to be performed.* Testees who have been to school are used to blackboard exposition of verbal or numerical questions and answers. But with figural materials like Matrices, large cardboard diagrams, or the flannelgraph, are preferable.

---

* In the writer's investigation of coaching and practice effects in three subtests, a major difficulty was that pupils continually turned on or turned back pages. In giving figural tests individually to very backward testees, the NIPR finds it helpful to print only one item to a page.

5. *Explanations necessary to support the demonstrations should be given through oral instructions. Such instructions must take account of idiosyncrasies in local patterns of speech and expression.* Even with groups taught in English, many of the tester's phrases may not convey the intended meaning as well as would the vernacular. On the other hand it is difficult to standardise what interpreters tell the testees.

6. *The training session should include supervised practice in doing the test problems, with a specific provision for feedback to the examinees.* Such practice and feedback must cover not only the basic task but also any variations that may be incorporated in certain of the test items. Although it was stated, above, that coaching does not add a great deal to practice, it is desirable that testees should know whether their practice is successful or not. Schwarz makes the good point that this is especially necessary in Africa where it is part of the culture pattern that children do not ask questions. Thus even when encouraged they will not admit that they are confused, or don't know what to do.

7. *To get maximum examinee cooperation, the testing procedure should differ sharply from the routines to which they are normally accustomed in school. Elements of the dramatic or flamboyant inspire the peak effort that is necessary for effective aptitude measures.* Again this sounds dangerous because of variations between examiners. However, G. C. Scott, in 1950, observed that the best way of getting good cooperation and understanding of a group oral intelligence test among Sudanese pupils was to turn it into a jolly game, while yet ensuring uniformity in the crucial instructions and test questions.

One further principle suggested by MacArthur, Irvine and Brimble is that: *Tests containing items close to immediate experience should be given first followed by more unusual and/or abstract tests.*

CONSTRUCTION OF TESTS FOR NON-WESTERN GROUPS
While western tests have often worked well in other cultural groups especially when slightly adapted to increase their intelligibility and acceptability, it is generally preferable to devise new ones locally to suit the modes of perception, the language background and concepts of the particular culture. Many psychologists have advocated this,* though few have had the time, or sufficient knowledge of the local culture, to attempt it. Too often it has been assumed that merely by cutting out language items and using pictures of local objects, animals, etc. or abstract shapes, it is possible to arrive at a suitable intelligence

* E.g. J. L. Dawson; J. Silvey (1962, 1963); Grant & Schepers.

test for Africans, Asians or others. This ignores the probability that the form of the item—the way the subject is called on to display his ability—may be unfamiliar, and that subjects may not recognise pictures as western children do. Moreover such attempts to reduce cultural bias also reduce validity. The test fails to exploit the strengths either of western or of non-western groups (as happened with the Eells Games test when given to different social-class groups). It is essential, then, to validate any such new test, to show that it predicts some useful criterion better than available western tests. To rely on internal evidence that the test is reliable, or that it shows high factor loadings, is not enough.

Even if it is decided to retain a well-known western test, on the grounds of promising validity, this could usually be improved by item analysis, since it is more likely than not that some items are misplaced for difficulty, or are less valid in the new setting and would be better eliminated or replaced. This means, of course, that direct cross-cultural comparisons will no longer be possible, and the same applies to new tests. But we have seen that such comparisons should be confined to limited purposes: there is far more scope for test development *within* cultures. Moreover if comparisons are of interest, it would generally be useful to base the test in the first instance on the more retarded group, and then find how the less retarded score, rather than the other way round. For example it would be better to use local materials and familiar operations as a starting point, instead of always resorting to designs, blocks, mazes and pictures. Alternatively it should be possible to validate a new test, and pick items that work well, in both or all the cultures concerned. This does not seem to have been attempted yet, but could well be tried out among different social classes within a western nation. Equally a single set of tests might prove feasible within most of the anglophone African countries, instead of each one trying to produce its own.

Schwarz has enunciated two further principles relevant to test construction:

8. *It is seldom possible to predict on logical grounds which tasks foreign examinees can and cannot do. Each new test should be subjected to thorough experimental investigation.* This we have already stressed.

9. *Preference should be given to items that are reasonably independent of individual differences in the tactics or strategies of the examinees. It is usually not possible to enforce a uniform strategy that will be followed by the whole group.* Here he is particularly referring to long tests, where unsophisticated testees may not budget their time wisely; hence his preference for short ones, each with its own instructions.

A few examples of sound procedure may be quoted. G. C. Scott translated the Ballard Oral Group Test for Juniors into Arabic, but found it quite unsuitable in Sudanese schools. Many items were unintelligible or non-discriminating, or failed to show any improvement in performance with age. There was the additional difficulty that conversational and written (classical) Arabic differ considerably: the children often did not know the latter, and had not seen the former written down. Scott therefore started afresh from a small pool of the more promising items and devised and tried out a very large number of new ones which got across easily, which showed suitable difficulty and improvement with age, and which correlated with total score. He also introduced a long 'warm-up' and practice period. As a result, good correlations were obtained between test scores and teachers' estimates of the capacity of the pupils for more advanced education. Similarly, at a higher level, a Moray House verbal group test worked very badly, particularly when given with a time limit. There was no correlation at all between number of items attempted and number right. But by rebuilding it and by successive trials of additional items, a satisfactory instrument was obtained, which also correlated highly with the oral test.

More recently, Brimble has constructed a practicable pictorial group test for selecting illiterate African adults who might benefit from adult education classes. While retaining conventional item-types such as Analogies, Classification, Series, Absurdities, etc. (on the basis of previous validatory evidence), he took the precaution of submitting all the pictures to illiterate villagers and rejecting those that they failed to recognise. Though direct validation was not possible, the test gave a promising correlation of ·68 with English and arithmetic marks among Standard IV pupils.

In a very different context, Doppelt and Bennett set out to produce a test of general employability or trainability for disadvantaged youths and workers, based as far as possible on culturally familiar materials, e.g. reading notices such as 'No Parking', picture vocabulary, following street maps, etc. These are given orally by tape, both so as to reduce educational difficulties and to avoid the anxiety and resentment engendered by a superior-class tester; and many easy items are included so as to increase confidence. Note that there is no assumption that the test is measuring g or other defined faculties; it is based more on a job analysis showing that adaptable workers do need to understand oral, and sometimes written, instructions, to find their way about, to cope with numbers in bills, and so on. Silvey (1963) similarly urges the abandonment of the notion that a conventional intelligence test is the most useful addition to the English and arithmetic tests or examinations commonly used in selecting for African secondary schools; likewise the belief that one and the same intelligence test can validly predict both educational and vocational aptitudes. A better test, or battery, for educational purposes might be based on an analysis of those academic skills that secondary schooling requires (or ought to require if it was less formal and syllabus bound). Thus it should tap imaginative, creative ideas as well as logical thinking; it should encourage discovery – what information is needed to solve problems, and judgment as to which deductions are true. Note however that all such tests do require external validation, however difficult to obtain; otherwise they may measure quite different abilities from those intended. Also there is still plenty of room, especially in research studies, for tests aimed at particular aspects of perception and thinking.

The major difficulty in local test construction is, of course, that the underdeveloped countries possess very few trained psychologists. Nevertheless some are coming forward, and there are many others, e.g. teachers and inspectors, who could help in the initial formulation of items which would be more appropriate to local modes of thought than items produced by westerners. The western psychologist could then apply the standard techniques of item analysis, validation and standardisation. The Educational Testing Service, Princeton, N.J., has helped to set up training centres in certain countries such as Malaysia;* and many teachers and others from all over the world have obtained training, particularly in achievement testing, at Princeton or in British or American universities. There is some danger, of course, that they may imbibe too many western conventions about tests, such as the American notion that almost all tests must be multiple-choice ones with machine-scored answer sheets.

In standardising new tests in developing countries, it would be quite unrealistic to attempt to provide national norms for successive age groups as in western countries, even if accurate records of age were available. The best that can be done is to collect distributions of scores for specified groups of reasonably homogeneous background and education. But the tester will still be faced with tricky problems when members of different groups are to be compared, and will need to tackle them along the lines discussed by Langenhoven (Chapter XIV). In the limited circumstances of selection for secondary schools, where all candidates have completed top elementary Standard, Irvine (1965)

* Cf. Chapter by M. J. Wantman, in A. Taylor's book.

points out that a correction could be based on the number of years needed to reach that Standard, instead of on age.

TESTING IMMIGRANT PUPILS OR OTHER MULTILINGUAL GROUPS

When teachers in Britain, or elsewhere, are faced with an influx of children from other cultures of any age from 5 to 15, speaking little or no standard English, but a variety of foreign tongues, they naturally ask whether the psychologist can assess these pupils' potential educability. Are they permanently handicapped, either genetically or because they have been brought up under deprived conditions, or can they be expected to make good progress as soon as they have become more fluent with the English medium? Which children, if any, would be better placed in Special Schools, or in remedial classes? For various reasons which have been elaborated in earlier Chapters, the psychologist cannot provide reliable answers, but obviously he should try to help. Usually his thoughts tend to turn first to non-verbal materials such as WISC Performance, Progressive Matrices, or to picture tests such as Moray House and Sleight. Some of these, at least, can fairly readily be adapted to be given by mime, or better by a tester who has some facility in the children's mother-tongue. But clearly the rationale of this approach is unsound; the psychologist is still thinking in terms of some mental entity, intelligence which, if elicited through a non-language medium, will enable him to predict the child's capacities in highly verbal tasks. Ortar (1963) has been faced with much the same problem of assessing multilingual immigrants of varied cultural background in Israel, and concludes that, among the following types of test materials, (a) and (b) are the most culture-bound and most unsuitable:

(a) Pictures or models (as in the WISC Object Assembly).

(b) Abstract performance materials (Cubes, Formboards, etc.) are slightly less dependent on cultural interpretations.

(c) Abstract paper-and-pencil materials.

(d) Language materials can be translated and can much more successfully convey similar meanings to different cultural groups.

(e) Number materials seem to be most 'universal' across groups who have been exposed to any schooling.

This also, of course, fits in with the suggestion, above, that for educational predictions it is preferable to sample educational skills. An example may be quoted from the writer's investigations in Jamaica: five tests which could be got across with very little language – Matrices, WISC Kohs, Porteus Mazes, Design Reproduction and Draw-a-Man (cf. Chapter XVII) yielded an average correlation of ·59 with the school achievement in English and arithmetic of 10–11 year boys. Or if all five were combined, the figure rose to ·74. But a simple group test based on the rote learning of a list of monosyllables gave a correlation of ·83. Presumably the latter could have been applied in a non-English language by a tester who could speak it. Moreover in some of the writer's other groups, e.g. Ugandans, the non-verbal tests were considerably less predictive of educational performance than with Jamaicans, and this might well be true of Indian and Pakistani immigrants to Britain.

It follows that the safest basis for assessing the immigrant child's future educability is to observe the actual progress he makes in acquiring the new language and in school achievement and adjustment over a year, or indeed as long as possible. But of course this is unstandardised; it depends greatly on the teacher's subjective impressions, and will be much affected by the kind and amount of help the pupil has received over the period. In the case of pupils who have enough English to be able to communicate with a psychological tester, the ordinary individual intelligence test such as WISC Verbal and standard attainment tests are likely to be highly diagnostic, though their results must be interpreted in the light of the child's background, how long he has been in the country and what kind of schooling he has received in the country of his birth as well as here. But when communication is virtually impossible, testers who can speak the mother-tongue should be recruited and trained, and similar tests constructed in the appropriate languages, for example tests of vocabulary, general information, comprehension, arithmetic (mechanical, problem and number series), and probably the word-learning test just referred to. There is not much evidence regarding the validity of such tests couched in the mother-tongue for predicting learning in a second language. But, in a very different context, E. T. Prothro showed that an Arabic vocabulary test, given to Arab students at an English-medium university, correlated slightly better with their course grades than did an English vocabulary test.

However tests such as these would take a long time to prepare, hence there is a case for limited and cautious use of performance or non-verbal tests, generally avoiding pictures. Probably the five already mentioned are among the most promising for immigrant children of about 8 to 13, but few if any are available below seven years.* The

* The individual Coloured Progressive Matrices will go down to lower ability levels than the writer's test, but takes longer to give. Ord's two-dimensional

investigations described in Part V show not only that all-round test performance is lowered by adverse conditions such as poor cultural level and planfulness of the home, and lack of encouragement of initiative, but also that specific cultural factors may affect particular tests – for instance the structural characteristics of the mother tongue, practice in artistic expression, access to toys and comics, familiarity with tracking, etc. Hence a rather varied battery of tests will help to offset such specific biases. Another advantage of performance tests is that they provide the tester with opportunities to observe the child's mode of response to difficulties. His understanding of instructions, the way he tackles problems, and his persistence may be to some extent diagnostic of the way he reacts to schooling. But whatever tests are used, the interpetation of their results must be largely a matter of clinical judgment, of weighing the scores against the likely effects of abnormalities of home upbringing, linguistic history and education. There is no point in trying to assign a single IQ to a child whose abilities are, one hopes, improving rapidly. But the scores on a range of tests, combined with observations of current adjustment and a thorough case study of the child's history should make possible some extrapolations to the future.

ATTAINMENT AND SPECIAL APTITUDE TESTS

The development of objective achievement tests is forging ahead especially rapidly in African and West Indian countries, where the numbers of pupils wishing to enter secondary schools, or to take General Certificate of Education examinations, are becoming so large that it is hardly possible to mark conventional examinations with sufficient speed and reliability.* Although most schools are geared to a UK grammar school type of syllabus, it is obvious that local variations in content and approach can be better allowed for by tests constructed on the spot than by taking over British ones, especially as published norms for the latter will have little meaning. When first introduced the objective form of test will give rise to difficulties, especially among pupils in the smaller, more backward, schools in remote areas, though these can be overcome fairly readily by allowing reasonable practice. The short-answer type of item (cf. Vernon, 1960) is generally preferable to the multiple-choice,

---

Kohs should be made available, and renormed for English children. A standard scoring scheme should be worked out for Bender-Gestalt or other Design Reproduction test and norms accumulated. The Draw-a-Man test revised by D. B. Harris, and Porteus Mazes can be used according to the authors' instructions.

* Cf. D. W. Grieve; and A. Taylor.

though it requires somewhat more skilled and lengthier scoring; and there is seldom any need to impose time limits that require working at speed. In fact the scoring of multiple-choice tests is not as straightforward in developing countries as western educationists might assume; poorly qualified office workers and even elementary teachers are liable to make a lot of mistakes. Several countries are tempted to try machine-scored tests because of the enormous burden of hand-scoring. Obviously this greatly exacerbates the difficulties of the not-too-bright pupil in entering his answer in the right box on the separate answer sheet; hence this system has never been adopted even with top primary pupils in England. Though prior training would no doubt help, a better compromise seems to be to let the pupil indicate his responses on the question paper and then have a clerk or teacher transfer these to the appropriate spaces on the machine-scorable sheet or punched card.

There is a great need for tests of aptitudes for particular trades or for technical training in underdeveloped countries. But this is particularly difficult to meet because of inadequate development of relevant skills among most of the eligible population. The situation is similar to that in intelligence testing where, as is well known, we cannot predict future reasoning capacities by means of infant tests which mainly sample perceptuomotor schemata. We have to wait till children have acquired the rudiments of verbal thinking. Again musical ability cannot be predicted as accurately by Seashore's tests of auditory sensitivities as by tests based on musical materials. Hence we cannot expect to predict ability at mechanical jobs except by tests that sample the skills involved in these jobs. Any test of so-called aptitude is, in fact, a test of achievement in the slightly lower-level skills that will eventually be integrated into the required ability. But Africans have had far less opportunity than westerners of gaining experience of materials and their properties, or of handling and working with mechanical or similar objects. Tests of spatial judgment, of general reasoning, even of verbal and arithmetical attainments may be of some help, but they will not separate off the boy who would do better in technical than in academic courses. Most skilled jobs do involve working with ideas, numbers and spatial concepts, hence paper-and-pencil tests of the type Schwarz has developed show useful validity in selecting moderate to high grade technicians. Manipulatory tests such as those used by MacDonald and Biesheuvel may also contribute, though it is more likely that they are measuring acculturation and general intellectual development than relevant practical skills. Probably better tests could be constructed by searching for operations already familiar within the culture where the candidates have had opportunities to develop practical facility. Even in fairly primitive peasant societies, quite a wide range of operations in agriculture, house-building, making utensils and ornaments, might be sampled. This does not seem to have been attempted. There is of course the further difficulty that manual abilities tend to be highly specific; there are *dexterities* rather than a general dexterity for working with things, handling tools and machines. A better alternative might be to provide more opportunities for hand-work and constructional tasks in the upper elementary classes and lower secondary forms, so that boys could begin to build up the necessary contributory skills, and discover their own inclinations towards technical jobs. This would probably provide a better basis for selection for more advanced training than any aptitude tests.

PART IV
Studies in Britain

XVII

THE TESTS

Parts IV and V are largely concerned with detailed methods and results. Though written as simply, and with as few Tables, as possible, the general reader may prefer to skim most of Chapters XVII–XIX, XXII, XXIV and XXVII.

The battery of tests used in the present writer's studies was chosen chiefly with a view to covering a wide range of intellectual abilities in a fairly short space of time. Each test should be brief, though reasonably reliable, and should be suitable for a (British) Mental Age range of roughly 6 to 13 years, so that it could be got across to 11-year-boys who might be considerably retarded. The groups to be tested would all have had several years of schooling in the English medium, hence it was possible to include some conventional group tests of educational attainments. But the main weight was placed on individual tests, since it was felt that individual testing, along the lines of the Stanford-Binet, would make it easier to ensure that the instructions were properly understood by the boys, and the boys' responses by the tester, and that they were well motivated and interested. Most of the written group tests and individual verbal tests were given by Mrs D. Vernon, whose experience as a teacher and whose facility in picking up local accents were valuable in securing the cooperation of suspicious pupils, or those weak in English. Group sessions were usually confined to 20 boys or less at a time, and an additional tester was there to help any who appeared not to understand. Most of the non-verbal or performance tests were given by the writer. But in each field trip outside England, one or more local students or members of the staff of Education Departments were enlisted, who had a good knowledge of the boys' background. They undertook the interviewing, which was designed to find out something of the home conditions, previous schooling and interests of each boy; also they gave the 'creativity' or other tests which raised the greatest difficulties of communication. Only one test was speeded, though most of the group tests had time limits sufficient for practically all boys to reach their limits. Note that no so-called intelligence tests were included, since the main emphasis of the investigation was on contrasted patterns of abilities in different groups, not on whether one group was generally superior or inferior to another.

The total battery normally occupied two group sessions of about an hour each, and three individual sessions of about three-quarters of an hour though much of course depended on the 'quickness in the uptake' of the particular group or individual. Thus by going all out it was just possible to deal with a sample of 50 in two weeks (ten working days), provided careful arrangements had been made beforehand for picking a representative sample of boys who fell within the required age range, for getting them to suitable testing rooms on time, and provided absences and illnesses did not interfere – as they often did. Naturally we usually arranged to have more leeway.

VERBAL AND EDUCATIONAL TESTS

1. *Arithmetic.* The first 40 items from Vernon's Graded Arithmetic-Mathematics test, covering the four rules, weights and measures, elementary operations and problems (items of similar difficulty were substituted for £.s.d. in Canada). This provided an easy opening to the sessions as all pupils had done similar work in class. The test was unspeeded, but almost all had reached their limit in 16 minutes.

2. *English.* Three subtests were taken from a test constructed by L. H. E. Reid for surveying attainments in Jamaica:

(i) Reading comprehension: sentences with one missing word to be written in.

The skies are blue and the sun ——— brightly all day.

(ii) Usage: sentences representing common errors, with four-choice alternatives for one word.

He (swim, swam, swum, swimmed) across the harbour last week.

(iii) Parts of Speech: the appropriate modification (past tense, plural, etc.) of the word in capitals to be written in the blank space.

(DRAW) I ——— water from the tank yesterday.

Each subtest was thoroughly demonstrated at the blackboard, and individual help given where needed. Total working time was 16 mins. for 50 items.

3. *Spelling*. Twenty sentences with one word wrongly spelt, to be underlined and written out correctly (six mins).

I told the gerls to sit. ——

4. *Vocabulary* (Group). Mill Hill Junior Form A, containing 33 multiple choice items. Ten minutes were found sufficient.

5. *Vocabulary* (Terman-Merrill), given individually in the usual way, the pupil supplying his own definitions in his own time.

6. *Word Learning*. After preliminary practice in learning and writing out a list of 6 monosyllabic verbs, pupils were given a list of 20 verbs, which they studied for 5 mins. and then wrote out as many as they could, if possible in correct order. Another 2 minutes' study was given and another reproduction (See Appendix D).

7. *Information Learning*. After some practice items, the tester read out slowly a list of 15 'facts' (App. D), emphasising the critical words, e.g.:

A barrel of beer holds 36 gallons – 36 gallons.

Thereafter a question was asked on each fact, in a different order:

How many gallons are there in a barrel of beer?

A further reading and a set of questions in another order followed.

INDUCTION TESTS

8. *Abstraction*. A simpler version of the Shipley test of letter, number and word series, where the subject writes 'what comes next'. One letter or number is to be written over each dot:

9   8   7   6   5   .
bad B   sad S   lad L   had .
hot cold   wet dry   fast slow   down . .

There are 40 items; pupils reach their limit by 13 to 15 minutes.

All the remaining tests were given individually, except that Draw-a-Man, the Gottschaldt Embedded Figures, and Design Reproduction were sometimes done in group form with more sophisticated groups.

9. *Matrices* (creative response, see Fig. 4). A similar set of 24 non-verbal items based on Xs and Os, or on abstract shapes. These had been tried out and item-analysed in an English primary school. The subject draws in 'what comes next'. When he fails an early item, it is explained

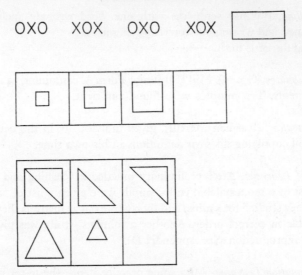

Fig. 4. Items from Creative-Response Matrices Test.

to him in order to instruct him how to tackle later ones. Thus in both Induction tests, the initial task is extremely simple and the subject learns how to do the test as he goes along.

CONCEPT DEVELOPMENT

10. *Sorting* (cf. Goldstein & Scheerer). Twenty common objects were spread out randomly, namely: a pencil, cigarette, box of matches, bar of chocolate, wooden bear, plastic cow, woollen tiger, orange, leaf, twig, plastic flower, nail scissors, watch, toy motor, pingpong ball, plastic cup, spoon, penny, large nail, and metal wheel. (Other more appropriate animals were substituted in Canada.) The subject was instructed to put together into groups any things which are alike in some way, to add others that 'belong', and to name the groups or say why they are alike. If further regroupings do not occur spontaneously, the tester picks out various sets (up to a total of ten), asks if they are alike and why, and if any more can be added.

Various methods of scoring were tried;* eventually the most reliable seemed to be to distinguish three grades of abstraction:

Class Names, e.g. wild or four-legged animals, models (scored 2)
Common Concrete Properties, e.g. make noises, fight, move, in zoos
(scored 1)

* Cf. M. Annett; J. Kagan *et al.*

Associations or Common Use, e.g. You use the match to light the
cigarette (scored o).

The number of objects in each group* was multiplied by 2, 1 or 0 and
totalled.

1. *Piaget Battery.* A set of 13 tasks was selected, representing a wide
range of concepts which, according to Piaget's writings, and the studies
by Lovell (1961), Hyde, Goodnow and others, show a clear progression
in stages of response between about 6 and 11 years. They were also
chosen for brevity and for ease in evaluating the response without
extensive 'clinical' enquiry; that is, they were given with sufficient
questioning only to ensure that the subject had or had not grasped the
concept.†

(a) *Time Concepts,* including day after tomorrow, day and time in
another town, why a watch has two hands.

(b) *Left and Right,* pointing to tester's right ear, and stating whether
each of three objects is to the L or R of another.

(c) *Equidistant Counters,* placing a number of green counters equidistant from the tester's and the subject's red counters.

(d) *Logical Inclusion.* White and blue squares and blue circles;
several questions such as – 'Are there more circles or more blue things?
Why?'

(e) *Tilted Bottle.* A half-filled bottle is seen upright, then half-hidden
and tilted, or on its side. S draws the water surface on an outline picture.

(f) *Conservation of Liquid.* Water is poured from one of two half-
filled beakers into a tall glass or a flat dish. Which has more? Why?

(g) *Conservation of Plasticine.* Two equal balls: S rolls his into a
sausage. Who has more? In addition one ball is flattened into a plate
and S is asked, if both were dropped into the water beakers, what would
happen to the level of water.

(h) *Insect Problem.* The tester draws an insect on top of a circle
representing the edge of a jar. S is asked to draw what it would look like
if it walked round the rim to the bottom.

(i) *Number Concepts.* Cards are presented with the numbers 3, 2 and 5.
What is the biggest number you could make with these? Also with the
numbers 28493.

(j) *Conservation of Lengths.* Two equal-sized rods; does alteration of
their relative positions affect the length?

* Up to a maximum of five objects. Where a grouping was suggested by the
tester, one was subtracted from the number of objects in that group.

† Detailed questions, and the responses of English and Jamaican boys are
given in Vernon 1965a.

(k) *Dot Problem*. S is asked to make a dot in the same position on a sheet of paper as one drawn on the tester's sheet. Scored for left-right reversal, and for use of ruler or other means of fixing the correct position.

(l) *Shadow*. S inserts the shadow on a drawing of a lamp and a man; scored for correctness of position, and length.

(m) *Conservation of Area*. Two fields (green blotting paper), 2 cows and 12 houses (white blocks); houses are scattered on one field, along the edge of the other. Which cow has more grass to eat, and why?

'CREATIVITY' TESTS

These were introduced into the battery, not so much because it was thought that imagination or originality could be meaningfully measured across cultures, as because it was hoped that the tests would give low correlations with the more conventional tests, i.e. they would measure an independent factor or factors. Four tests were given individually, taking about five minutes each, but with no stress on time.*

12. Three of the *Rorschach Inkblots* (Nos. V, III and VIII) were used as a test of imagination, not a projective device. Total responses and proportion of unusual responses (given by less than ten per cent of normal subjects) were scored, together with certain other categories: A per cent (animal), H per cent (human and anatomical), Dd per cent (rare detail), P per cent (perseverative).

13. Six of *Torrance's Incomplete Drawings*, which the subject is asked to make into pictures of anything he likes. Each one is scored for unusualness or cleverness vs. unimaginativeness, and for degree of elaboration (U and E scores).

14. An empty, clean dog-food or baked bean *Tin Can* is shown, with lid attached, and the subject is asked what he could do with it, and encouraged to produce as many uses as possible. This is scored for total different suggestions (N), for proportion of rare or clever uses (U per cent), and proportion of perseverative suggestions, involving no change of category (P per cent).

* Thus the conditions resembled those recommended by Wallach and Kogan, as conducive to creative responses. Fuller details of scoring these four tests have been published elsewhere (Vernon 1966b).

15. 'If you had *Wings* and could fly, what would you like to do and see?' The subject is encouraged to produce as wide a range of suggestions as possible. Scoring is for N – total responses, P – perseverative or repetitive suggestions, Ae per cent – proportion of activities involving own enjoyment or profit, Ah + As per cent – activities involving helping others or studying things, and U + E per cent – proportion of clever or unusual responses and of responses with elaborate descriptions.

PERCEPTUAL AND SPATIAL TESTS

16. *Porteus Mazes*, the standard series from V or VI to XIV. With a group of 100 English boys, the usual procedure, where a fresh maze is given as soon as an error is made, was applied to half the cases at random. But the other half were given only one copy of each maze and allowed to correct their errors. Since the two methods were found to yield almost identical score distributions, the second, more economical one was followed elsewhere. Possibly this was a mistake, which altered the essential character of the test, even if it did not make it too easy.

17. *Picture Recognition.* Ten drawings of objects or scenes are presented, whose recognition requires the interpretation of perspective, superimposition or other three-dimensional cues; for example, a nearby aeroplane and a distant airport, a boy walking along a road and a man further back, a chain of mountains in a valley. Some of Hudson's (cf. Fig. 2) and J. L. Dawson's series were included, and redrawn for Canadians. Errors of perception were scored 1, ½ or 0.

18. *Gottschaldt (Embedded) Figures Test.* A 21-item test was constructed and item-analysed on the basis of trials in English schools. In each item a simple figure is shown on the left; the subject has to perceive this

Fig. 5. Item from Gottschaldt Embedded Figures Test.

within the more complex figure on the right (cf. Fig. 5), and trace it out there with red pencil. Note that the procedure differs both from Witkin's, where the simple figure has to be memorised, not compared perceptually, and from Thurstone's, where multiple-choice responses are offered. There is no time limit, though most boys complete all they can do in under 12 minutes.

19. *Design Reproduction*. Four drawings (A, 4, 5 and 6) from the Bender-Gestalt test are copied, followed by the two Memory for Designs items in Terman–Merrill (M.IX.1 and L.IX.3). When given as a group test in the UK, the demonstration drawings were magnified to about six times the original size. For each of the eight figures, four to six common structural errors were listed and carefully defined, and each subject was scored for the total of such errors.

20. *Kohs Block Designs*. The WISC designs were used, but with certain modifications in procedure suggested by Goldstein & Scheerer, and developed by McConnell, and Jahoda (1956). Models A and B and Card 1 were given as usual, but if the subject failed on Card 1 or any later card:

(a) The tester demonstrated the model, destroyed it and asked S to try again.

(b) The tester made the model and left it for S to copy.

(c) The tester made it again and if S still failed on two successive cards, the test was abandoned. Wechsler's scoring according to time was applied, but if (a) was needed 1 point was given, (b) or (c) 0 points.

21. *Draw-a-Man*. The standard Goodenough instructions and scoring were used, D. B. Harris's more reliable version not having appeared when the work started. In addition, a scale of 20 points was extracted from Witkin's description of the field-independent child's drawings (See Appendix D).

22. *Vernon Formboard*. This consists of seven wooden triangles or rectangles, and seven different matrices into each of which all the pieces can be fitted. The median times for solving successive matrices range from 15 seconds to about 2 minutes, and scores from 0 to 5 are awarded for various speeds of completion of each matrix. If a subject works unsuccessfully at filling any one hole for over 30 secs., he can be shown the location of a key piece, and 30 more secs. are added to his total time for that matrix. This was the only speeded test, and it was usually given at the end as being the most popular.

23. *Mischel's Delayed Gratification Test*. Although no attempt was made to test personality qualities or attitudes, W. Mischel's chocolate

test was included as a form of reward to the boys. At the first individual session each boy was offered a 6d. or 10c. bar of chocolate now, or one double the size if he waited till the tests were completed a week or so later.

INTERVIEWING

A semistructured interview with each boy was designed to supply information from which ratings could be made of the background variables listed below. The questions were adapted to suit local conditions, and supplementary information, e.g. on health, school attendance and home conditions, was obtained from the Head or class teacher.

A. *Regularity of Schooling:* age of starting school, moves, absences through illness, truancy, withholding, etc.

B. *Health and General Physical Development,* illnesses, malnutrition.

C. *Unbroken Home* (Nuclear Family) vs. step-parent, desertion, father-absence, mother at work. Questions were asked on family structure, who lives in the home – grandparents, additional relatives, etc., and who looks after the boy.

D. *Socioeconomic Status.* Father's job, others employed in the family, type of housing, overcrowding.

E. *Cultural Stimulus.* Parents' and siblings' level of education; books and periodicals in the home, use of library, visits to places of interest; parental aspirations for the boy; cooperation with the school and help with homework.

F. *Linguistic Background.* Language predominantly spoken at home, or with peers; if English – encouragement of good speech.

G. *Initiative.* The emphasis was intended to be on parental encouragement vs. over-protectiveness. In practice the rating referred chiefly to the adventurousness of the boy's leisure pursuits and vocational aspirations vs. passivity.

H. *Male Dominance.* This was intended as an assessment of identification with the father (or male substitute) vs. stronger influence of the mother; but it was difficult to dissociate this from the person who made the main decisions in the household.

I. *Planfulness.* Rational, democratic home atmosphere and upbringing vs. improvident, feckless, impulsive. Being based mainly on indirect clues from the boy's description of the home, his household responsibilities, what he did with his pocket money, vocational plans, etc. and on teachers' assessments, this was particularly impressionistic. Indeed G, H and I are all likely to be fairly unreliable.

It might be thought essential to evaluate all these factors by means of parental interviews and home observations. But apart from the expense and time, it would be virtually impossible to obtain the cooperation of many parents. This is especially true in England where, owing to the natural caution of head teachers and Education Officers, the questioning of boys had to be confined mainly to such 'safe' topics as leisure time activities, including household chores, books and cultural activities and vocational plans. Moreover, on general psychological grounds the writer (cf. Vernon, 1964) would contest the fruitfulness of enquiring into details of training in early infancy, which has been stressed in many researches on child development. The general climate and values of the home throughout childhood and up to the present time are likely to be more relevant to the current level of intelligence, and these can be judged fairly effectively by questioning a 10–11 year old boy and his teachers.

SCORING

Each of the above tests is scored on a different scale, and for only a few of them are norms from western sources available. In order to find whether any group was more advanced or retarded in one type of ability than another, it was essential to refer them to some common scale, and this was provided by the score distributions in the group of 100 10–11 year boys in S.E. England. This group represents the level of ability achieved when boys are reared in an economically prosperous and reasonably healthy environment and receive good, up-to-date schooling from the age of five. Each test score in the English group was therefore converted to a Deviation Quotient for this age group, with a Standard Deviation of 15, so as to be comparable to a conventional IQ. In other words the English average was fixed at 100 for every test, and lower or higher scores were equated with DQs ranging from about 140 to 60 (cf. Appendix D).

APPENDIX D

TEST MATERIALS AND SCORING

Word Learning. The practice series of words was:

do
send
fix
walk
hit
show

The main list was:

burn	fly
eat	love
bite	miss
begin	call
add	buy
blow	live
break	say
try	jump
run	tie
come	give

Each correct word, regardless of spelling, counted 1½, but only 1 if it followed a word *later* in the list. Thus the total for two reproductions was 60.

Information. The practice items were:

1. In America you have to pay 2 *dollars* to get your hair cut.
2. There is a beautiful flower called a begonia which has bright *red* blossoms.
3. The distance from London to New York is about *3,000* miles.

The main list was:

1. In 1962, Christmas Day fell on a *Tuesday.*
2. A grown-up dog usually has *42* teeth.
3. There is a famous gorilla in the London Zoo, whose name is *Guy.*
4. The first three letters on the bottom row of a typewriter are *ZXC.*
5. Cadmium is a *yellow* colour.
6. A barrel of beer holds *36* gallons.
7. By combining hydrogen and oxygen in the right proportions we can make *water.*
8. The ordinary air fare from London to New York is *£85.*
9. Easter Day next year is on *April* 10*th.*
10. A hydrangea is a kind of bush with *blue* or *pink* flowers.
11. Helium is a *gas.*
12. The bible tells us that Noah's ark landed on Mount Ararat. The height of this mountain is *17,000 feet.*
13. Mozart's 40th symphony was written in the key of *G.*
14. There are *39* books in the Old Testament of the Bible.
15. The Civil War in America began in the year *1861.*

Draw-a-Man. Body sophistication scale based on Witkin: 1 point is awarded for each of the following.

1. Trunk better than circle, oval, rectangle or triangle.

2. Trunk shaped, e.g. waist shown.
3. Shoulders clearly shown.
4. Head and neck shaped, integrated with trunk.
5. Arms better than sticks or ovals; no gross asymmetry.
6. Legs better than sticks or ovals; no gross asymmetry.
7. Arms integrated with body, not misplaced, overlapping or detached.
8. Legs integrated with body not misplaced, overlapping or detached.
9. Nose better than dot or line.
10. Eyes ditto, e.g. with brows and/or pupil.
11. Ears, fair proportion and detail.
12. Hands, distinct from fingers and arms.
13. Fingers better than claws or prongs.
14. Clothing better than belt or buttons.
15. Complete and consistent clothing.
16. Complete and consistent shoes.
17. Reasonable proportioning of head and limbs to trunk.
18. Some facial expression.
19. Figure in action.
20. Consistent accessories, e.g. cigarette, gun, etc.

Though precise standards for passing or failing these points are not laid down, all the scoring was done by the writer in order to maintain consistency.

Score Conversions. As an example, the median scores on the English test of English boys and Eskimos were $40\frac{1}{2}$ and 22 respectively. Now only 16 per cent of English boys score at or below 22, and in a normal distribution the 16th percentile is 1 SD or 15 DQ points below the mean. Thus the Eskimo score is equivalent to an English DQ of 85. Similarly in this test it was found that a score of 46 corresponds to a DQ of 115, a score of 3 to a DQ of 70, and so on. The conversion tables for several of the tests are listed below, in Appendix F, Table 10.

The actual technique of preparing the tables was to calculate the SDs of the English distribution *below the median*, and then to adjust these to 15. The simpler method of going direct from percentiles to DQs was unsatisfactory since, with a group of only 100 it is obviously impossible to fix DQs in the 60 to 75 or so range with any accuracy. Above the median, however, few of the tests had a high ceiling, hence the SDs were curtailed (i.e. the distributions were mostly negatively skewed). And as few conversions above 100 were needed, the percentile level of each score was obtained and its sigma-score equivalent read off from Normal Curve Tables.

This mode of scoring might seem open to criticism in so far as it suggests that we are chiefly concerned with measuring the inferiority of non-western groups. For example the Indians' Vocabulary DQ of 70 indicates that they average at the mental deficiency borderline on English standards. But this is not the prime intention; rather it provides a means of showing that, in terms of western standards, Indians are much better at Mazes, Draw-a-Man and other tests than at Vocabulary. We could perhaps have based a DQ scale on the combined distributions from nonwestern groups by themselves, but this would obviously be affected by the particular choice of groups, whereas the English sample is well-defined. Incidentally the result would have been to push up the English medians to various figures between 100 and say 120, which would not be very meaningful.

In the writer's view a more serious drawback than using the English medians on each test as a baseline is using the English variances. For example, English boys seem to range very widely on the Sorting test, whereas they are relatively homogeneous in Vocabulary. The result is that no non-western group scores very low on Sorting, whereas Vocabulary medians are all near the bottom of the English range. Presumably there is stronger cultural pressure towards Vocabulary development in England, but of course we have no means of attaining absolute measures of variance. What might be preferable would be to refer scores on all tests to an age scale, instead of to the distributions in a single age group. Thus we might conceivably have found the Indian Sorting test performance equivalent to English 7·0 year level, like their Vocabulary performance, instead of to DQs of 91 and 70 respectively. This would have been advantageous in so far as the chronological ages of the various samples were not entirely uniform, and age differences had to be ignored throughout. But if the writer had attempted to give every test to representative samples of English 6- to 12-year-olds, say, he would never have got started on testing abroad.

XVIII

What the Tests Measure

When using a number of varied mental tests, it is always tempting to guess at the underlying abilities.* For example Word and Information Learning *appear* to involve memory, and it is easy to assume that they will reflect the emphasis laid by the education system of the country on mechanical learning. Similarly Picture Recognition may be assumed to measure the three-dimensional perception which is necessary, not only for interpreting line drawings, but also for technical jobs. How far it is possible to generalise to abilities in daily life, at school or in jobs can, of course, best be determined by follow-up correlations with external criteria; and most of the tests (or closely similar ones) have been studied in this way in numerous previous researches so that we have a fair idea of what they measure, at least in western cultures. Also the results reported below on group differences, for example the high score of Jamaicans on Word Learning and the low score of Ugandans on Picture Recognition, supply confirmatory evidence, though obviously here one is in danger of arguing in a circle.

But in addition it is helpful to analyse the correlations among the tests themselves, in order to find the main underlying dimensions. As shown in Chapter IV, we want to know if Picture Recognition depends largely on *g* or general ability, or if it measures much the same spatial factor as the other perceptual and practical tests. It may quite possibly involve other minor group factors, say three-dimensional recognition, which are not yet fully identified. And we can be sure that there is a considerable specific element – ability at this particular test – together with chance errors, which have no interesting wider reference.

Unfortunately the factorial approach is less convincing than it should be because of the differing views both on techniques of factor analysis, and on the main factors to be accepted. However in this instance the factor pattern in the English group was pretty straightforward; and though there were important differences in other groups

* Cf. Vernon 1961, pp. 46–8.

(showing that the same tests do not always measure the same abilities in other cultural contexts) there was also considerable resemblance.

The detailed figures for English boys have been published elsewhere (Vernon 1965a), and a specimen analysis for one of the samples – the Eskimos – is presented in Table 13. As always happens in a representative age-group like the English sample, the spread of ability is wide, and this results in a large *g* or general ability factor, present to a greater or lesser extent in every test. *Abstraction* and *Matrices* are generally the most highly loaded; they are fairly pure *g* tests, though the former often shows some verbal, the latter some spatial, component. Arithmetic, Kohs Blocks and Piaget Total run them very close; whereas most verbal and perceptual tests have lower loadings around ·5 to ·6 and 'creativity' measures lower still. In other groups the same wide-ranging *g* factor does not always appear, but these five tests always tend to cluster, i.e. to measure a reasoning ability or what Thurstone calls Induction. Abstraction and Matrices in particular involve grasping new relationships and their implications. The writer's Matrices is similar to Raven's famous test, though designed to get across rather more readily to unsophisticated and duller boys. We have seen in previous chapters that the value of the Progressive Matrices in non-western cultures, particularly in relation to educability, is rather doubtful. But it worked quite well as a test of general trainability of British Navy and Army recruits, of widely diverse education, during the Second World War (cf. Vernon and Parry); and it is much used in clinical practice.

All the educational attainment and learning tests, together with vocabulary, show a strong *v:ed* component. Moreover this is highly consistent across cultures. As Irvine (1968) points out, all educational systems using English as medium of instruction tend to follow a common sequence in teaching English and number. Also, since our non-western groups are linguistically handicapped, their attainments on all these tests are affected by how much English they have acquired. In certain groups – Hebridean, Jamaican, and Ugandan – there was clear evidence that the factor enters into many tests of a non-educational nature.

In no group was it found that the two learning tests measured a common memory ability. Instead it often appeared that the *v:ed* tests tended to subdivide into:

(a) Spelling, Word Learning, Arithmetic and sometimes English attainment, i.e. skills which can be drilled at school.

(b) Vocabulary, especially the oral form, and Information Learning which depends largely on comprehension of oral statements. This sub-factor links up, rather irregularly, both with the Sorting test and with oral fluency or productivity in the creativity tests.

Word Learning is interesting since, though mainly measuring school-taught English, it was clearly affected by the cooperation the tester was able to elicit, and by the pupils' willingness to concentrate on this rather dull task. *Arithmetic* was mainly a g or induction $+ v{:}ed$ test, i.e. it seldom yielded any distinctive results. However many studies in western countries and in Africa (cf. Irvine, op. cit.) show that, when several number tests are given they do measure a largely distinct ability. That is, some individuals or groups may be better or worse at it than they are in verbal abilities.

The Sorting test was disappointing, although it was attractive to the boys and yielded a wide spread of scores, indicative of good reliability. But its correlations with other tests, i.e. its factor structure, were rather unstable, and it gave few meaningful group differences. One got the impression that facility in categorisation depends largely on linguistic accident. For example the Eskimo tongue may lend itself to general categories which can be translated into English much more readily than the Indian languages.

The *Piaget battery*, when scored for total errors, mainly acts as a general intelligence test, though giving additional small correlations with verbal, fluency or spatial tests, indicating that different items measure different things. When the 13 sets of items are themselves intercorrelated they show a strong general factor, and similar tasks tend to cluster, though rather irregularly. The four Conservation tasks + Time Concepts (also involving conservation) yield the most consistent group factor. Less clearcut are a spatial or visualising group (Left and Right, Tilted Bottle, Insect, Dot, and Shadow), and a number group (Number Concepts, Equidistant Counters, sometimes including Left and Right). If these three sets are scored separately,* Conservation should give some indication of mental maturity – the attainment of Piaget's stage of concrete operations, though in practice this differs little from Induction ability. One would also expect the Number and Spatial sets to be relevant to number and spatial abilities, but again more confirmation is needed.

---

* In this case the Logical Inclusion subtest is omitted. Perhaps because of its linguistic complexity, it was always the least reliable and most specific of the tasks.

'*Creativity*' *tests.* These were troublesome to apply, score and interpret. Often it was difficult for the tester to know whether he had got across the desired 'set'. For example Ugandan boys seemed incapable of accepting the notion of 'suppose you could fly'. And yet, because the tests were unspeeded and the boys strongly encouraged, they eventually produced more answers than their apparent fluency would warrant. On the other hand there was more community in responses across cultures than had been expected; both Eskimos and Africans saw the same kinds of things in inkblots, or used the Tin Can for similar purposes. A major problem is that all scores except the N or fluency totals tend to be small and therefore highly unreliable; and they are all affected by the size of N. Obviously it is only those who give numerous responses who can produce appreciable numbers of original, perseverative, or other types. It seemed preferable to employ proportional or percentage scores, e.g. U/N per cent rather than U. But this was unsatisfactory also since it is easier to get, say 3 unusual answers out of 5 than it is to get 12 out of 20.

A preliminary factor analysis among 100 English and 40 Hebridean boys (Vernon 1966b) gave promising results. The various scores showed little dependence on g or $v:ed$, and there was a clear productivity factor, corresponding to Thurstone's Ideational Fluency. In addition a distinctive originality factor appeared in the U and some other scores, contrasted with the P or perseveration scores. However in no subsequent group was this finding replicated. Once the fluency factor had been extracted there was no consistent tendency to produce original answers to several tests, and the correlations with all other tests were extremely variable. Perhaps a more useful way of using the tests in future would be to score Rorschach, Wings and Tin Can for number of responses, omitting P, and to give each U response double weight. This could be interpreted as a measure of imaginativeness + oral fluency.

The *Incomplete Drawings* test was even more useless, since neither the U nor E scores correlated consistently with anything except to a small extent with g, and with drawing ability as measured by Draw-a-Man and Design Reproduction. Whatever kind of creativity it taps bears no relation to orally expressed imagination.

Non-verbal Tests. The various perceptual, drawing, spatial and pictorial tests always show something in common distinct from g and $v:ed$. But as Irvine (op. cit.) noted in Africa, the results are apt to be more inconsistent than those of verbal tests, presumably because the kinds of experiences that stimulate abilities with shapes, blocks, pictures, pencil and paper, are more obscure and less uniform across cultures. Moreover the underlying abilities are quite complex: that is the tests subdivide irregularly. Sometimes those involving drawing yield a partially distinctive factor; sometimes the more practical tests, Formboard and either Kohs or Mazes, split off from the more perceptual.

The *Porteus Mazes* test has probably been applied to a wider range of ethnic groups than any other test in existence. Porteus himself claims that it can be got across readily to illiterate adult samples, and provides striking evidence that it measures some kind of planning ability, adaptability to the environment, foresight and self-control. He quotes mean scores ranging from $7\frac{1}{2}$ year level in Kalahari bushmen to $10\frac{1}{2}$ in Australian aborigines, and normal or above among acculturated N. American Indians. However many anthropologists are not too happy as to the validity of these findings. Possibly some samples have been small and non-representative; and the amount of contact they have had with whites appears to have some influence on their results. In the present researches it yielded scarcely any group differences (except between urban and rural Jamaicans). So far as factor content goes, the test showed a rather low g-loading and, in different groups, small $v:ed$ or small spatial loadings. The disappointing results may be due partly to not following the normal instructions. But in addition performance is probably affected, among children, by the current popularity of mazes in Comics. Thus the median score for English boys averaging $11\cdot0$ years was $13\cdot0$. D. M. Hyde likewise obtained exaggerated scores among six to eight year European children in Aden, but much lower among Arabs, Indians and Somalis. It differentiated ethnic and age groups at least as well as Kohs Blocks, Coloured Matrices and Piaget Conservation tasks.

Picture Recognition. Previous work with Hudson's test has been referred to in Chapter VI. The present test actually yields quite a similar factor pattern to the mazes. Though showing some spatial content, the loadings are not so high as to suggest that it is measuring a very fundamental feature of 3-dimensional comprehension. Nevertheless it certainly tends to differentiate some ethnic groups from others.

Gottschaldt Figures, like Kohs Blocks, has an unexpectedly high g-loading, but shows a consistent spatial component as well. No evidence was obtained that the field-independence which it is supposed to measure can be differentiated from spatial or visualisation factors.

Indeed it yielded rather poorer differentiation between our cultural groups than did Kohs.

Design Reproduction. The Bender-Gestalt is chiefly used to diagnose possible brain damage, but can also be given as a test of general perceptual development and intelligence over about the 4–11 year range. Billingslea quotes a study in which it was found useful with Israeli immigrant children. The present version is of moderate reliability and, like the Gottschaldt, chiefly measures *g* and spatial ability. But it shows some effects of drawing skill and of experience at school in using a pencil for accurate copying.

Kohs Blocks. As we have seen, this has been widely used cross-culturally, though it offers many difficulties of orientation and of grasping the relation between a 2-dimensional picture and 3-dimensional blocks. Among western adults it is a good spatial-technical test, but among children it seems to be mainly a test of general intelligence or induction, with only a small perceptual-spatial loading.

The Draw-a-Man test, when scored by Goodenough's schedule, is generally admitted to be a weak test of intelligence for children aged ten or more, but to give a fair discrimination at younger levels, i.e. over the Mental Age range within which most of our subjects fell. D. B. Harris interprets it as showing the level of conceptual maturity a child has achieved, but there was no indication in the present research of any marked correlation with, for example, Piaget scores. Rather it acted as an additional perceptual-spatial test, and often contributed to a minor Drawing Ability factor. The influence of schooling was sometimes noticeable: occasional schools encouraged impressionistic action pictures rather than static detail and therefore obtained lower scores. Performance also seems to be affected by lack of social adjustment.

Though the test has been found acceptable in many ethnic groups, its limitations are apparent from W. Dennis's (1960) finding that Bedouin Arab adults and children obtain a mean Goodenough IQ of only 53. Undoubtedly such people have very acute perception of detailed features in the desert, yet in their drawings they frequently omit eyes, mouth and clothing. Dennis ascribes this mainly to their lack of exposure to representational art.

The scores obtained with the Witkin schedule correlated around ·90 with the Goodenough scores. But they were generally more diagnostic and showed higher *g*, spatial and drawing factor loadings.

Vernon Formboard. This involves an element of manual dexterity and thus appeared to be particularly affected by malnutrition and/or lack of experience with toys. But it depends chiefly on spatial perception, or seeing how the bits can be rearranged to yield a new shape; thus it obtained moderate *g* and considerable spatial and practical loadings.

Mischel's Delayed Gratification. Mischel presents some evidence, from work in the West Indies, that this test of willingness to delay gratification is associated with a secure family background, and with masculine salience in the home. The present writer's results suggest that it depends more on the extent to which the subjects trust the testers to keep their word. It gave small, but very variable, correlations with some ability factors and environmental ratings, some of which will be mentioned later.

XIX

The Influence of Background and Personality Factors on the Scores of English Boys

The English sample was collected in three main areas – North London industrial, Hertfordshire small-town, and Hertfordshire rural. The differences between these subgroups were unexpectedly small and are hardly worth reporting. It would seem that bad slums snd primitive rural conditions are difficult to find in present-day S.E. England (so far as the non-immigrant white population is concerned). The villages are occupied more by car workers in factories 15 miles away than by agricultural labourers, and even in our poorer London schools it was rare to see a raggedly dressed boy, or one who did not get at least half a crown a week in pocket money. The rural group scored a little lower on most tests, but the only difference significant at the ·05 level was on Abstraction, where its median quotient was 88.

Nevertheless socioeconomic and cultural conditions vary considerably within the homes in all three subsamples, and the following

TABLE 5. *Correlations of Environmental Ratings with Ability Factors, and Delayed Gratification, in English Group.*

	g	Educ.	Verb.	Perc.	Prac.	Delayed Grat.
Regularity of Schooling	−·15	·31		·21		·14
Unbroken Home	−·11	·30			·14	·24
Socioeconomic status	·38	·18	·24			·08
Cultural Stimulus	·56	·29	·16			·14
Linguistic Background	·49	·31	·24			·16
Initiative	·13			·13		·21
Masculine Dominance			−·30		·39	−·17
Planfulness	·32	·26			·11	·13

N.B. Correlations of ·195 are significant at the ·05 level.

loadings of the environmental variables on the ability factors are generally in line with those of previous investigations. The correlations of the Delayed Gratification test are added.

Regularity of Schooling particularly affects educational attainment, though also the perceptual and drawing tests; but it is unrelated to the g factor. Broken vs. Unbroken Home also does not affect general intellectual development, but is related to school attainment. Socioeconomic level and Linguistic background are considerably associated with g and with educational and verbal performance, but Cultural Stimulus in the home gives an even higher correlation ($r = \cdot56$) with the g factor. Planfulness likewise affects g and attainment. The rating for Initiative has insignificant loadings only, and Masculine Dominance is puzzling since it is positively related to practical ability (as measured chiefly by Piaget Visualisation and Formboard), though antithetical to the factor based on perceptual and drawing tests.

The Delayed Gratification test correlations are small, but it appears to go with the good, stable (unbroken) home, which encourages initiative. Mischel's suggestion that lack of masculine influence reduces willingness to delay clearly does not apply to our group.

MALADJUSTED AND DELINQUENT BOYS

Because of the difficulties of getting reliable background information on English schoolchildren, the tests were given to two other small groups for whom there existed rather detailed case notes compiled by psychologists, psychiatrists and social workers. These were 25 delinquent boys in a Home Office Approved School, and 20 boys in two Residential Schools for Maladjusted Children. In so far as these tend to come from rather abnormal and extreme home environments, and to present serious personality problems, they might throw further light on the influences of such factors on the development of abilities. Naturally the boys often needed tactful handling, but there was no real difficulty. Indeed the testing sessions proved very popular, and there was some jealousy as to who should be taken first.

One problem, however, was that these schools contain rather few boys within the age range of the normal group (10:5–11:3), hence the age limits had to be extended from 9:10–13:5, and the medians were 12:10 for delinquents and 11:4 for maladjusted. The latter group's quotients can reasonably be compared with those of the normals, and a rough age correction was applied to the quotients of the older group. But this lack of precision does not generally matter since it is the relative level of quotients on different tests within each group that chiefly concern us.

Fig. 6 provides a simple presentation of the median quotients for both groups compared with the normal figure of 100; but it does not of course indicate the range of individual differences within each group, which was quite wide, though no wider than among normals. For

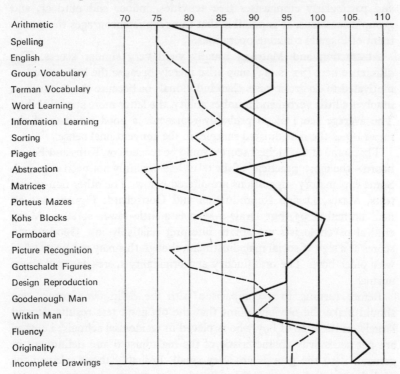

Fig. 6. Profile of Median Test Scores of Delinquent and Maladjusted Boys.

example Terman–Merrill Vocabulary, with a median in the maladjusted group of 93, ranged from 124 to 71. (The 90th, 50th and 10th percentile DQs are listed in Table 11).

As one might expect, by far the lowest score among maladjusted boys was Arithmetic (median 77, with none scoring higher than 92). Spelling is fairly backward at 85, but English improves to 89, and the two Vocabulary scores are little below normal at 93.* Information comprehension and learning is similar, but Word Learning is a little lower

* The level of significance of differences is considered in Appendix E.

(88), probably because the majority of boys have not settled down to concentrated work in class. Particularly striking is the Piaget mean of 98, indicating no appreciable retardation in the development of verbalised concepts of the world, quantity, space and time. (The only item in which they were noticeably weak was the one involving handedness.) Most of the boys attend a school which minimises formal instruction and particularly emphasises free activities, indoor and outdoor, and group discussions. It is possible that this regime encourages the attainment of Piaget's concrete operations.

Abstraction and Matrices usually yield very similar scores. The difference here (87 vs. 93) may arise merely because the boys were less motivated to do group tests than individual; or because the former test involves a little verbal and number ability, the latter more spatial ability. The average score of 90 probably represents a good estimate of the mean IQ of the maladjusted sample, in the conventional sense.

That some of the highest scores would be reached on Kohs and Formboard – the most 'practical' of the tests, had certainly not been expected. Some explanatory suggestions are offered below. The other non-verbal tests, Mazes, Design Reproduction and Gottschaldt Figures, are all near normal at 95, but Draw-a-Man is a little lower at 88–9. Many clinical psychologists are apt to interpret relatively low Goodenough scores as a sign of social maladjustment, though this may not be justified with older boys. The oral fluency and originality scores are well above normal.

Before turning to a comparison with the delinquent group, one should make the obvious point that the obtained test results depend largely on the type of boy who is placed in residential schools; i.e. they are not necessarily characteristic of the maladjusted and delinquent in general. Also the groups are very small. Probably those selected for Maladjusted Schools are chosen to be not too much below average in intelligence, though often backward in attainments. Whereas Approved Schools, though taking many of the same type, also accept boys of much lower-grade ability.

DELINQUENTS

The delinquents are equally poor in Arithmetic, but also at much the same low level in English skills. The great lack of cultural stimulus in many of their homes is reflected in the median of 80–81 on Vocabulary tests. On the other hand they are only six points below the maladjusted in the two group learning tasks, probably because their present school provides them with a secure environment in which they are relatively well adjusted to classroom learning, and to attending to a teacher or tester.

There is a big difference on the Piaget tasks – 15 points. They are behind mainly in Conservation. Their mean failure rate on 12 questions in this area is 21 per cent, compared with 10 for maladjusted and 14 per cent for normals. Thus a considerable proportion are lacking stable concepts of amount, size, etc.

The Induction test results are even lower, in fact as low as their Arithmetic attainment, suggesting that it is characteristic of the delinquent that he fails to generalise or see an underlying principle and to apply it in deciding on a course of action. Evidence will be presented later that a deficit on these tests is associated with repressed upbringing and discouragement of initiative. Perhaps something of the same kind characterises the English home that produces the delinquent rather than the maladjusted boy.

Mazes, Design Reproduction and Formboard show fairly small differences between the groups. Porteus's Q (Quality) score was not applied, but the tester did record slapdashness and pencil-lifting and found them occurring just as frequently in the maladjusted. Gottschaldt Figures shows a bigger difference of 15 points, and Kohs and Picture Recognition the greatest discrepancy of all, namely 20–21 points. In the light of many researches such as Bernstein's one might have expected relatively good nonverbal and spatial scores in a verbally retarded group drawn mainly from low socioeconomic grades. But this result seems to link with that obtained on the Piaget tests* in suggesting that the maladjusted have reached a more independent and integrated schematisation of the world of objects than have the delinquents, perhaps in compensation for their difficulties with the world of people.

Though the delinquents' Draw-a-Man scores were a little higher than those of the maladjusted boys, their drawings on the whole showed less character and were more conventional. Particularly noticeable among the maladjusted, both in this and the Torrance Incomplete Drawings, was the frequent aggressive or sexual content, and each boy's productions were rescored for this projective feature. Forty percent of maladjusted and 12 per cent of delinquents showed marked aggression or sex. However this could be attributed merely to the greater encouragement of uninhibited drawings in one of the schools for maladjusted.

* Factor analysis showed the Piaget scores to have an unusually high spatial factor content in these groups, and no verbal loading.

There were no appreciable differences between delinquents, maladjusted and normals on Incomplete Drawings. But the delinquents were at least equal to normals in Rorschach N and U per cent, Tin Can N and P per cent (not U), and 'Wings' Activity and E + U per cent scores. The maladjusted were high on all N and U scores. Thus despite their below-average verbal and reasoning capacities, both deviant groups – and especially the maladjusted – produce more ideas and more unconventional ones than normal boys.

A more detailed series of background and personality variables was assessed from the boys' case notes than those listed in Table 5, though in many instances the information was too scrappy for the ratings to be very reliable. Correlations were obtained between all the test scores and these ratings, and while they are mostly small, they do throw some additional light on the factors that influence test performance (cf. Appendix E).

Socioeconomic level gives correlations of ·30 and over with all the educational, verbal and learning tests, ·47 with Terman Vocabulary, but much lower r's with Abstraction and Matrices (·15), and scarcely any with the Piaget or spatial tests. There was a slight relation with drawing (·20 with Witkin score). Planfulness or providence of the home yields quite similar figures, but those for Cultural Stimulus are smaller, mainly because information on this aspect was incomplete. In most homes the Stimulus appeared to be virtually nil.

Regular previous schooling likewise correlates in the ·30's with the $v:ed$ tests and some of the creativity scores, ·51 with Vocabulary, ·21 with Induction tests, but very low with spatial tests and negatively with Piaget. However the Induction tests are as successful as the attainment measures in predicting Settling Down and Making Good Progress in Present School.

Neither Broken Home nor Tension between Parents show any generally adverse effects on abilities, if anything the reverse (as occurred, too, in the normal group). The patterns of child-parent relations were very difficult to quantify. When the father was dominant and had most influence on the boy, most test performances were adversely affected, particularly spatial and inductive (Matrices −·31, Piaget −·26). Whereas Father Affection vs. Rejection gave mostly small positive coefficients, the most striking being ·36 with Witkin Draw-a-Man. Mother Affection vs. Rejection was more puzzling, perhaps because affection could not be distinguished from over-protectiveness. It gave negative correlations with almost all tests, ranging up to −·35 with Information Learning. Criminal Background (among parents or sibs) showed small, nonsignificant, negative correlations with verbal-educational tests, but positive with non-verbal, ranging up to +·29 with Porteus Mazes. A rating of Seriousness of Boy's Delinquency yielded a similar pattern.

Boy's Neurotic Traits tend to associate with high verbal ability (r's of ·27 to ·29 with Vocabulary, Spelling, Abstraction and Rorschach N). Curiously, the amount of enuresis gave some of the highest coefficients, namely ·41 with Kohs, ·36 Gottschaldt, ·29 Matrices. Social Adjustment to Peers has no significant r's, but reaches ·24 with Witkin Drawing. Tendencies to Aggression give —·31 with the same test, and smaller negative r's with all the $v : ed$ tests, especially the drill subjects, Arithmetic, Spelling and Word Learning. Fantasy Tendencies and Possible Psychotic Symptoms show no significant trends; nor does a rating of the boy's Initiative vs. Apathy.

Though the battery was not intended to be used projectively, certain scores show projective possibilities. Thus Aggression in Drawings correlates ·43 with Neurotic Traits, ·35 with Aggression, ·31 with Fantasy, ·35 with Tension in Home, —·38 with Social Adjustment, —·29 with Father Dominance, —·25 with Delinquency. In the 'Wings' test the Ae (activities for self-enjoyment) and Ah (activities for others or for study) gave numerous correlations of ·20 to ·38 in opposite directions. The Ae-type were more mother-protected, enuretic, less sociable and showed less initiative, less fantasy and less home tension than the Ah type. Finally the Delayed Gratification test went with better Schooling (·34), and with Father Affection (·21), but not Mother Affection (—·11).

Summing up: with such a small and oddly constituted group one could not expect very definite conclusions on the relations between home influences, personality and abilities. Indeed many studies with the Wechsler intelligence scales have shown that score patterns cannot yield reliable psychopathological diagnosis (cf. Rabin and Guertin). Nevertheless many of the difference between delinquents, maladjusted and normals are meaningful, and both these and the correlational data suggest that background factors have significant associations with cognitive performance, which would be worth following up on a larger scale. Note that it is not only verbal-educational abilities which are affected, though the influence on these of home stimulation and schooling are naturally the most consistent. Spatial and inductive abilities also seem to be lowered by the conditions that lead to delinquency (not maladjustment), by the over-dominant father or protective mother, though the effects of parent-child interactions are certainly not simple.

No very clear support was obtained for Witkin's hypotheses, but the Draw-a-Man test scored for field independence did show considerable clinical significance with its positive relations to Father Affection and Social Adjustment, negative to Mother Affection and Aggressive tendencies.

APPENDIX E

SIGNIFICANCE OF GROUP DIFFERENCES

With groups of 20 and 25 any group differences are obviously rather unreliable. Since several of the tests tend to yield irregular or skewed distributions in some of the subgroups, we have preferred to present median rather than mean scores throughout, and to avoid burdening the reader with long lists of Critical Ratios or t's and probabilities. Since, however, all results are converted to DQs with a constant Standard Deviation, it is possible to indicate what level of differences reaches a given level of significance. In any one subgroup the range tends to be restricted, i.e. the SD is about 13 for most tests instead of 15. In this case a DQ difference of 8 points is likely to be significant at the 5 per cent level, of 6 points at the 10 per cent. For differences between 20 maladjusted boys and 100 normals, the corresponding figures are about $6\frac{1}{2}$ and $5\frac{1}{2}$ points.

However when differences are quoted between two tests *within* the maladjusted or other subgroups, much smaller figures are significant, depending on the correlation between the tests. For example a mean difference of 5·8 DQ points between Abstraction and Matrices ($r = ·44$) in the maladjusted is significant at the ·05 level, and one of 3·4 points is significant for Arithmetic and Spelling ($r = ·78$).

Correlations

The groups were too small for separate intercorrelations to be worth reporting; hence the averages of within-group coefficients were obtained. This gives us 45 cases, for which the S.E. of zero r is ·15. Hence only coefficients of about ·30 up are conventionally significant. They are not reproduced here, though the larger coefficients are mentioned in the text.

A factor analysis of the correlations yielded much the same pattern as in other groups, except that the g factor was relatively smaller than usual, probably because the range of ability is restricted. g was highest in Matrices, Abstraction, Terman Vocabulary, substantial in all the verbal tests, in Piaget and most spatial tests, but low in Sorting, Mazes, Formboard, Picture Recognition, Draw-a-Man and the creativity measures. There was a prominent $v:ed$ group factor, including small loadings for the verbal creativity tests, also a spatial-perceptual factor in all the non-verbal tests and Piaget. The creativity N and U measures yielded a single productivity-originality group factor, and a small group factor remained in the various drawing tests, together with Sorting and Picture Recognition.

XX

Testing in the Hebrides

There are many subcultures in the UK which might be expected to differ widely in attitudes and customs, and perhaps in abilities, from S.E. England; notably the industrial North, the rural Southwest, Wales and Scotland. The application of a wide-ranging battery of tests in any of these would be of interest. But for lack of time it was decided to concentrate on one rather extreme sample. The Hebridean islands off the west coast of Scotland are one of the most remote areas geographically, and probably have least contact with modern urban civilisation, though obviously this is breaking down with easy air travel and the advent of television. The use of Gaelic is dying out rapidly in all parts of Scotland,* yet it is still the main language of the rural parts of the Hebrides. Children normally speak it with their parents and friends, and it plays an important part in the school curriculum, though almost all teaching is conducted in English. The Isle of Lewis has one large town, Stornoway – a fishing port, centre of commerce and the tweed industry. It has many contacts with the mainland, and here the predominant language is English. The countryside, however, consists largely of barren and stony moorland, and most families live from crofting, i.e. smallholding and sheep-rearing, from weaving tweed in the home, or from fishing. The families are closely knit and hardworking; for example the mother helps with the tweed, the boys with the sheep. And there is a strong Puritan tradition, with a bias towards the more rigid Scottish sects. Naturally, though, the more progressive attitudes and interests of the urban community are gradually percolating outwards. As in all the non-industrial areas of Scotland, there is a tremendous respect for education, and the teaching tends to be much more formal and thorough than in postwar England. A remarkable proportion of the brighter pupils reach the university and enter the ministry, teaching or other professions.

In 1948 Christina Smith reported an investigation in which the Cattell Scale I (pictorial test) was applied to representative samples of

* Cf. survey by the Scottish Council for Research in Education.

8- to 12-year-olds in all parts of the island. Form A was given with instructions in English and Form B in Gaelic. The average IQ was found to be decidedly low, namely about 85 and, contrary to expectation, it was no higher with the Gaelic version. There was, however, a large practice effect at the second testing, regardless of language, presumably due to the initial unfamiliarity among the children at that time with any objective tests. The author paints a vivid picture of the conditions that may have lowered the scores, apart from any influence of the language factor: the unsuitability of much of the test material (e.g. pictures of trains, lamp-posts, watering cans, scooters), and the rarity of picture books in the homes, the weather conditions that often inter-fere with school attendance, and the amount of time that has to be taken from ordinary schooling to teach most of the pupils English. She comments on the shyness and suspicion of Gaelic children at the novel situation and their anxieties at revealing their difficulties with English. She was particularly struck by their reluctance to work at speed, and attributes this to 'the unhurried, untrammelled mode of existence', which makes them 'temperamentally unresponsive to the pressure of time'. No doubt there have been many changes in the ensuing 20 years, but there may still be differences in abilities and attainments between 11-year boys reared in a relatively isolated and restricted environment from boys of the same age in S.E. England; also differences between the predominantly Gaelic-speaking and English-speaking cultures.

In 1965, all the boys in the age-range 10:6–11:7 in one large primary school in Stornoway and three country schools were given the battery of group tests and a questionnaire on the language used with parents, friends, etc. (Head teachers' assessments of language were also ob-tained.) Forty boys were picked for individual testing whose group test distributions were representative, and of whom 20 came from pre-dominantly English-speaking, 20 from Gaelic-speaking, homes. The latter, however, often used English with their peers, as well as in the classroom. Almost all the testing and interviewing was carried out by Scottish (though not Gaelic-speaking) testers. None of the Gaelic-background boys showed any difficulty in understanding them, and there was little sign of the suspicion of strangers that Miss Smith encountered, though sometimes their Highland canniness was mani-fested in over-logical or argumentative reactions to test items that struck them as silly.

Almost all the English-background boys were urban, the Gaelic-background country-dwellers. But it was necessary to confine the work to schools which were easily accessible from Stornoway, hence the latter are probably not typical of the rural culture in the more remote parts of the island. Differences in the socioeconomic level of the fathers were small: both groups contained the occasional professional, business or clerical parent, and the van-driver or labourer. The majority were mill-workers, tradesmen or shopkeepers, though at least half the country families carried on crofting or weaving part-time.

Cultural stimulation by the homes may have been somewhat less than in Southern England, in so far as few parents had received senior secondary education. Only half the boys had ever been outside the island, and access to libraries or TV among the country dwellers was rare. On the other hand, lack of cooperation of the home with the school was very rarely reported. Regularity of attendance was superior in both groups to that recorded in England. The proportion of unstable or broken homes was as low as in England, but according to our subjective ratings there were fewer feckless parents. The boys' existence seemed well-organised: most of them showed a lot of responsibility and initiative in their out-of-school activities. The country ones, for example, often looked after the sheep, or wound bobbins. More of them than of English boys had thought about possible vocations and had reasonably realistic ideas.

The atmosphere of the island is still peaceful, with no sense of rush – more a sense of having all the time in the world. But many more parents nowadays are wage-earning so that to a much greater extent people live by the clock; and Miss Smith's phrase 'lackadaisical acceptance of whatever may transpire', could hardly be applied to the present day younger generation, though of course it may be more true in the outlying areas.

RESULTS

Fig. 7 shows that there is no general retardation corresponding to a low IQ; nor are there large differences between the subgroups, except on three tests that depend most on oral English – Terman Vocabulary, Sorting and Piaget. Most of the variations could well be due to chance.*

The median scores on Spelling and Word Learning are considerably above the English average, and these are the tests that involve most rote learning. It is interesting that the Gaelic-speakers are actually

---

* Unless a Hebridean-English difference exceeds five points, or a Gaelic-English subgroup difference exceeds eight points, it is hardly worth considering ($P = \cdot 10$).

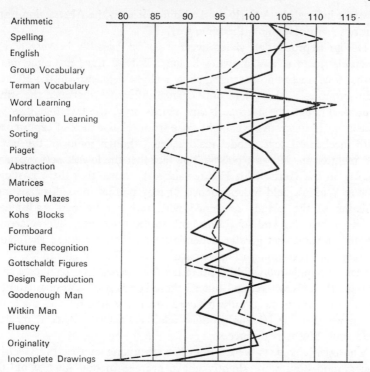

Fig. 7. Profiles of Median Scores of Gaelic- and English-speaking Hebridean Boys.

better on these than English-background boys, suggesting that they compensate in this direction for their difficulties in using English. They tend to be superior also in Information learning. In arithmetic and written English both groups are close to normal, though the Gaelic-background boys begin to drop behind on Group Vocabulary and show quite a serious deficiency when they have to supply their own definitions in the Terman-Merrill Vocabulary. Presumably the same difficulty affects their ability to categorise objects in the Sorting test; and it is most marked in Piaget where the median quotients are 86 and 102 respectively. The Gaelic boys were not retarded on conservation of amounts, but dropped heavily on various items concerned with time (Day after tomorrow, Time in a different town), number, logical inclusion, and conservation of lengths and areas. Thus some of their concepts of the world are less mature than those of Stornoway or English boys. More generally, they do not easily think, classify or abstract in English. A fairly marked difference on the Abstraction test, but not Matrices, points the same way.

Design Reproduction yields average scores, possibly because of its resemblance to school drawing lessons. But all the remaining non-verbal tests, including Matrices, show a slight deficiency in the Hebridean group as a whole, and only chance differences between the sub-groups. Though the average is five points only, the fact that it is so consistent is suggestive. It might arise from relative lack of experience with mechanical toys, model-making, etc., though many of the boys did mention models as a hobby. The fact that the lowest performance (91) is on the Gottschaldt Figures suggests rather that there is some lack in Witkin's field-independence. It may be that the still-persisting isolation of the island, combined with rather rigid and traditional family-upbringing and schooling both in the town and country areas, produce a somewhat greater dependence on the family and the community than is common in other parts of the UK. It might follow that the island population would yield rather fewer scientists, engineers and artisans than elsewhere, and indeed there is less need and opportunity for them than in more industrialised areas. An attempt was made to check whether the Islands produce relatively fewer science than arts graduates, but without success.

The creativity tests were somewhat surprising in that the Gaelic-background boys were slightly above average in oral fluency on all three verbal tests, the English-background boys about average.* Though very slow in responding, when pressed they did produce a wide range of ideas. For example in Rorschach the content of responses was more varied than the usual Animal or Human answers which pre-dominate in English boys. The Gaelic-speakers excelled particularly in 'Wings', quite possibly because country boys are more observant of birds. On the other hand they showed poorer originality and much more perseveration in the Tin Can and 'Wing' tests. Since this is not due to any lack of linguistic fluency, it suggests that their rural and home environments tend to restrict creative imagination. In the Incomplete Drawings (U and E scores), both groups were much below average, especially the Gaelic. As pointed out above, the test seems to have little psychological value, and the probable explanation is that Hebridean boys are unwilling to let themselves go, or display their lack of skill, in an unfamiliar medium.

A final difference was observed on the Delayed Gratification test, where 80 per cent of the English-speaking, but 50 per cent of the Gaelic,

* Fuller figures are published in Vernon 1966b.

waited for the larger bar ($P = <\cdot05$). Since there is no reason to think that the Gaelic homes are more insecure or father-deprived, the obvious explanation is that these boys were more distrustful of strangers than those with English backgrounds.

All the tests and environmental ratings were inter-correlated and analysed both by centroid and group-factor techniques, with very similar results. The outstanding feature was that no g factor, nor inductive or reasoning ability could be distinguished from the verbal-educational factor. There was a single large $g:v$ which yielded loadings of ·75 and over on English, Spelling, Information Learning, Group Vocabulary, Abstraction, Matrices, Piaget and Gottschaldt Figures. In other words, verbal, reasoning and spatial abilities are less differentiated than usual. However this finding is not attributable merely to the linguistic heterogeneity of the sample, since the correlation of the factor with English vs. Gaelic speaking was only ·29. Nor was there any correlation with Regularity of Schooling, probably because this is so uniform throughout the schools. In contrast there were high correlations with Cultural Stimulus (·72), Planfulness (·63), Socioeconomic (·51), Initiative (·50) and Delayed Gratification (·34). Thus the factor probably chiefly represents modern sophistication and cultural stimulus vs. more traditional and restricted environments which tend to retard mental growth in any direction.

In addition there was a distinctive, though fairly small spatial factor in the perceptual and practical tests (not in Matrices, Porteus Mazes or Picture Recognition). This gave no positive correlations with environmental ratings. A strong fluency factor appeared in the verbal creativity N scores, also loading the U per cent and some other creativity measures, and this gave small positive correlations with Initiative, Cultural Stimulus and Masculine Influence ratings, not with English vs. Gaelic. This suggests an extraverted, outgoing factor, like Cattell's Surgency, rather than purely an ability factor. English vs. Gaelic did however show large positive residuals with Terman Vocabulary, Incomplete Drawings U and Delayed Gratification, also negative ones with Arithmetic, Spelling and Word Learning, i.e. with tests that showed the biggest differences between the two groups. Most of the Piaget items, especially those involving Conservation, contributed to a fourth factor.

In conclusion, the application of our battery to quite small groups of considerable interest which plausibly link up with their home, linguistic and educational environments. This suggests that it can be profitably employed in wider-ranging enquiries.

The findings should not be construed in any sense as an attack on the Gaelic culture or language. It is true that the pressures of modern civilisation threaten the survival of minority cultures and languages all the world over, and that members of such cultures are likely to achieve most success in a technological world if they become completely assimilated. But there is much of value in the maintenance of a variety of cultures, each adapted to its particular geographical environment, and giving greater support, security and stability to its members by its own traditions and ways of life. Though our boys from Gaelic homes are handicapped in certain respects, we have seen that they develop a remarkable fluency with English by the age of 11; they do well in elementary school subjects, and are the equal of the English-background boys on spatial-perceptual tests. It should, however, be borne in mind that rather greater deficits might have been found, had it been possible to sample the more typical rural population.

PART V
Cross-Cultural Studies

XXI

Jamaica

The West Indian communities are of special interest to the social scientist since they bridge the gap, as it were, between West African and British-North American cultures. In many respects the populations still resemble those of the countries from which their ancestors were abducted to work as slaves on the sugar plantations. There is appalling poverty, malnutrition, low standards of housing, not only among the rural smallholders and seasonally employed labourers, but also in the slums surrounding the larger cities. Adult illiteracy, magical beliefs and practices are widespread; schooling is not available for all children and is often irregular and of poor quality; and the language of the majority of homes is a dialect or kind of pidgin which differs so markedly from Standard English that children virtually have to learn a new language to be educated. But at the other end of the scale, there is considerable industrial development (e.g. oil and pitch in Trinidad, bauxite in Jamaica), in addition to agricultural exports and a lucrative tourist industry. There is too a comparatively large middle and upper class who run the economy, and who – unlike Africans – successfully operate political democracies, and have generally absorbed western ideas and values, as has the middle-class negro in the United States. Thus a fuller understanding of the intellectual and emotional development of the West Indian should be relevant to the psychology of the United States negro, and particularly to that of the large body of West Indian immigrants and their families in Britain.

Jamaica is a tropical island of great beauty and luxuriant fertility, not much larger in area than Devon + Cornwall. The population is over $1\frac{1}{2}$ million and is rising rapidly owing to the high birth rate; hence the pressure for migration. About one quarter live in the capital city area of Kingston, whereas some mountainous and jungle-like areas are very sparsely populated. There are very small percentages of East Indians,*

---

* In other Caribbean countries, notably Trinidad and Guyana, the proportion of East Indians, descended from indentured labourers rather than slaves, constitutes nearly, or more than, half the population.

Chinese and whites and others, but some three-quarters are classified as negroes, and one fifth as mixed, i.e. having some white blood. This latter group ranges in colour from almost pure negro to almost white (they are sometimes referred to as 'the browns'); and it is of the utmost importance as constituting the bulk of the middle-classes who provide most of the country's commercial and professional leadership. Indeed lightness of colour is one of the major criteria of social class (cf. D. R. Manley, 1959).

After the emancipation of slaves in 1838, Jamaica remained under colonial administration until responsible self-government was ceded in 1944. During that period, education for the mass of the population was looked on as a welfare service, to be carried out as cheaply as possible. Though elementary schooling was eventually made available in all areas for 7–15-year-olds, either by the churches or the government, even now there are school places only for some three-quarters and, with the population explosion, it is impossible to keep up with the needs for additional buildings and staff. Attendance is nominally compulsory in urban areas, but is very irregular in the country, so that the *average* daily attendance is about 50 per cent of the whole age-group. Children are frequently kept at home for household and agricultural chores, and older boys in particular drop out through lack of interest. Many of the older buildings consist of little more than a roof, and the classes of up to 60 to 80 per teacher (on good attendance days) are separated merely by blackboards; and children are often crowded five or six to a four-foot desk. The teachers themselves were educated at elementary schools, and although most of them have passed additional examinations, only a minority have undergone a full three-year training. In view of their own poor education, the overcrowded conditions, the serious lack of books and equipment and the bad traditions of formal education (probably inherited from the Scottish missionaries), the methods of teaching are sadly mechanical. Learning is regarded as doing or saying what the teacher wants, and getting the right answers through chanting and drill, not finding out something by one's own efforts. Even reading, as Elsa Walters has described, becomes a meaningless rigmarole. Ask a pupil what he has been reading and he is likely to reply 'Page 16', as it does not occur to him that the content has any significance. Because of the irregular attendance the teacher can hardly know what stage any one child has reached or give him individual attention; so she does practically all the talking. Children's needs for physical and mental activity are repressed, since this is the only way in which most teachers, themselves brought up in the system, can handle over-large classes. The frequency of corporal punishment, at home or at school, is greater than in any other country known to the writer.

Many Jamaican educationalists deplore these conditions and this type of teaching, and much is being done to provide more up-to-date schools and train better teachers. But resources are severely limited, especially in view of the investment in secondary education. The astonishing thing indeed is that many children do manage to survive such treatment, and do well in secondary schools and the university.

Secondary education had quite different origins from elementary, much as in England. During the nineteenth and twentieth centuries, private and preparatory schools, day or boarding, were established for white children residing in Jamaica, and these gradually opened their doors to the emerging middle-class Jamaican. They have now come under State control, and admission is based almost exclusively on ability, i.e. on passing the Common Entrance Examination, similar to the English '11+'. There has been a vast expansion since independence and some 8 to 9 per cent of each age group nowadays gain places, as compared with about 1 per cent in 1940. This is a very high figure for a developing country. The majority of places are free, and in 1960 these were awarded to candidates with an average score of close to 100 on Moray House Verbal Reasoning, English and Arithmetic tests. The remaining places, called grant-aided (though in fact the parents paid fees) went to the next 'slice' in the ability range.* However there is a tremendous disparity in the results of different social classes, and of different parts of the country. Over 50 per cent of candidates with professional and upper-class parents as against three per cent of farming children gained free places in 1959 (cf. Manley 1963). Also there were doubtless far more children from the lower classes who did not sit the examination, or even attend school at all. Thus despite the objective technique of selection, and despite the amount of cramming and pressure that elementary schools apply to their pupils, only a tiny percentage of the negro peasant children reach the (not very high) standard required for admission. Moreover it has been observed that the few who do succeed often have great difficulties in settling down, their background and speech being inferior to those of the predominantly urban and better-class children. Another point of interest is that girls do very much better than boys (cf. the similar situation among US negroes); and a lower

---

* The writer's data were mostly gathered in 1960, when he was preparing a Report on 'Selection for Secondary Education in Jamaica' for the Jamaican Ministry of Education. No doubt there have been changes since then in selection policy and methods.

standard of entry is applied to boys in order to admit roughly equal numbers. The discrepancy is much greater than that observed in England at 11 years, and is probably due to the greater irregularity of attendance among boys and their resentment of the nagging of female teachers. Also there are in fact greater vocational opportunities for the educated girl, and hence more incentive to take an interest in schooling.

The secondary schools are much better equipped and staffed than the elementary, and closely resemble the English grammar school. However, many of the staff are untrained, or non-graduates, and the numerous expatriate teachers usually stay only for a few years. Pupils make a fair showing at the Cambridge Overseas School Certificate or GCE, but with their still noticeable language difficulties, and the bad teaching they experienced at the primary level, too much of the instruction deteriorates into mechanical drilling in the examination syllabus. The same difficulties persist even among those who go on to university, i.e. inability to think readily in Standard English and inability to work on their own without spoonfeeding. But, as always, there are wide individual differences, and the Jamaican educational system clearly produces many graduates whose intellectual capacities are fully comparable with those of western students. A start has been made in the provision of technical, commercial, agricultural and other less academic types of schools for some of the large numbers of pupils who fail the Common Entrance Examination, instead of leaving them to linger in the old-fashioned elementary school till 15, or to drop out of their own accord. But obviously this is an extremely expensive development, and in a relatively low-income country (especially one which has not yet had much time to outgrow British educational traditions), it is almost inevitable that scarce resources should be concentrated mainly on the selected few.

SOCIAL DEVELOPMENT OF CHILDREN

The outstanding characteristic of West Indian family life is its instability. Until the father feels able to support the wife – often not till middle-age – marriage of the parents is the exception rather than the rule. And though there are many stable 'Common Law' unions, both parents live at home only in some 40 per cent of households.* Very frequently, then, the father is promiscuous and the mother is left with the children. Often she becomes the main breadwinner, and the children are brought up by the grandmother, or farmed out to relatives. In part

* Cf. E. Clarke; M. Kerr; and Smith and Kruijer.

this system probably derives from the matriarchal system of many African cultures, but it was exacerbated by the conditions of slavery which suppressed family life and the recognition of paternity; (the planter, in effect, became the only father figure in the community).

The Jamaicans love children and indeed have far too many of them, since the men regard fecundity as a sign of virility and many women believe that restriction is bad for health (cf. J. Blake). But they bring them up in what can aptly be described as a Victorian manner, suppressing their natural needs and consciously aiming to 'break their wills'. For example, when the children become mobile, the mother or substitute may tie them to a table leg to prevent wandering. They beat them severely if they behave 'rudely', or even if they don't do well at school. The middle-class families are of course more stable, and more likely to be patriarchal, though equally authoritarian; and many of their children are largely reared by lower-class domestics. This tendency to female-domination and absence of a respected father figure, coupled with the repression of initiative and emphasis on external restraints rather than inner standards, must play a vital part in the emotional development, particularly of boys. It contributes to the apathy and disinterest that they so often display at school, though masked by an ebullient and outgoing temperament outside school.

The sheer poverty of smallholders, plantation and other labourers and slum-dwellers, has other serious effects. In families on the borderline of destitution, the immediate gratification of hunger and sex naturally takes precedence over long-term purposive planning, or Freud's Reality Principle. Rational and objective thinking are not likely to develop well when the basic needs are unsatisfied, and the organisation of personality is unintegrated and insecure. The tumbledown shacks in which many live contain little furniture, let alone any toys, books or other stimuli to the spatial sense and to imagination. M. Kerr gives a sympathetic picture of rural life in Jamaica, with its superstitions and magic, and she comments particularly on the absence of fantasy play among children. Yet another handicap is inadequate diet, partly because nature so lavishly provides starchy foods. Few schools can arrange midday meals, and many children come long distances. Hence their apparent passivity is hardly surprising.

STATISTICAL DATA

In view of the regular use of tests standardised in England for selection purposes, a good deal is known of the distribution of abilities among

Jamaican school children (cf. Manley, op. cit.). However, barely one fifth of all children eligible by age take these tests. From their results one can estimate that the top five per cent of the population obtain Verbal Reasoning quotients of 100 and over; and then by extrapolation that the population median is roughly 75. The corresponding results for some other tests are shown below, including a mixed Abstraction and Matrices test set by the writer, and an English test devised by L. H. E. Reid, a Jamaican psychologist, to suit West Indian conditions.

TABLE 6. *Estimated Median Quotients (Standard Scores) of Jamaican 11-year Population*

Moray House Intelligence (Verbal Reasoning)	75
Moray House English	72
Moray House Mechanical Arithmetic	82½
Moray House Problem Arithmetic	70
Reid's West Indian English test	78
Inductive Reasoning	69

Note that performance is far highest on mechanical arithmetic, but lowest for problem arithmetic and induction. Moray House English test quotients are somewhat below Verbal Reasoning ones; but with the more appropriate Reid test, they do better. Ample reasons have been given above for this general retardation in intellectual development, compared with white standards. Sheer linguistic handicap must be a major factor, though not the only one since performance is lowest on the least verbal test. In addition, what with school entry at seven and irregular attendance, the average Jamaican candidate will probably have spent only half as long in school as the average English pupil by the time he takes his 11+.

A very extensive survey of performance in Arithmetic, English and Inductive Reasoning, and of relevant environmental conditions was carried out by L. H. E. Reid, covering 63 representative schools. The various measures or indices were intercorrelated, taking school means as units, and the loadings of all variables on the most prominent general ability factor are shown in Table 7.

It is clear that home conditions – parents' reading and their interest in education, together with occupational level, and the progressive vs. backward rating of the community, yield the highest correlations with attainment and reasoning ability. The superiority of schools with predominantly two-parent rather than mother-only families must be interpreted with caution, since the former might well be more common

TABLE 7. *Loadings of Jamaican School Scores and Environmental Variables*

Mean school attainment	0·90
Mean Inductive Reasoning	0·86
Occupational Grading of Parents	0·62
Progressiveness Grading of Community	0·71
Parental Reading Habits	0·76
Parental Interest in School	0·68
Small Family Size	0·12
Per cent Children Living with Both Parents	0·36
Per cent Children Living with Mother Only	−0·43
Size of School (Total Enrolment)	0·76
Mean Pupil Length of Schooling	0·60
Modern Buildings	0·35
Good Equipment	0·55
Space per Pupil	−0·11
Large Playground	−0·15
Small School Classes	−0·44
Qualifications of School Staff	0·48
Male Head Teacher	0·15

among more intelligent and better-class parents. The biggest schools produce much better results, being mainly in urban areas, and they are fed more by skilled working and middle-class families. They are apt too to have better buildings and equipment, and *larger* classes, but smaller playground space. Qualifications of staff seem important, but these may also mainly reflect school size.

So far there has been little research on West Indian immigrants in England, though it is widely recognised that children of school age have considerable difficulties in adjusting to the unfamiliar conditions of English schooling, and are severely handicapped by their inability to understand Standard English, or to be understood.* Those who arrive at younger ages, and particularly those born in this country, are thought to do better. A Report by the Inner London Education Authority gives results on the 11+ Verbal Reasoning test and English and Arithmetic examinations for some 1,200 immigrants who had attended English primary schools from a matter of months up to six to seven years. The writer has attempted to convert the Verbal Reasoning figures into quotients relative to those of English children, and estimates a median of roughly 82 for West Indians, 87 for Cypriots, Pakistanis and other immigrants. However for all immigrants combined there is a rise from about 76 for those with two years or less schooling to 91 for those with

* Cf. Goldman & Taylor, also Inner London Education Authority.

six-seven years. There is no reason to think that the quality of immigrant families was superior seven years ago to what it was one year ago, hence this remarkable increase can be attributed safely to the better schooling, knowledge of Standard English, and the rather better environmental conditions in London.

XXII

Main Investigation in Jamaica

The full battery of tests described in Chapter XVII (excluding Abstraction and creativity) was given to a carefully chosen group of fifty $10\frac{1}{2}$–11 year Jamaican boys in 1963. Representative groups of ten were taken in each of five schools:

(i) better class urban,
(ii) poorer class urban,
(iii) country market town,
(iv) sugar estate,
(v) isolated rural small-holding.

This sample would be somewhat superior to the general population in so far as large urban schools are over-represented and only attenders were included; but not very greatly, since the median score on Reid's English test was 81, compared with the estimated population median of 78. Testing often had to be done in the playgrounds through absence of space, amid distractions from noises of chanting and corporal punishment in neighbouring classrooms, but there was excellent cooperation and no insuperable language difficulties. The median scores of the whole sample are set out in the form of DQs* in Fig. 8, and the dotted lines show the medians for the urban schools (i) and (ii), and the rural (iv) and (v), respectively. In almost all tests the order of means was the same as the order in which the schools are listed.

Clearly the best performances are in the top half of the Figure which contains the most drill-like tests, Spelling and Word Learning. Boys in School (i) were fully up to the English mean, though the rural boys fell a long way behind, having greater speech difficulties, poorer attendance, etc. Arithmetic is more backward, with a median of 83, since the test includes verbally stated problems as well as mechanical sums. The

* These figures often differ by one or two points from those published previously (Vernon 1965a), the reason being that the conversion tables from test scores to DQs were later revised. The 90th and 10th percentile figures are given in Table 12.

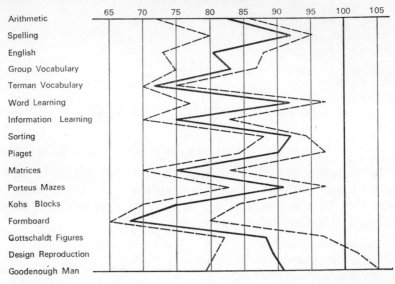

Fig. 8. Profiles of Median Test Scores of Urban, Rural and Combined Jamaican Samples.

median is equivalent to 9·0 year level on English norms. The score distributions for English and Arithmetic indicate that, despite the intensive drilling at school, nearly one third of Jamaican boys at 11 years are still virtually innumerate and illiterate. It is generally recognised moreover that there is a great deal of 'lapsed literacy' in the community (cf. C. A. Moser); i.e. that many adults fail to retain what was forced into them at school.

However the English and Group Vocabulary medians of 81 and 83 are higher than might have been anticipated considering that the boys were unsophisticated to standardised tests and multiple-choice items. But all our linguistically handicapped groups were able to deal better with these than with oral vocabulary and with comprehending and retaining oral information. The median individual vocabulary of 72 is very low, being equivalent to a Terman–Merrill M.A. of 7·0 years. Also there was little difference between the five schools; although the urban boys were clearly more fluent than the rural, none of them were accustomed to explaining their concepts orally (i.e. to Bernstein's formal language). On the other hand there were quite high scores on the Sorting test (median 92), also closely bunched. As McFie and Jahoda have claimed of Africans, Jamaican boys are not particularly retarded in classifying and describing familiar objects.

The Piaget performance is also quite high at 90, but the range is much wider and the rural boys drop to 83. In so far as the test reflects rational concepts of the world, this would be expected. However the boys varied considerably on different tasks and were generally most retarded on Number Concepts and the Conservation items.* The rural group was still lower on these items and in addition failed very frequently on some of the orientation items – Left and Right, Insect and Dot problems.

One of the most striking deficiencies was on the Matrices test, although this involves minimal use of language, and every effort was made to explain the easy items as simply as possible. The low scores of a larger sample on another Induction test have already been referred to. These tests call for resourceful thinking in tackling new problems, and it seems probable that the repressive atmosphere of home upbringing and schooling are at least partly responsible. Kohs Blocks, which involves the same kind of ability combined with spatial sense, was equally poor, and the majority of boys in the two rural schools scored three points or less, indicating that they were unable to break down any of the printed designs. Actually the poorest performance of all, relative to English boys, occurred on the Formboard, thus contradicting any easy generalisation that backwardness arises primarily from linguistic or educational handicap. However the lack of energy displayed by many, in addition to their poor spatial sense, suggested that inadequate nutrition and fatigue were partly at fault. Kohs and Formboard are both manipulative tests, and our remarks on lack of identification with a father, and lack of adventurous, male pursuits, may well be relevant.

However not all spatial-perceptual tests are so low, and the Gottschaldt Figures, Picture Recognition,† Porteus Mazes and Draw-a-Man are all around 90. Admittedly our group is somewhat above average, but these scores on quite a varied range of non-verbal tasks certainly gives a better impression of Jamaican intelligence than do tests more dependent on language comprehension. At the same time they lend even more point to the low scores on Induction, Kohs and Formboard, indicating that home and school upbringing can inhibit reasoning and spatial abilities.

The Draw-a-Man test was of interest for two other reasons. Not a single drawing attempted to portray skin colour or other local cultural

* Detailed figures are given in Vernon 1965a.

† The final series of Pictures for 3-D recognition had not been prepared at this time, hence exact comparisons with English or other scores is not possible; but the performance was certainly superior to that of Ugandan boys (Chapter XXVI).

features, apart from occasional palm trees. A large proportion were cowboys, suggesting that the current younger generation is by no means isolated from western culture. Secondly the gap between urban and rural schools was larger on this test than any other. The drawings of the latter, though also influenced by Comics, etc. were exceedingly primitive in their conceptions of the human figure, and equivalent to 7·0 year level on Goodenough's norms. Design Reproduction too showed a wide range. Though likely to be helped by the stress on accurate work at school, many of the rural boys had little experience of owning and manipulating pencil and paper; their school exercises were often done on broken slates.

The chocolate test yielded 54 per cent who delayed gratification – considerably lower than the 75 per cent in England. But surprisingly, boys from the best school waited much less frequently than those in the two poorer town schools (the rural ones were intermediate). Since the former were certainly more forthcoming and more likely to trust the tester, the probable reason is that chocolate would be fairly commonplace to them. A small bar would be nice now, and they would very likely get more from other sources next week. Whereas in Schools (ii) and (iii) a large bar was considered a rarity, worth waiting for. In other words the responses to the test may arise from superficial social attitudes rather than deeper motivations. However it was also observed that children with unstable backgrounds, in the sense of frequent shifts of residence, very seldom delayed ($P = ·05$).

ANALYSIS OF CORRELATIONS

Analysis of the correlations between the tests, and of the tests with environmental ratings, yielded fairly similar results to those in England, but some differences (cf. Vernon, op. cit.). All the tests had much in common, i.e. a large general factor, but the purest measures (with lowest group-factor content) were Matrices, Sorting and the Piaget Conservation + Visualisation items. These are all tests which were given individually, with the simplest instructions. Arithmetic, Information Learning and Kohs Blocks are also strongly loaded. The factor yields correlations of ·25 to ·33 with Cultural Stimulus, Planfulness, Socioeconomic status, Initiative and Male Dominance, thus confirming the importance attached to these conditions in the preceding Chapter.*

* A rating of Linguistic Background gave an even higher correlation of ·47; but this probably reflected the child's present fluency rather than Speech in the Home, and can hardly be interpreted as a causal influence.

However it was not adversely affected by Broken Home. As in many other researches, the cultural level of the home, parental education and encouragement are more important than socioeconomic level as such, and here they affect all types of ability.

The verbal-educational component was strong in all the written tests, and further affected several perceptual tests, particularly Design Reproduction and Draw-a-Man. The implication would seem to be that, when most homes provide little or no stimulation or relevant experiences, such abilities can hardly develop without some schooling, albeit poor schooling. (It will be remembered that in the Hebrides also $v:ed$ ability appeared to be involved in a much wider range of tests than usual.) Individual Vocabulary gave a different pattern of loadings from the written tests, suggesting again that understanding of oral English is different from doing English at school. This factor correlated ·46 with Cultural Stimulus, ·41 with Linguistic Background, ·28 with Socioeconomic, and ·24 with Unbroken Home.

A single spatial-perceptual factor was found in the drawing and practical tests, chiefly in the former. This correlated ·27 with Male Dominance rating, thus giving some support to Witkin-type hypotheses of the dependence of spatial abilities on male identification. Though there was no distinctive practical subfactor in Kohs and Formboard, the Formboard did give a considerable residual r of ·21 with the Initiative rating. The spatial factor also correlated with Regular Schooling, Cultural Stimulus and Linguistic Background, suggesting again that schooling of any kind helps, and uneducated parents hinder, the development of other abilities besides the scholastic.

XXIII

East African Culture and Education

Social anthropologists frequently emphasise the immense diversity of language, culture and social organisation in Sub-Saharan Africa, and criticise the over-simplified stereotypes of European residents and visitors: e.g. that the African is naturally indolent because of the hot climate, that he is too inferior in brain power to be capable of more than elementary education, or that he thinks 'concretely' and cannot cope with 'abstractions', and so on (cf. Ombredane). And yet one cannot but be struck by the number of similarities in reports by psychologists and others who are well aware of the dangers of ethnocentric frames of reference, and who have worked in many different parts of the continent: to name but a few – Biesheuvel and Hudson in S. Africa, Jahoda in Ghana, Doob in Kenya, Uganda and elsewhere, Ombredane and Faverge in the Congo, Dawson and Berry in Sierra Leone.* Particularly among the partly acculturated there are similarities in patterns of test scores, in problems of education, in modal personality characteristics, even in many child-rearing practices and values. Thus although the writer's sample of 50 Ugandan boys is obviously not typical, even of Ugandans, it adds something to the picture.

Many of the factors relevant to mental development in Africans have been discussed in Part 2, but some will be recapitulated here or expanded. Let us commence with Jomo Kenyatta's statement: 'To the Europeans, individuality is the ideal of life, to the Africans, the ideal is right relations with, and behaviour to, other people.' This exemplifies the emphasis on social integration and conformity, mentioned in Doob's description of the simpler, 'less civilised' peoples of the world (Chapter XIII), where he was referring particularly to the traditional, subsistence economies of Africa.

In earliest infancy the African baby has close physical contacts and warm relations with the mother; he is usually breast-fed, carried on her back, and sleeps with her or with other children. Quite probably these

* Cf. also E. L. Klingelhofer; E. B. Castle; L. J. Lewis.

conditions heighten the shock of weaning, but they also lay the foundations of gregariousness. African upbringing is appropriate to a static
society, as though designed to promote harmony, dependence and continuity. From the start children are trained through practical experience
in the skills and good manners appropriate for their age, including sub-
servience to their elders. Throughout society there is a strong sense of
status – everyone knows his place, and it is taken for granted that all
members want to behave alike. Children are severely punished for non-
conformity, and this may underlie the later rebelliousness to authority
commonly observed among those who escape to the towns or go to
secondary schools. Naturally there are wide tribal differences. For
example in Sierra Leone, Dawson contrasts the more aggressive
Temne people whose upbringing is very strict, with the more humane
and friendly Mende. The former make poorer workers and have greater
difficulties in adjustment to urbanisation. Systems of controlling adult
behaviour vary likewise. Often authority is vested in hereditary chiefs;
or control over deviancy may be exerted through communal disapproval, or through witchcraft sanctions. Since however all controls
tend to be external, not internalised, the sense of personal responsibility and the conscience (with the consequent neuroses) of western
civilisation are lacking. Sin does not exist in the abstract; actions are not
wrong if not found out, only if they affect the relations of the individual
with his group. Disasters or failure are ascribed to spiritual beings or
witchcraft rather than to natural causation or personal shortcomings.
Thus the urbanised, partly acculturated, African is left without the
support of either external or internal controlling mechanisms.

Another major difference between African and western societies lies
in their work routines and attitudes to work. In a subsistence economy,
all work is directly related to satisfying the primary needs, or to social
and religious observances. Thus, as Biesheuvel (1966) points out, work
is generally leisurely and periodic, depending on the climate, the
rhythms of nature and local custom. Regularity or an accurate sense of
time are unimportant, and even eating and sleeping tend to occur
irregularly, on demand as it were. This is one of the reasons why, to
Europeans, the African seems indolent, others being of course the widespread malnutrition and debilitating diseases to which we have already
referred (Chapter VI), and the prevailing tropical conditions which dis-
courage sustained effort. Normally, also, it should be remembered, the
African does not work for gain or personal advancement, but as a member of a tribe or an extended family; hence he is not motivated to do jobs
(or take tests) as we expect. Modern progress however is creating new

needs. Previously the agrarian community was self-sufficient, but now taxes, school fees, bride prices have to be paid, and there is an increasing demand for shop goods, which necessitate some compromise with a cash economy, usually through temporary or permanent migration of the younger adults to wage-earning jobs. Both the employment of adults and the education of children involve working to the clock, together with more continuous effort under somebody else's direction; and the work itself has no intrinsic relevance to biological or social needs, hence there are serious difficulties of adjustment.

So much for some of the characteristics of outer behaviour among Africans. Only a brief and obviously superficial indication of their religion and philosophy will be attempted, in so far as these are relevant to intellectual development. E. B. Castle points out that Christianity has a considerable influence, especially on the educated, and that Muslim beliefs are even more widely accepted. But for the majority religion is part of the whole way of life, rather than a set of beliefs to be accepted or rejected. Supernatural beings are ever-present, determining men's destinies. Good or evil forces inhabit places, animals and other humans, living or dead. Such a religion on the one hand fosters a spirit of resignation over present misfortunes and hope for the future, and on the other hand leads to deep-seated fears of the unknown – of sorcery and spells, of Europeans, of strange places and foods, of darkness and the jungle. Though modern medicine may be welcomed, most believe that illness is better treated by witchcraft and the medicine-man. According to Musgrove, one of the great difficulties in the higher education of Africans is their inability to see causation as the natural interplay of geographic, economic and historical factors. Where the western mind fragments and analyses the world in which it lives, the African mind tries to achieve harmony with the visible and invisible worlds. There is surely more than a chance resemblance here to the magical beliefs and animism which Piaget has described among western children, and which precede the attainment of operational thinking. The urbanised African has outgrown many of the rituals and taboos, but he has nothing to put in their place. Hence, to cite Biescheuvel again, the stresses of adjustment and culture-conflict are increasing rather than decreasing his dependence on magical practices.

EDUCATION

It follows that when formal education first came to Africa, the prospects of its growth were pretty unpromising; and it was further handicapped since, initially, it was propagated chiefly by missionaries, whose professed aim was to eliminate savagery by imposing western-type schooling and religion. Unable to see any value in African culture or sense of community, they introduced the highly formal and mechanical approach, characteristic of nineteenth century education in the UK (or France or other colonial powers). That this has persisted long after its value began to be questioned in Europe and America is by no means the fault only of its founders. We have already mentioned the linguistic heterogeneity which necessitates all but the most elementary teaching being given in a second or third language (Chapter VIII). The local teachers themselves are mostly poorly qualified in speaking and teaching in the foreign tongue. In East Africa they may have had merely six years primary education and two years training, though nowadays four years training and/or some secondary education is required. Few textbooks are available, and these cannot cover a wide range of interesting content because of the need to reduce verbal complexity. Such conditions naturally reinforce the tendency to stick to a narrowly defined syllabus and to drill rather than to explore. Unfortunately, again, the authoritarianism of European education, and its use of corporal punishment, accorded only too well with the passivity of the African child, his desire to conform, and his expectation of harsh treatment from adults.

Another, rather surprising, reason for educational backwardness is that Africans – especially boys – are so strongly motivated towards education. Except among some of the more remote and primitive tribes, it is seen as the avenue to a well-paid job. The office worker or civil servant is likely to earn as much cash in a month as the peasant family does in a year. Great sacrifices may be made to pay school fees; (in East African primary schools these are around £2 per year). Thus not only the parents but the extended family expect to reap the benefits. Primary pupils, therefore, feel a very strong obligation to gain a secondary school place, and secondary pupils to pass the examinations which give entry to a career. They work extremely hard and, with their linguistic difficulties, concentrate all their efforts on memorising the textbook and the teacher's notes. They take little interest in artistic or practical subjects, or extracurricular activities which do not directly contribute to passing examinations, and they tend to reject any attempt to liberalise teaching as a waste of precious time. Apart from the few brightest students they do not want to be helped to think.

Notice the difference from the situation in Jamaica and among negroes in the USA. This is due largely to the current shortage in developing African countries of trained personnel for non-manual jobs.

There is relatively less opportunity, therefore, for girls though it is beginning to be realised that an educated daughter may also be an economic asset. Traditionally women existed for work in the fields, motherhood and child-rearing, hence they had no need of education. Far fewer girls were sent to school and their drop-out rate was higher. But the numbers are now beginning to catch up with those for boys. Traditionally again the men are the talkers, who settle the affairs of the community. These differences in sex-roles and attitudes, compared with those of the western nations, have interesting effects on test performance. Both in Zambia and Rhodesia it has been shown that boys perform appreciably better on vocabulary and attainment tests which depend heavily on language, whereas there is little difference from girls on non-verbal tests (cf. Irvine, 1968).

It would be most unfair, of course, to leave the impression that all African schooling is equally bad, although everywhere financial resources are limited and there are far too few well-trained teachers. But with the increasing number of African educationists who gain experience abroad, and the help of expatriate teachers in the schools and university Education Departments, many more progressive ideas are infiltrating. Particularly notable is the experiment in Kenya of teaching English from the start of primary schooling by direct methods, based on activity and on locally produced primers. These aim to make English a medium of meaningful oral communication, rather than just a translating skill, and to give confidence in its use.* Already the Kenyan project is said to have led to a great improvement in primary work in general, though long-term follow-up is needed. If it could be applied more widely, by adequately retrained teachers, it might be one of the most significant single steps in raising the effective level of African intelligence. Little progress, however, has been made with the wider problem of integrating African needs and traditions with a modern educational system. Unfortunately the governments are still obsessed with European-type academic education and resent suggestions that this is unsuitable for the 90 per cent or so who will have to remain predominantly in agriculture for many years to come.† Insufficient attention is paid, also, to the seven per cent or so of sorely-needed skilled and semi-skilled tradesman. At the present time only some two per cent are required with educational qualifications comparable to those of

---

* From experience in West Africa, O. M. Ferron concludes that, when there is a felt need for communication in English, the language is picked up much more readily than when it is taught by conventional methods.

† Cf. C. Cox; G. Hunter; and H. Houghton.

European secondary school leavers and university graduates, who will become professionals, teachers, administrators and clerical workers. And it is probable that these too could be better produced by a type of schooling less closely modelled on the English grammar and public school of 50 years ago. Indeed there are already signs of overproduction and of a shortage of jobs for academically trained leavers. Moreover the gap between the educated élite and the masses is widening, and leading to serious social discord in some countries.

EAST AFRICA

The three countries of E. Africa all gained their independence from British rule in the early 1960s. Though they retained few economic or other ties with each other, they are relatively homogeneous geographically, culturally and particularly in their education systems. Each, however, is made up of numerous distinct tribes, differing greatly in their economic and educational advancement. Uganda is roughly the size of Britain, Kenya twice and Tanzania four times as large, and each has a population of eight to ten million Africans and a high birthrate. In addition there are some half-million people of Asian descent, living almost entirely in the towns, and less than 100,000 Europeans. Their economies are still basically agricultural, only some three per cent of the population being urbanised (as against nearer 50 per cent in South Africa). Though the countries are vast, much of the land is infertile, and as agricultural techniques are mostly oldfashioned, living standards are very low.

Primary schooling is available for roughly half the children aged six upwards – more in the towns and in areas inhabited by the most progressive tribes, far less in desert and more primitive areas. It lasts seven years, and as entry to the higher standards is usually restricted and there is still a large drop-out, only about half of those who start complete the primary course. They are then eligible to sit the selection examination for entry to secondary school which, in Uganda, takes the form of English and arithmetic tests. In spite of tremendous expansion of secondary schooling in recent years, there are secondary places only for some ten per cent of school-leavers, i.e. about two-and-a-half per cent of the child population. In Tanzania, Swahili is very widely used as a lingua franca, and has become the main medium of instruction in the early primary years. But in Uganda there is no common language and English is introduced as early as possible in the primary school, though the local vernacular may be used in the lower standards, especially of rural schools.

XXIV

Testing of Ugandan Boys

While the great bulk of the Ugandan population lives by subsistence agriculture, in the towns the Africans are engaged in the whole range of occupations normal to an urban community (except that the bulk of the commerce is in the hands of Asians). Particularly is this true of Kampala, the capital city, which also adjoins the capital of the Buganda, the largest and most advanced of the tribes. Here too is established the oldest university of East Africa, Makerere College, with a mixed expatriate, African and Asian staff.

With the assistance of the University Faculty of Education and the permission of the Ministry of Education, a sample of 50 boys was tested in two primary schools in Kampala during Sept.–Oct. 1966. In order to secure reasonably fluent English speakers, they were chosen from the 12-year age group (that is, so far as was known to the schools, since there were no exact records of ages). One of the schools was in a poor central area, but it has a high reputation and can afford to pick and choose its intake; 11 out of 19 fathers were in clerical or higher-grade jobs. The other school was on the outskirts of the city, and accepted all comers whose parents could afford the fees. They came mostly from nearby housing estates and from the surrounding countryside. The overall parental occupational distribution was:

Professional – lawyer, university lecturer, teacher	6 per cent
Clerical-supervisory – police inspector, probation officer, bank clerk, small business owner	28 ,, ,,
Skilled trades – lab. assistant, painter, tailor	20 ,, ,,
Police, driver, small shopkeeper	32 ,, ,,
Peasant, night watchman	14 ,, ,,

Clearly this sample is much superior to the East African population in general, as well as being rather older than samples tested elsewhere. But no psychologist, to the writer's knowledge, has ever secured anything like a representative sample in any one African country, both because of tribal and linguistic diversity, and because of the fact that scarcely 30 per cent of this age group attend school. However the sample would be more nearly typical of the whole range of urbanised Africans. Moreover, on the basis of Irvine's (1965) findings in Rhodesia, it was expected that socioeconomic class would have less effect on abilities and attainments among Africans than in western countries, though this expectation was not confirmed.

Among 56 per cent of the boys the mother tongue was Luganda; 15 other tribal languages were represented in the remainder. Only in 26 per cent of homes was any English spoken, and in none was it the dominant medium. An attempt was made by the interviewer to elicit household compositions, though the intricacies of African family relationships are notorious. However it appeared that in this group 52 per cent of households approximated to the western nuclear family, consisting of father, mother and siblings with sometimes a few additional blood relatives and/or servants. The boys' teachers were generally aware of, and disapproved of, polygamous households. In a few cases one or both parents were dead, or the boy was living with an uncle or grandparent. Length of schooling could not be elicited reliably, but the great majority had started at six or seven years. They were mostly in the 5th or 6th Standards, though 4 of the brightest had reached Standard 7, and 7 of the most retarded were in Standard 4. Among the latter there were some difficulties of communication, but these did not appear to arise from suspicion or unwillingness; indeed some of the boys' friends who had to be excluded were greatly disappointed.

RESULTS

The median DQs are shown in Fig. 9, and the percentile ranges in Table 12. By far the lowest score is on Terman-Merrill Vocabulary, the quotient of 57 being practically off the scale. The median of three-and-a-half words correct might be equated to five year American Mental Age, and is much below the seven to eight words achieved by Jamaicans, Eskimos and Indians. The difficulty was not just one of speech, since the test was applied by an African student (in English); nor even primarily comprehension, since the median on Information Learning was 78. It seemed rather that the notion that words can be isolated and defined in the abstract was unfamiliar, except to the most intelligent. On the other verbal-educational tests, including Arithmetic, medians are in the 80s to 90s, that is they generally surpass those of other overseas groups (though it should of course be remembered that this was a more highly selected sample of the total population). It is not surprising that Word Learning at 94 is one of the highest performances, and that Arithmetic and Spelling are good, in view of the emphasis in the schools on rote learning. However the Information Learning result is more typical of the basic difficulty the boys have in understanding and thinking in a foreign language, which explains why relatively few are capable of secondary school work, and then only of a very formal nature.

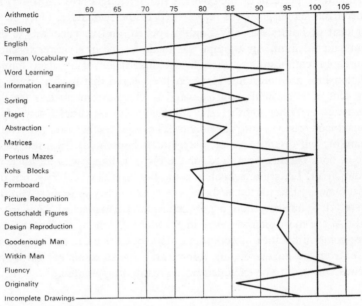

Fig. 9. Profile of Median Test Scores of Ugandan Boys.

The Sorting test at 88 was also quite well done, indicating that schooled Africans have no special difficulty in 'abstracting' and naming classes. This confirms Price Williams's study in Nigeria of classification of familiar objects, and Bruner's report of well-developed equivalence grouping of pictures of common objects among Senegalese children who attend school, though not among unschooled bush children. The Piaget score at 73 is much lower, through the tester made every effort to get the tasks across simply, and to accept any formulation of the correct response, however halting. The worst deficiencies were in all the Conservation tasks, over 50 per cent being non-conservers in every item; they were very low, also, on Number Concepts. Working with much younger children – five-year-olds in Rhodesia – Hendrikz found her Africans well developed in counting tasks, but much behind white children in number concept tests. Cowley and Murray compared the spatial concepts of 5–12-year old Zulus and whites, and found the former very greatly retarded in tests involving topological or projective space. In Euclidean space, e.g. simple matching or reproduction of two-dimensional shapes, they had much less difficulty.

According to Duckworth, Piaget himself has reported that children in Teheran are about two years retarded, whereas in Martinique they are some four years backward in causal thinking, i.e. in tests involving realism and animism. The testing in Martinique was conducted by Dubreuil and Boisclair, who attribute their findings to the primitive features of an African culture, particularly its permeation by superstitions. While our results show considerable variations on different kinds of Piagetian tasks, it would seem plausible that magical beliefs might especially affect the attainment of conservation and the concrete-operational stage. On the other hand Bruner and his colleagues obtained good results with schooled children in Senegal who were given a water jar conservation task in the vernacular, suggesting that much of the difficulty may be one of communication of ideas.

The Induction test scores were also low at 84 and 81, though nowhere near so low as Piaget and Vocabulary, and not so noticeably depressed below the level on other tests as among Jamaicans. Actually these figures are very similar to those of urban Jamaicans (cf. Fig. 8). The creativity tests were difficult to administer but, with encouragement, the numbers of responses, i.e. the Fluency scores, were similar to those of English boys. Indeed in the Rorschach blots, N was well above average, but the quality was poor, the responses consisting almost entirely of animal and human details. Hence the U per cent score on this test fell to 69. The other tests – 'Wings', Tin Can and Incomplete Drawings – revealed little of interest, though the Ugandan boys notably failed to exploit the possibilities of wings, e.g. for helping others. Likewise, while they found as many uses for Tin Cans as English boys, they scarcely ever suggested making toys or models.

Turning to non-verbal tests: Porteus Mazes yielded a median quotient of 99, largely because the boys were extremely slow and careful, and often lifted their pencils in spite of checking. Draw-a-Man also gave results within the normal white range, whether scored by the Goodenough or Witkin schedules. Though several of the drawings were extremely primitive, others showed considerable skill and sophistication. Picture Recognition and Kohs Blocks give two of the lowest scores (79 and 78), as foreshadowed in our discussion of three-dimensional perception among Africans; and the Formboard is similar at 80. Picture

Recognition is much poorer than in any other group. Yet there is not an all-round deficit on spatially-loaded tests. Design Reproduction is quite high at 93, since most of the boys showed meticulous attention to detail. More surprising was the Embedded Figures test (94); many who failed abysmally at Kohs or at grasping the spatial relations of the Form-board pieces were quite quick in breaking the Gestalt of the complex figures, even when seen upside-down. R. Schwitzgebel found a greater deficiency among young adult male Zulus on a version of the Witkin Embedded Figures than on several other perceptual tests. But they were a lower-grade as well as an older sample; and the writer's version is much easier to explain. Clearly, though, much more work is needed to isolate the crucial features in perceptual tasks that create special difficulties for Africans.

ANALYSIS OF CORRELATIONS

When the test intercorrelations were calculated, virtually no relation was found between verbal tests and Kohs Blocks, and very little with Porteus Mazes or Formboard. In other words there was no g factor comparable to that of the other samples. Verbal ability (in English) is relatively distinct from other aspects of cognitive functioning. This $v:ed$ factor is very prominent in Information Learning, Vocabulary, Spelling and English, and fairly strong in Arithmetic, Word Learning and Piaget.* But the loadings for Abstraction, Matrices, Concept Formation and Design Reproduction drop to around ·40, and for other non-verbal and most creativity measures lower still. This means that Matrices, Draw-a-Man and Kohs (with a loading of zero) would have even less predictive value for school work than they do in western cultures, since education depends so heavily on the specialised ability of acquiring the English language. The relevant background factors are, however, the familiar ones: Socioeconomic status has the highest loading (·51), followed by Cultural Stimulus in the home (·44), Planfulness (·38), Unbroken Home or nuclear family – presumably another index of acculturation (·35), English in the home (·33), and Initiative (·28).

There is in addition an Induction factor, though less pervasive than the usual g. It chiefly loads Abstraction, Matrices, Arithmetic, Piaget (especially Number Concepts), and Kohs. The only significantly loaded environmental ratings are Buganda vs. other tribal affiliations, and boy's

* The figures quoted were obtained from a group-factor analysis. Very similar results were obtained in a centroid analysis, published in Vernon 1967b.

Initiative. One might interpret this as a factor of intellectual resource-fulness and advancement vs. primitiveness, a characteristic in which the Buganda tribe notably surpasses others.

Next a broad perceptual-practical factor is most prominent in Kohs, Formboard, Gottschaldt, Porteus Mazes, Picture Recognition, and Conservation and some other items in the Piaget battery. It gives smaller loadings for Design Reproduction, Draw-a-Man, Matrices and Abstraction. On the environmental side it is significantly associated with Socioeconomic status and Initiative rating, and slightly with Cultural Stimulus and English in the home. Finally it correlates ·34 with Mischel's Delayed Gratification test. Only 32 per cent of boys delayed (less than any other group except one of the Canadian Indian tribes); but they were superior on almost all the non-verbal tests just mentioned, though not on most verbal or inductive tests. This factor may be inter-preted as an ability for coping with perceptual analysis, concrete operations and the world of objects, quite distinct from educational attainments. Though there is no direct evidence of its relevance to vocational capacities, it may well be similar to the general adaptability measured by Biesheuvel's battery of tests for mineworkers.

Other factors were less clearcut, though there were indications of a distinct Drawing Ability (in Draw-a-Man, Incomplete Drawings, Design Reproduction and Formboard), and of a fluency or productivity factor in most of the creativity N, and some U scores. The latter corre-lated with English in the home and Cultural Stimulus. It also loads several of the Piaget items, confirming our suspicion that lack of oral fluency accounts for some of the failures of Africans in Piaget-type con-cept development.

XXV

Canadian Indians and Eskimos

There are roughly 190,000 Indians and 12,000 Eskimos in Canada, though any estimate must be imprecise because of considerable inter-breeding with whites. They are thought to be originally of Mongolian stock, their ancestors having crossed the Bering Straits between the last ice age, 20,000 B.C. and 3,000 B.C. (cf. Jenness, 1963). They came in numerous waves and spread out over the American continent, forming a number of subcultures largely distinct in their economies, customs and languages. The Eskimos were presumably the last wave, and they remained in the north, mostly above the Arctic circle, though spreading over the 4,000 miles from Alaska to Greenland.

The impact of white civilisation on these stone-age people was catastrophic. It brought many amenities such as the horse, the wheel and the rifle, but it also brought diseases and drink, which exterminated thousands. The virtual extinction of buffalo and caribou destroyed the traditional livelihood of many tribes and led to widespread starvation. In his determination to exploit the natural wealth of North America, to cultivate, to build up his towns and trade, the white man callously disregarded the needs of the indigenes, fought against them when they objected, and eventually herded the remainder into reserves on such land as was no use to him. In Canada there was, in fact, little warfare, and peace treaties were signed ensuring that Indians would be wards of the Crown on their reserve lands within the provincial boundaries. Some tribes took to ranching, farming or trapping, but with the break-down of their natural hunting economy, demoralisation ensued, and to a large extent they exist on reservation funds and social welfare allowances. Many other Indians, loosely referred to as Metis,* together with the Eskimos, were left free to eke a living from hunting, trapping and fishing in the northern parts of the provinces and the vast North-west territories. But in the twentieth century, the fur-market fluctuated so violently that even this source of income ceased to support more than

* More strictly, Meti means a half-breed of partly French descent.

a fraction of the population. Many have moved into white settlements or trading centres and become hangers on, apathetically expecting the white man to provide. The very fact that, nowadays, none need starve seems further to have undermined their traditional independence.

However, this sorry story was mitigated to some extent by the efforts of humanitarians who gradually awakened the public conscience of white Canada to the plight of the indigenous peoples. Increasingly, therefore, the federal and provincial governments have been pushed into attempts to relieve the situation. But official policy has vacillated, and there is no easy solution. Often it would appear that politicians and civil servants, working thousands of miles away in Ottawa, have merely done their best to avoid trouble and keep things quiet. Others have preached the maintenance of the indigenous peoples' natural way of life, community development, and the building up of native crafts and trades. Admirable as these are, they only touch the fringe of the problem. Many others believe in progressive acculturation and integration with the white culture, and this process has indeed gone much further among some of the peoples in the USA and Alaska.* In Greenland also the Danes have instituted a policy of gradual adaptation which seems to be working relatively well.

Assimilation in Canada has been notably unsuccessful. The reserve Indians, Metis and Eskimos who have moved to centres of employment are commonly regarded as untrustworthy workers, not because there is much racial prejudice, but because of their improvidence, instability and tendency to drunkenness. Thus, with rare exceptions, they tend to become a depressed class of casual labourers and unemployed, in the slums of the big cities. For the same reason, efforts to set up mining, building, trading, whaling or other industries in the Indian and Eskimo territories, have had but a limited success, although the few non-whites who do obtain steady wage-earning employment are said to make good mechanics, labourers, etc.

CULTURE AND VALUES

There is a tremendous range of different cultures and languages, for example between the prairie Indians, the Pacific Coast fishing tribes, the Metis and the Eskimos; hence generalisations are always dubious. Nevertheless they seem to have shown in the past some outstanding

---

* Cf. G. MacGregor; Jenness, 1964; Hobart and Brant. Other groups of US Indians and Eskimos show at least as severe poverty and demoralisation as those in Canada.

common characteristics which help to explain the present. In primitive hunting societies the fundamental units of social organisation were the nuclear family, and the small band of interrelated families. The products of the hunt were freely shared among members of the band, and there was no point in conserving for the future. All would feast on what was available now, believing that, from the unlimited resources of nature, other kills would be made before long. Likewise time was freely available for making weapons, utensils, decorations, etc., and for enjoyment, when not employed on the chase. In so far as property was recognised, it applied to a man's names, songs, dances and spirits rather than to his material possessions. There was no organised legal system, nor allegiance to outside authority; decisions were generally based on informal consultations among heads of families. A man achieved status in his group by his skill in hunting, and – in the case of the more warlike Indian tribes – his bravery and leadership in fighting. (The Eskimos were always too scattered, too occupied in wresting a living from the Arctic, and too easygoing, to indulge in warfare.) Naturally, therefore, the indigene does not readily adapt to the Puritan ethic which stresses work as a duty, competition rather than cooperation, the virtues of acquiring property, and saving for oneself and one's family, combined with obligations to the community and nation. The white man expects that time and money should not be squandered, and is suspicious of sharing with others since it undermines the initiative of the recipients.

The maladjustment of reservation Indians to white society is enhanced by their continued resentment of injustices, past and present, and nostalgia for the days when they were the proud hunters (cf. E. H. Erikson). The older men, particularly, who have the greatest influence on tribal decisions, hang on to as much of the customs and language as they can, spurn any moves towards acculturation and seem deliberately uncooperative except with the rare white man who has won their trust. The younger adults, both Indian and Eskimo, are more Canadianised, have generally had elementary education and speak enough English for trading and employment purposes. They even encourage their children to get a full education, in preparation for a wage-earning job, though they do little to maintain attendance and often take the boys away on hunting expeditions. However this naturally varies from school to school, and parental cooperation was generally good in all those studied by the writer.

Zentner (1963a) has conducted extensive questionnaire enquiries among Indians and whites in both Oregon and Alberta, and claims that the two races of adolescents are nowadays very much alike in their educational and vocational aspirations and values. Though the Indians do not identify completely with whites, and show much pride in their race, many of them believe that Treaty rights should be abolished in order to encourage fuller integration and economic self-sufficiency. Similarly Worsley* obtained essays from senior Meti students in northern Saskatchewan on 'What I want to be when I am grown up'; and when these were analysed by Knill, they revealed that a majority aspired to professional, commercial or skilled occupations, as did whites, though very few of their choices were likely to be realised. But these authors do not sufficiently recognise that their informants represent the most able five to ten per cent of Indians. It is unlikely that a survey of the whole range of the age group would show anything like the same enterprise and desire for assimilation with white society.

Although this forthcomingness of the most educated minority is a hopeful sign, one is even more struck by the apparent inability of the indigenous peoples to throw up leaders, who would represent the needs of their groups, and get them to cooperate in working towards economic, educational and political ends. There is the occasional minister, teacher, entrepreneur, etc., but far fewer outstanding or upwardly mobile individuals than among American negroes, despite the added handicap to the latter of colour prejudice. Even the underdeveloped African countries, with far poorer educational facilities and, as our data have shown, poorer practical skills, produce more spokesmen and organisers. It may be that the more progressive Indians tend to intermarry with whites and to become completely absorbed into the white culture. Most of those who are left, it would appear, have become too introverted, rigid and apathetic to try to raise their own standards.

UPBRINGING AND SCHOOLING

Both Indian and Eskimo cultures are highly permissive towards, and fond of, young children, despite the occurrence in occasional tribes of such practices as binding to boards (cf. Erikson). They tend to be weaned late and greatly indulged; corporal punishment is never used and there are no angry reactions to misbehaviour, though gentle restraints are imposed on aggression and, later, shaming is used for control. From quite early the children are guided towards responsibilities and adult roles, and there is clear sex differentiation. Thus boys are encouraged to play at hunting and fighting (or riding in ranching communities), and by 10 to 12 are accompanying adult males and achieving their first kills.

* This investigation is described by Knill and Davis.

Generosity and sharing within the group are still prominent. The Eskimo particularly realises his extreme dependence on others for help in adversity. At the same time, family cohesion seems to be more fluid among the Eskimo. Illegitimacy and irregular unions are condoned; children are adopted freely (even when their fathers are white) and sometimes interchanged. Thus, although there is always affection and support, there seems to be less personal involvement of the parents in the particular child than in western societies.*

Though day and boarding schools have long been established on Indian reservations, education in the outlying areas was extremely patchy till recently, depending mainly on the efforts of missionaries. But in 1945-7, the provincial and federal governments took over responsibility for education in all except the most inaccessible settlements.† In the Northwest, for example, there is a school for 900 Eskimos, Indians and whites at Inuvik, and a large proportion of Eskimos are brought in, if need be by air lift, from up to a thousand miles away, and boarded in hostels from September to June. Interestingly, this does not seem to produce much emotional disturbance (cf. Vallee), perhaps because of the looseness of family attachments already referred to. Whether it is beneficial to abstract them from their natural habitat and interfere with the acquisition of traditional skills is more debatable. For the syllabuses and textbooks are the same as those of the provincial educational systems, with little concession to local needs and interests; and practically all teachers are whites.

When children enter at six to seven they are considered to make good initial progress, though they may have to go into beginners' classes to learn English before starting Grade I work. Some do not start till a later age and they show more learning difficulties. However, in all types of school there is much retardation; the average $10\frac{1}{2}$-year-old is more likely to be in Grade III than Grade V (cf. Knill and Davis). The majority never achieve beyond Grades V–VI (say, English top junior) standard. The drop-out rate is high, though a few proceed to Grade IX–XII work, in secondary or technical boarding schools, and a tiny percentage even achieve university, all without cost to their families. Though motivation is excellent in the early years, it is commonly observed, especially among Indians, that by 12 or so they fall off in keenness and tend to become introverted and suspicious. A plausible explanation is that, with adolescence, they come to realise how little the world holds for them, and they react to the clash between tribal and

* Cf. W. E. Willmott; D. J. H. Clairmont.
† See Department of Citizenship and Immigration: Indian Affairs Branch.

white values with apathy and withdrawal. In recent years observers in many areas have noted a serious growth of delinquency among unemployed school-leavers, both Eskimos and Indians,* characterised by a pose of toughness and resort to the three F's – fighting, fornication and fraud. These youths are disillusioned with the traditional way of life, and aspire to the high living standards of whites, but their upbringing has done nothing to build up the internal moral controls of the white. They exemplify Merton and Cohen's theory† that delinquency arises when certain success goals are accepted as desirable by society, but the means to the attainment of these goals are denied to a segment of the population.

Nowadays, rapid changes are taking place in the economic circumstances and the adaptation of indigenous peoples to Canadian education and society. Living off the land is fast disappearing (cf. Jenness, 1964), and this process must accelerate since, with the high birth rate and good medical services, the land will support an ever-declining proportion. Nevertheless it would be fair to say that the traditional values of the indigene and the aspiration to hunt and trap still play a major part in the upbringing of boys until adolescence. True, they are likely to be severely handicapped in the growth of abilities by poverty, lack of cultural stimulus, language difficulties, family instability and lack of purpose; yet they have the advantage of living in an affectionate and permissive atmosphere, and of encouragement to cope actively and resourcefully with their physical environment.

* Cf. J. D. Ferguson; D. J. H. Clairmont; Knill and Davis; Zentner 1963b.
† Cf. Cloward and Ohlin.

XXVI

Background Data on Indian and Eskimo Boys

The general discussion in the preceding chapter will be amplified by some concrete details collected on 90 Indian and Eskimo boys in 1965. Five small groups aged 10:1–11:11 (median age 11:1) were studied, with the kind assistance of the Education authorities concerned. The Indians were drawn from the prairie tribes of Stoney and Blackfoot, living on reservations at Morley and Cluny respectively, near to Calgary, Alberta. Both schools have small hostels, but collect most of their

TABLE 8. *Social and other characteristics of samples of Indian and Eskimo boys*

| | Indian | | | Eskimo | |
	Morley	Cluny	Tuktoy-aktuk	Inuvik	Hostel
Numbers	18	22	12	13	25
Per cent Delayed Gratification	50	32	58	69	48
Median Size of Household	7	8½	8	8½	10
Per cent Broken or Unusual Homes	50	23	0	8	40
Median Socioeconomic Index	5	5½	4	5½	5
Median Cultural Index	4	5	4	4½	4
Linguistic: per cent rated 1–2	61	35	8	38	40
Per cent Schooling Delayed till 7+, or Great Irregularity	50	45	17	46	72
Mean Planfulness Rating	3·2	3·1	4·1	3·5	3·2
Mean Initiative Rating	2·8	3·0	4·3	3·8	4·0

pupils by bus from a few miles around. The Eskimos live in the North-west Territories, above the Arctic circle, and were tested in the large school at Inuvik, on the Mackenzie Delta, or at the Arctic seaport of Tuktoyaktuk. Table 8 shows the numbers in these subgroups: the Inuvik group is divided into Inuvik residents, and hostel boys or boarders. The latter tend to come from less acculturated families, living more from the land than from wage-earning.

About a quarter of the Indians and an eighth of the Eskimos were very slow and difficult to test and interview, usually through lack of English or general dullness (they were mostly in Grades I or II). But the others were extremely keen and generally forthcoming. The Eskimo boys were particularly jolly and easygoing, and there was little sign of the reputed shyness and suspiciousness among most of the Indians, once they had learnt that the testers came from the land of the Beatles, and had seen the Queen and the Duke.

Parental Occupations

Seventy per cent of the hostel and half the Tuktoyaktuk boys (but only one Inuvik resident) claimed that their parents lived off the land, trap-ping, hunting or fishing. Many of these would be highly skilled, though often classified at the bottom of the socioeconomic scale.* The remain-ing hostel boys' fathers were chiefly DEW line employees – mechanics, labourers – while the majority of Inuvik fathers were government or school employees, e.g. janitor. A few were employed at an oil company, bakery, etc., but none appeared to be skilled or non-manual workers. In Tuktoyaktuk and Inuvik at least 20 per cent were unemployed, though sometimes the mothers earned a fair wage as fur garment workers or school cooks. Several men obtained occasional labouring jobs, interspersed with trapping, but probably existed mainly on relief. No boys mentioned soapstone carving or other artistic work, though these are sometimes profitable.

The commonest occupation of Morley Indian fathers was log or post cutting. Most owned a few cattle or horses, and a few made a living from this. Some were called carpenters by their sons – probably not highly skilled. Some fathers were janitors or mothers cleaners, and several mothers made ornaments or moccasins. At Cluny there was a wide range from casual labourer to housebuilder, farm or ranch owner,

---

* According to B. R. Blishen, in the 1951 Census 72 per cent of Indians and Eskimos fell in the bottom grade of his 7-point occupational scale, as contrasted with 25 per cent of French-speaking and 17 per cent of English-speaking Canadian whites.

and two administrators on the reserve, though again there was a good deal of unemployment, especially in winter.

Housing and Possessions

In all groups the commonest type of house was a fair-sized lumber or log cabin, with a large (though poorly furnished) living room, oil or wood heated, and from one to four bedrooms. One Eskimo, a janitor and part-time broadcaster, had built a house of lower middle-class white standards (with government aid); a few families lived in what can best be called shacks, a few in tents. Western Eskimos do not use igloos, though they may cover a tumbledown shack with snow for insulation.

Almost all the Cluny but scarcely any Morley houses had electric lighting; half the Inuvik and hostel boys claimed to have electricity. Despite the poor furnishings almost all Morley Indians had one or more ancient cars, and most Eskimos a boat with outboard motor; and many possessed 'luxury' equipment such as washing machines, record players, tape recorders, which illustrate the tendency to spend extravagantly when in funds, rather than save for a rainy day. Only in Cluny homes (73 per cent) was there television.

Every boy was asked what he would do if the interviewer gave him $10.00, and the answers are classified below:

	Indian (per cent)	Eskimo (per cent)
Clothes	33	24
Food	16	3
Give to parents or buy something for them	16	10
Hockey stick, bike, books, guns, visit relatives, etc.	10	10
Save	16	28
Sweets, toys, 'shows'	8	25

The Indians especially stressed useful equipment, clothing and food, admitting that their families were sometimes short of necessities. The Eskimos were more willing to save, but also more likely to squander on immediate pleasures.

Delayed Gratification

The results of the Chocolate test, shown in Table 8, should be compared with those quoted in earlier Chapters. There is no doubt that the Cluny group, with the lowest per cent waiting for the larger bar, was the most uncooperative, while the Inuvik residents were most used to cooperating with whites. However the overall low average of 49 per cent possibly reflects the Indian and Eskimo tendency to improvidence, to living for the present rather than the future.

Family Size and Makeup: Overcrowding

The interviewers tried to extract the numbers and relationships of persons living at home, though this was often difficult as the numbers ranged up to 14, possibly 20 in one instance. Frequently there were married brothers and sisters, or the boy might be living with grandparents or show no clear affiliation, particularly among the Morley Indians and the Eskimo hostel groups. From Table 8 it may be seen that size of family was greatest in the latter. Broken or unusual households, including others besides the nuclear family, grandparent or married sib, are shown in the same Table. They total 28 per cent for all groups combined, whereas the corresponding figure for English and Scottish samples was eight per cent. Overcrowding ranged up to nine persons in a two-room cabin, though the average persons per room was close to two.

Socioeconomic Level

An index with a possible range of 0–12 was based on skill of parental occupation, type of house and equipment, overcrowding and number of wage-earners. While direct comparison can hardly be made with the scale used in England, the English mean would be roughly 10 on this scale. Less than 10 per cent of the most prosperous Indians and Eskimos would overlap with the poorest English scores. Note that the five subgroups do not differ greatly, though on the whole Cluny and Inuvik were a little better off, Tuktoyaktuk the poorest.

Cultural Level: Health

Similarly a Cultural Stimulus index ranging from 0–8 was based on parental education, school standard reached by older sibs, evidence of parental interest in schooling and amount of reading at home. The English median would be seven on this scale. Again the Cluny Indians are slightly the best; 16 per cent of the Eskimo hostel boys had lower scores than any member of the other four groups. Almost every boy claimed that his parents wished him to get a good education and expected him to complete a secondary course or better. Few, however, said that their parents asked them about what they did at school, or that they received any help with homework other than from older sibs.

Although most Canadian Indian and Eskimo children are clearly living in much poorer economic and cultural conditions than English or Canadian lower class, it is worth pointing out that these have advanced considerably over the past 20 to 50 years. Sizes of families are increasing, the birth rate being some three times that of whites, but health and educational provisions have also improved. Some families are earning substantial wages, even if few are fully self-supporting. Many children were shabbily dressed and some inadequately for the climate; but the majority would scarcely be distinguishable from poorer class Canadians except by features and speech. It was not possible to collect reliable assessments of health and nutrition. Doubtless there is underfeeding, poor management and choice of diet in many families (e.g. carbohydrates and tinned foods rather than the traditional protein and fat which the climate demands). But defective health or nutrition were certainly less obvious than in the West Indies and Africa. The Eskimo hostel group contained the greatest number judged as above average in health, possibly because of the good food and care they had received over the last three years or more.

Linguistic

A one–five rating was made of the amount of English used in the home, three representing half English and half Stoney, Blackfoot or Eskimo. The percentages with little English, given in Table 7, show that the Morley group was most handicapped in this respect, Tuktoyaktuk the least. The Indians commonly used their own language on the playground, the Eskimos almost always English. The hostel group had little language difficulty, despite their home background, since older boarders (up to 16 years or more) used English all the time, and the younger ones picked it up quickly. Also the Inuvik school consisted to about one third of white Canadians. Thus when an Eskimo testee was held up by, say, the Formboard problems, he could often be heard thinking out solutions in English.

Irregular or Delayed Schooling

Only rough records of attendance were available, but age of starting school was known, and the percentages starting more than one year late (or missing a lot subsequently) are shown in Table 8. Only five per cent of English pupils show comparable irregularity, and in addition they have the extra year from five to six. Clearly schooling has been most regular at Tuktoyaktuk, most irregular or delayed among the hostel Eskimos.

Planfulness

The rating of purposiveness of the home vs. improvidence and irrationality was based on informal conversation about the house, belongings, parents, food and clothing needs, boy's duties and interests, savings, etc. The mean would certainly be low by English standards, but no quantitative comparison is possible. There is little to choose between the subgroups, but the Tuktoyaktuk community is more stable and better organised than most.

Boys' Leisure-time Activities

All boys had recognised duties such as bringing in water, chopping wood, feeding or rounding up animals, taking out the garbage, babysitting, etc. Interests cannot be readily tabulated since very varying numbers of activities were mentioned. All the Eskimos and 68 per cent of Indians clearly regarded hunting, trapping or fishing with adults as a major interest, though the animals varied: at Morley, deer, elk and fish predominated; Cluny – deer, ducks; Inuvik – musk rats; Tuktoyaktuk – ptarmigan, geese; hostel boys – seals, caribou, ducks, fish. Hunting or fishing on their own was also frequently mentioned by Eskimo boys, especially the hostel subgroup. Among Indians, horse-back riding was listed by 45 per cent, but ice-hockey, skating and swimming were also much more popular than with Eskimos. Ball games were referred to by one sixth of both groups, but miscellaneous 'playing with friends' occurred much less frequently than in England.

Reading was claimed by 34 per cent of Eskimos and 55 per cent of Indians, but it was clear that few boys or families had more than, or even as many as, half-a-dozen books and that most reading was confined to comics or an occasional magazine. Nevertheless there were one or two in each group whose reading is comparable with that of an English boy who has passed the 11+. Under the constructional heading, 80 per cent of Eskimos claimed to make boats, bows and arrows, guns, airplanes, etc. (no subgroup differences), and eight per cent did carving; whereas 45 per cent of Indians mentioned more large scale carpentry such as bird-houses and corrals. Model kits could probably not be afforded by either. Very few indoor games were mentioned, though observation during home visits revealed that there were various traditional sleight-of-hand and gambling games, and often some toys.

Boys' Occupational Aspirations

Boys were asked what they thought they would be when grown up, rather than what they would like to be. On the whole the answers, classified below, are pretty realistic (more so than their educational aspirations), the

	Indian (per cent)	Eskimo (per cent)
Professional (doctor, priest), office, store	5	12
Mechanic; bus, lorry or boat driver	6½	4
Builder or carpenter	25	8
DEW line or Government work	—	12
Ranching, raising cattle	12½	—
Farming	12½	—
Log or post cutting	17½	2
Trapping, hunting	—	38
Police, cowboy, army, pilot	11	24
Don't know	10	0

majority choosing the same as their fathers or else jobs which they had actually observed among adults in their communities (cf. C. L. French). The penultimate category might be regarded as fantasy jobs, but the rather high proportion of Eskimos in this category is due mainly to the popularity of 'police' in Tuktoyaktuk where, indeed, a few adults are employed by the RCMP. Very few boys, it will be seen, envisage skilled trades. Over three-quarters of all choices represent outdoor jobs. Among the Eskimos 52 per cent of hostel boys and 24 per cent of town ones think they will be trappers or hunters. J. D. Ferguson, working in Tuktoyaktuk, points out that although life on the land is nowadays likely to be less profitable than wage-earning, it still has the highest prestige. Next in order of appreciation are occupations such as boat-building, which are carried out by Eskimos themselves, independently of white supervision.

Initiative

No rating was given by the interviewer for male vs. female influence or dominance, as in England, since masculine identification was obviously predominant in every case. However, an attempt was made to assess initiative on the same 1–5 scale as with English and Hebridean boys, on the basis of active, resourceful interests and vocational aims, and self-reliance. The mean rating in England was 3·0, and it seems fair to credit the Indians with similar, the Eskimos with distinctly higher, scores (Table 8), though obviously any comparison must be highly subjective. It is deplorable that, as these boys get older, nothing could be better calculated to depress such initiative than life on an Indian reservation, or in a white settlement in the North.

XXVII

Indians and Eskimos: Test Results

The median scores for Inuvik + Tuktoyaktuk combined (i.e. 25 town boys), and for 25 hostel boys are shown in Fig. 10, those for Morley and Cluny Indians in Fig. 11. In order to ensure that English test standards could reasonably be applied, the group tests were also given to 75 Canadian white boys and 86 girls in Calgary schools (median age 10:6½, i.e. a little younger than the indigenes). The boys scored 101 on

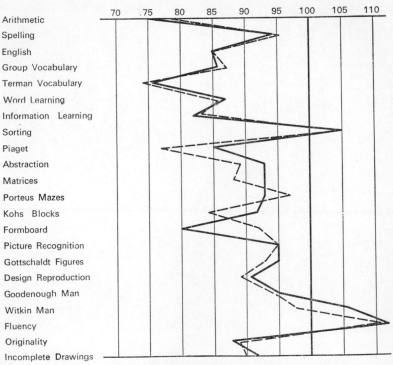

Fig. 10. Profile of Median Test Scores of Eskimo Boys.

English, 98 on Group Vocabulary, 97 on Abstraction and 100 on Gottschaldt, showing that they were closely similar to the English standardisation group in most respects.

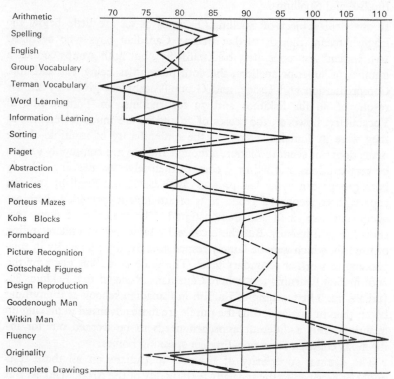

Fig. 11. Profile of Median Test Scores of Indian Boys.

Arithmetic

All groups are very backward around 76, but the best Eskimos were noticeably superior to the best Indians, the 90th percentile DQs being 94 and 84 respectively (cf. Table 12). However the test used emphasises conventional fundamentals, and the Albertan educational authority has recently introduced the new mathematical approach, which gives less practice in these elementary processes. Thus the white Calgary boys' median was only 91, and one could reasonably say that the Indians and Eskimos are 15 points below this figure rather than 24 below the English figure. Teachers of Eskimos and Indians have often stated that they do better at arithmetic than on more verbal subjects; but our observations indicate that they are seriously handicapped by the new approach, because of its high verbal content.

English and Spelling

In the drill subject of Spelling, Eskimos at 94 are little below the English mean, though further behind Canadian boys who averaged 105. Indians are moderately backward (85), but both groups contain a number of superior spellers, the 90th percentiles being 111 and 106. Comprehension and Usage, and Group Vocabulary give very similar results of 86 for Eskimos and 79 for Indians. In Terman-Merrill Vocabulary, however, the scores of 76 and 70 are much lower, just as they were in Jamaica. Here too the unfamiliarity of multiple-choice items does not seem to matter, although Indians are commonly said to be very cautious, not liking to commit themselves to guessing. Clearly both groups can make fair progress with classroom English, and can cope with conventional group tests of attainment, provided these are adequately explained and demonstrated. The majority of boys, too, show fair oral fluency. But these conceal a basic lack of understanding of English, which may be largely responsible for their difficulty in progressing to work at secondary level. The same point was made by the Information Learning test, where Canadians averaged 107, Eskimos 82, Indians 72. The teaching of English in Canadian schools is if anything better than in England, thus the pupils are more advanced in picking up meanings. But a different approach needs to be worked out for indigenous children from non-English-speaking homes.

The distinct superiority of Eskimos to Indians on all these tests might be ascribed to the specially high quality of the Arctic schools. But since the groups are so similar in Arithmetic, the difference is more likely due to the greater usage of English in the homes and in the Inuvik hostel. In addition there may be closer resemblance in grammatical structure between Eskimo and English (both languages involving agglomeration of elements) than between the two Indian tongues and English.

Word Learning

The white Canadian, Eskimo and Indian medians of 98, 87 and 75 respectively are similar to the results on English attainment tests. The pupils do not, like Hebrideans and Jamaicans, do as well at this test as at Spelling, since there is little emphasis on rote learning in Canadian education. The Cluny Indians were noticeably more sullen during the group tests than those at Morley, and this is reflected in their medians of 72 and 81 (P = ·05). On other educational tests there was little difference between these subgroups, possibly because the poorer home backgrounds at Morley were compensated by a particularly good school atmosphere and better teaching.

Sorting Test

The medians of 104 and 91 again indicate that this task depends little on linguistic capacity or on level of concept development. Morley and Cluny medians were 97 and 89. Since there was no lack of cooperation from Cluny boys on this test, the difference may be merely that Blackfoot language and thought structures are less favourable to this kind of categorisation.

Piaget Tests

Both the Indian groups and Tuktoyaktuk Eskimos sank to 73, but the hostel Eskimos were distinctly higher at 85. These results suggest severe constriction of intellectual development by the unstimulating atmosphere of the Indian homes and reservations, and possibly the remoteness and lack of variety in Tuktoyaktuk. Boys at the hostel would come in contact with a wider range of ideas and in addition have developed greater resourcefulness in living off the land. Note that performance in these subgroups does not depend simply on degree of acculturation.

All groups were weak on the conservation tasks; out of 12 questions, English boys failed 14 per cent, hostel Eskimos 40 per cent, town Eskimos 51 per cent and Indians 56 per cent. Both Number and Time concepts and knowledge of Right and Left were weak throughout. On the other hand Eskimos were similar to whites, Indians poorer, in understanding shadows and the level of water in the tilted bottle, and in drawing the Reversed Dot correctly. Indians were better in the Insect test. Neither showed much inferiority in Logical Inclusion or in the Equidistant Counters problem.

Creativity Tests

The Eskimos showed considerable fluency on the three verbal tests (DQ 111), though their responses were mostly of poorish quality, with more perseveration ‚than among English boys. For example, in Rorschach they might say, of Blot V: 'This could be a bat, a butterfly, a witch, a hawk, an eagle. . . .'; or with No. III: 'Here's a nose, a face, hands, legs, arms, a body', but fail to show whether these were seen as parts of a whole man. Nevertheless there were frequent touches of imagination or fantasy, particularly in 'Wings', and the median U score of 89 is higher than for most verbal tests. The subgroups were all quite similar.

The Indian performance was much weaker, although the fluency average is pulled up to 110 by the large number of perseverations and small-detail Rorschach responses. The 'Wings' test, asking for narrative-like responses, caused much difficulty, and many boys' answers consisted of nothing but flying to cities where famous ice-hockey matches are played. (However the Morley group surpassed Cluny in this test, probably because they live in more wooded and mountainous territory and may have more understanding of nature, while the Cluny boys live on more open, agricultural land.) In every test the U scores were very low, yielding an average quotient of 77. Linguistic fluency alone is not to blame; it was the quality not the quantity of responses that was lacking. Intellectual apathy in the homes and active discouragement of divergent thinking by the culture seems more likely to result in this extreme poverty of imagination.

Such tests also have projective possibilities, though they were not studied in detail. Thus in Tin Can, half the Indians and Eskimos suggested throwing the can away or destroying it, whereas only one English boy and no Hebridean thought of this. A further subtest was tried in this group, namely telling a story about: 'The Dog that Couldn't Bark'. This yielded much the same fluency differences as before, but in addition responses were classified into those imputing kindness to people or other animals, and those imputing cruelty or blaming the dog himself. Morley boys obtained the highest cruelty score, followed by Cluny; then the Inuvik residents; the other Eskimos still showed a preponderance of cruelty, whereas Hebridean and English boys more often imputed kindness. The Incomplete Drawings test was disappointing, showing slightly inferior U and E scores in Indians and Eskimos, but few differences of content except for rather more tomahawks and sledges.

Inductive Reasoning

Abstraction and Matrices gave rather uniform results averaging 90 in the Eskimos, 82 in the Indians. Though the latter are seriously retarded, their performance is better than that on verbal tests, and superior to that of the Jamaicans. On these tests, and on five of the perceptual-spatial tests, it is noteworthy that the hostel Eskimos score a little better than the town groups, averaging 95 and 90 respectively This fits in with the difference obtained with the Piaget tests and confirms the view that land Eskimos have to a greater extent developed self-reliance and participated in adult male activities. On the whole, also, the Cluny Indians do a little better than the Morley group, which accords with the observation that they represent a slightly more progressive tribe; however they drop behind on Abstraction as they did on most of the group tests.

Spatial Tests

In the Gottschaldt Figures test of field independence, in Kohs Blocks and Picture Recognition, the Cluny Indians come right up to the same level as the Eskimos with scores of 90 to 95, though the Morley group stay about seven points behind. In so far as these tests are predictive of technical-mechanical aptitude, they support the view that indigenous males have considerable aptitude as mechanics, though they seldom get the opportunity to display it, and are handicapped by linguistic and motivational weaknesses.

Reproduction of Designs

Here both groups of Indians do well (median 92, Eskimos 89). In Porteus Mazes, Eskimos and Indian scores are little below the white mean (95 and 98). Cultural experience in finding one's way in woods, waterways and snows may have contributed to this result. Actually the outstanding performance was at Tuktoyaktuk (median 102 vs. 92 for other Eskimos: $P = \cdot 05$), which is difficult to explain unless Porteus is justified in his claim that the test involves planning ability. The Tuktoyaktuk homes were rated relatively superior in Planfulness.

Draw-a-Man

The medians for both combined groups are 95–6 on Goodenough scoring and 101 on the Witkin score. These are high compared with most other tests, bearing out the reputation of N. American indigenes for artistic talent. In restandardising the Goodenough scale, D. B. Harris obtained drawings from 318 Alaskan Eskimos, and these showed one to two years superiority to white norms over the 8–14 year range. But as his samples were sent in by teachers in Eskimo schools, it is possible that they were not representative of the various age groups. Other studies (e.g. Havighurst) have shown average or superior scores on Goodenough among American Indians. The hostel Eskimos' quotient on Witkin (but not Goodenough) was again the highest, most of the boys drawing realistic seal-hunting scenes. The Morley boys were also good on Witkin but poor on Goodenough, mainly because their art teacher encouraged impressionistic action pictures with little detail.

Formboard

Here too the medians of 87 and 85, contrasted with the Jamaican 68, support the view that stronger male influence, and experience in coping with the physical environment (despite severe linguistic difficulties) are involved in spatial tests. However this test is exceptional in that the hostel Eskimos were the poorest subgroup, with a median of 80. We cannot invoke undernourishment as a factor (as in Jamaica), and it seems more likely that the town Eskimos and Indians would have had somewhat better opportunities to indulge in manipulative activities and games involving manual dexterity, in model-building, etc., than land boys.

ANALYSIS OF CORRELATIONS

The main ability factors underlying the test in the Eskimos seem to be much the same as in an English group (cf. Table 13). There is little indication of unusual features such as occurred in the Hebridean and Ugandan groups. The general factor is particularly large, relative to the size of the specialised abilities or group factors, quite possibly because the Eskimos were more heterogeneous in their abilities than the English. For example they ranged more widely in age (over a two year instead of a ten month span), and in amount of schooling; and this seems to have affected their development on the spatial-perceptual as well as the verbal side. As usual, Abstraction, Matrices, Piaget Total, Arithmetic, English and Embedded Figures show the highest *g* loadings. A series of half-a-dozen additional group intelligence tests was given by R. S. MacArthur, with special care to ensure adequate practice and understanding of instructions. The Lorge–Thorndike Non-verbal and Cattell's Culture-Fair tests turned out to be particularly good measures of the same general factor, with loadings of ·89 and ·87. The standard Progressive Matrices reached ·74 and obtained a moderate spatial factor loading of ·37.

The most unusual feature of the Eskimo figures was the absence of correlation of this general ability factor with the ordinary environmental conditions – Socioeconomic level, Cultural Stimulus and Planfulness. Presumably we did not know the right questions for eliciting more significant environmental parameters. However Amount of Schooling and Age were strongly loaded. Within about three years of starting school, the boys develop much the same structuring or organisation of abilities as English boys and, except for some linguistic difficulties, are not very backward. This would suggest that Eskimo children whose families are too isolated for them to attend school must be far more retarded than those we tested, although presumably they acquire skills in hunting and survival of a high order. It implies, also, that there is considerable potential going to waste though, as pointed out in Chapter V, this is not effectively available unless we can devise ways to bridge the gap between the traditional values of the race and those of modern civilisation.

Two overlapping English abilities were distinguishable, one mainly in the written tests, especially English, Group Vocabulary, Information Learning and Spelling; the other mainly in the Fluency N and other creativity scores, also giving small loadings of ·28 to Sorting and Picture Recognition. The former factor was definitely dependent not only on schooling but Cultural Stimulus in the home (·52), Use of English, Unbroken Home, and on Town vs. Hostel dwelling (all ·20 to ·25). Fluency, however, did not involve schooling and its highest correlation was ·37 with Initiative rating.

The spatial ability factor showed moderately high loadings for Kohs, Witkin Draw-a-Man and all the other practical and perceptual tests (except Picture Recognition). There was also a separate small Drawing or pictorial factor in Witkin, Goodenough, Incomplete Drawings, Picture Recognition and some of the Piaget drawing items. Spatial ability showed no appreciable environmental correlations, though hostel boys were slightly superior, while Drawing was the only factor to correlate with Socioeconomic level (·25). Finally the Piaget Conservation, and a few other, items provided an additional factor which was considerably higher in the hostel boys ($r =$ ·42).

The Indian sample is a bit more uniform in its schooling, but shows a wide scatter in English, a few boys being quite fluent, while others come from homes where the language is never used. The test intercorrelations again yield quite similar factors, though particular tests differ in their loadings. For example Abstraction and Matrices, while good g tests, were also found to depend largely on $v:ed$ and spatial ability respectively. The Sorting test showed no g-content at all, only $v:ed$ and Fluency, and all the creativity measures (except Incomplete Drawings) were similar. Porteus Mazes, Picture Recognition and Formboard too were relatively specific, with g loadings around ·20 only. In this group, Socioeconomic level makes much more difference, correlating ·38 with the general factor, and Cultural Stimulus shows a loading of ·47. But the outstanding figure is ·65 with Initiative rating, indicating that the development of all abilities is largely affected by the morale vs. apathy of the boy and his family. On the other hand Regular Schooling and Linguistic background are irrelevant.

The usual *v:ed* factor appeared in the written group tests and this correlates ·31 with Planfulness. The superiority of the Morley to the Cluny group was shown by a loading of ·38. A strong oral Fluency factor is present in all the creativity measures, while also affecting Terman Vocabulary and Sorting. This has high correlations with Socioeconomic level (·59), Linguistic background (·44), Initiative and Planfulness (·39).

The spatial factor is not very prominent, being practically confined to Gottschaldt Figures, Formboard, Matrices, Kohs Blocks and some of the Piaget Conservation items; here the Cluny group is much superior. But there is quite a broad Drawing + pictorial ability factor, also involving various Piaget tasks; this gives small correlations with good home conditions.

In conclusion, then, the Indian groups fairly closely resemble the Eskimos in many respects, particularly in showing relatively good spatial performance, though on a majority of tests their scores are around ten points or so lower. Yet they probably have more contacts with white society, or at least more opportunities, than Eskimos have, and quite comparable educational, medical and relief provision. True, the linguistic handicap is greater, though that is one sign of their resistance to acculturation. Perhaps it could be argued that the superior performance of Eskimos is due to natural selection and survival of the fittest, which have probably operated more severely in Arctic than in prairie habitats. But this seems less likely in so far as the Indian scores do equal the Eskimos on certain tests – Arithmetic, Design Reproduction, Kohs, Porteus and Drawing. Thus the most likely explanation of serious retardation in other aspects of intellectual development among Indians is the general maladjustment of the tribal cultures, and the inability of white society to organise acceptable goals.

PART VI
Summary and Implications

Summary and Implications

This book has ranged widely over several countries of the world, and it has drawn on many psychological theories and investigations. Throughout, however, it has drawn attention to, and expressed concern over, the differences between peoples in their level of technological advance, of education and civilisation or backwardness. Although the psychologist's tests are highly inadequate instruments for bringing out the full strengths and weaknesses of different groups or individuals, particularly when applied outside the cultural group for which they were constructed, they nevertheless tend to confirm our everyday observations. Each group certainly shows variations in patterns of abilities: members of an underdeveloped country may reach, or surpass, western standards on some tests, and fall below what we would regard as the borderline for mental deficiency on others. But the average performance on quite a wide range of tests only too strikingly fits in with the observed inequalities of mankind. Similarly, within any one western country, there are obvious differences in the status, vocational and educational achievements of subgroups such as the social classes, the coloured immigrants in Britain, the negroes and Indians of North America; and however open to criticism our tests of intelligence and other abilities may be, they tend to reflect these differences.

No one would deny the importance of geographical and economic handicaps, of disease and malnutrition in the production of such differences. But to a very great extent man makes himself and fashions his own environment, and it is he who must be changed if he is to achieve a more prosperous and healthy existence. We suspect that his offspring fail to develop the high-level skills and mental abilities required for adapatation and progress in the modern world because of the way he brings them up in the home and community, and the schooling or training he provides. It is not only the poor circumstances of the parents but their backwardness and resistance to change which result in the underdevelopment of their children's capacities. However in every group there are the more and the less able; and many of the former do achieve good education and positions of leadership. They influence their own societies, sometimes dramatically, usually more gradually, and bring up their own children less disadvantageously.

Changes are occurring too as groups and subgroups come in contact with and try to help one another, even if the influences they exert are often motivated by self-interest and political considerations.

These, however, are not matters for the scientific psychologist to dabble in. Yet he can make very real contributions by studying the present situation and trying to disentangle the main factors underlying the stimulation or retardation of intellectual growth, by clarifying the nature of the essential variables and developing and testing sound hypotheses, also by improving the diagnostic tools which he uses in his evaluations. He cannot, of course, claim to be wholly impartial or free from ethnocentrism and middle-class prejudice; inevitably he views other groups through the spectacles of the values and concepts of his own group. Indeed even these opening paragraphs sound as though the middle-class western way of life was being held up as the ideal to which all inferior groups aspire. True, there is a kind of universal scale of economic prosperity and technological advance; and psychologically there is a scale ranging from the relatively simple to the more complex and powerful types of mental process, and the two are interlinked. But the writer has been at pains to point out that the complex intelligence of the western middle-class is not the only one, and that its development is accompanied by serious drawbacks; that over and above variations in position on these scales there are, and doubtless always will be, countless variations which promote the adjustment and stability of different cultures. Also that although most tests, including those used in the writer's researches, do reflect western-type intelligence, there is no reason why psychological techniques should not be applied in studying the particular abilities and qualities of other groups, and the factor underlying their growth.

Part I shows first that much of the controversy regarding differences in abilities between ethnic groups and subgroups has arisen because the term 'intelligence' is ambiguous. It is used here to refer to the effective all-round cognitive abilities to comprehend, to grasp relations and reason (Intelligence B), which develops through the interaction between the genetic potential (Intelligence A) and stimulation provided by the environment. One must also distinguish constitutional equipment, that is the potential as affected by pre-natal or other physiological conditions; and Intelligence C – the results obtained on various intelligence tests, which provide merely a limited sample of the Intelligence B displayed in behaviour and thinking at home, at school, at work. There is strong evidence that differences in Intelligence B and C between individuals within one culture are largely – certainly not wholly – genetically determined. But when environmental differences are more extreme, as between ethnic groups, their effects predominate. This does not mean that there are no innate racial differences in abilities, but they are probably small and we have no means of proving them. Differences between subgroups such as social classes are partly genetic, not wholly environmental (Chapter II).

Current conceptions of cognitive growth derive largely from the work of Piaget, Hebb and Bruner. From the initial sensory-motor reflexes of the newborn, a succession of more complex and adaptive schemata or skills are built up through the impact of environmental stimulation on the maturing nervous system and through the infant's active exploration and experiment. Thus a series of stages or successive reorganisations can be recognised in the child's perception, speech and thinking, through which different children progress at different rates. (Bruner's enactive, iconic and symbolic modes of coding differ in important respects from Piaget's sensory-motor, preoperational, concrete and formal stages, but both are useful in describing intellectual development.) Moreover more backward groups typically fail to progress as far as others along this scale, and though they may develop lower-order skills which are highly effective for survival, their reasoning capacities remain similar in many ways to those of younger children, or even regress through lack of appropriate stimulation. That is they learn to be unintelligent, instead of acquiring the skills that constitute intelligence. An important implication is that man has by no means reached the limits of his mental powers; there is immense room for improvement at the lower end of the scale, and also the possibility of more effective 'techniques' at the top end (Chapter III).

General intelligence is merely the common element in a whole host of distinguishable, but overlapping, cognitive abilities. When dealing with homogeneous or highly selected populations, it is profitable to study different mental faculties and abilities along special lines, adopting the factorial models of Thurstone and Guilford. But with more heterogeneous populations, and particularly when considering different ethnic groups or subgroups, the common element or *g* factor tends to dominate. And there are advantages in following the hierarchical or group-factor model, which successively subdivides more specialised types of ability. This implies that, while we should certainly try to study a wide variety of mental functions in contrasted ethnic groups or subgroups, we are most likely to discover conditions that affect general or all-round ability; then those that favour or inhibit verbal and educational as contrasted with perceptual, spatial and practical abilities, and later the smaller (but still quite broad) group factors such as number, memorising, fluency or creativity, etc. Intelligence B cannot be precisely defined since it refers to the totality of our schemata, but its essence lies in the more generalised thinking skills, which can be applied to a wide variety of problems. An Appendix to this Chapter IV examines an alternative formulation of factors in intelligence, namely R. B. Cattell's theory of 'fluid' and 'crystallised' general ability.

What then do we mean by the potential ability of an underdeveloped group or individual? It is not Intelligence A or constitutional potential, since these cannot be assessed and are of use only in so far as previous environment has developed them. Equally the conventional expedient of contrasting achievement measures with intelligence test scores (verbal or non-verbal) is beset with fallacies. Abilities at different types of test often differ, and by surveying these patterns of abilities in the light of the individual's or group's physical and cultural background, education and motivation, the psychologist can often arrive at useful diagnoses and remedial proposals. If plausible reasons can be suggested either for general backwardness or for unevennesses in performance, and if the remedial measures at the disposal of the community can be shown to, or reasonably be expected to, work, then that person or group has potentiality (Chapter V).

Part II surveys the major environmental factors which have been found to influence the development of intellectual abilities, concentrating on recently published investigations. Most studies consist of cross-sectional comparisons of groups or individuals who differ in respect of many interacting conditions, and these do not readily demonstrate the effects of any particular condition. The methologically superior experimental approach, where one condition is changed and other factors are kept constant, and the longitudinal follow-up of a sample who undergo various conditions, have their own difficulties. Thus even in the case of relatively clear-cut conditions such as malnutrition during pregnancy or later, and debilitating diseases, our knowledge is scrappy and often indirect. The incidence of dietary deficiencies is worldwide, especially in the low-income countries, and it is found that they can cause permanent impairment to the brain at the formative stage of pregnancy and early infancy, and seriously reduce later intellectual capacity. After this stage, poor health and nutrition or endemic diseases, though often associated with poor performance, do not seem to affect mental growth as such (Chapter VI).

Particular stress is laid by most psychologists on the sensory stimulation, opportunities for activity, and the emotional relationships of the first year or two of life, as basic to later psychological development. But the evidence, apart from that of animal experiments, is unconvincing. While it is clear that extreme social deprivation has traumatic effects on human infants, probably the ordinary range of social and physical environments (even among relatively primitive groups) provides adequate stimulation. In other words, conceptual and linguistic deprivation during the period from about one-and-a-half years and throughout childhood, when children should be building up their concepts of objects and their relations, labels and thinking skills, may be more important than so-called sensory or perceptual deprivation. And while the preschool and early school periods are crucial, the modifiability of intellectual capacities by changed conditions even in adolescence has been underestimated.

Certain types of visual discrimination are strengthened in environments where they are important for survival. But the evidence for the effects of ecological environment (e.g. 'carpenteredness' vs. rounded, and open-vista vs. closely filled) on susceptibility to illusions is conflicting. Perceptual development seems to depend to a greater extent on social norms, education and acculturation. Clearly however many African peoples have difficulties with analytic perception of figures and pictures, and with three-dimensional interpretation. This deficiency is not found among other quite backward groups such as Eskimos. Its origins are obscure, and it may be remediable by appropriate training, but the main explanation would seem to lie in lack of visual-kinaesthetic experience and of encouragement of play and exploration throughout childhood (Chapter VII).

The interactions of language with thinking are highly complex and controversial. But a child's language, which is wholly shaped by his cultural group, must be intimately involved in his perceptions and conceptualisations of the world. Hence his intellectual development is highly vulnerable to poverty of linguistic stimulation, and to the inadequacies of the mother-tongue – in many societies – as a medium for education. Bernstein's analysis of 'formal' and 'public' language codes describes the extremes of a continuum which is typical not only of the British socioeconomic classes, but applies in many respects to technological as against more primitive cultures. Bernstein brings out also the close connection between linguistic training and cultural values: the formal code is associated with internalised controls (Superego formation), high educational aspirations and planning for the future; the public code with externally imposed discipline and with less purposeful attitudes to life.

Infant rearing practices and maternal deprivation may cause temporary emotional traumata, and seem to be associated with certain cultural traits. But their long-term effects on personality and particularly on the development of abilities, are more dubious. A number of investigations indicate that socialisation practices and the home 'climate' during preschool and school years are more influential. The 'democratic' but demanding home climate makes for better intellectual progress than the over-protective, the autocratic or the 'unconcerned' homes. The work in this area of Witkin and his colleagues provides important evidence that the encouragement of resourcefulness and independence in growing children leads to greater clarity and differentiation of perceptions and concepts, while maternal over-protection tends rather to favour verbal abilities. It is not clear whether it is general intelligence or spatial abilities which are chiefly affected, nor what parts are played in causation by social-class differences, by sex or temperament, or by masculine identification, etc. However Witkin's generalisations have fruitful applications to differences between cultural groups, e.g. Eskimos and certain African groups (Chapters VIII and IX).

Turning then to intellectual progress at school: the major researches in the UK of E. Fraser, Wiseman and Warburton, and J. W. B. Douglas, are outlined. These show that, although the handicaps of poverty are much less marked than 40 years ago, socioeconomic class and its associated conditions of child care, neighbourhood morale, and good or poor schooling, still make substantial differences to children's intelligence and achievement. Even between 8 and 11 years the differential between the middle-class and lower-working class child becomes progressively greater. But the most important factor of all appears to be the cultural level of the home and the parents' interest in and aspirations for their children's education. Hence the further improvements that we would desire in material conditions, social welfare and schooling, will not of themselves eliminate the handicaps of the lower working and less educated classes.

Much the same factors are shown to be significant by research in the USA, though the major differences there are not so much between socioeconomic classes as between ethnic and linguistic groups, i.e. between whites and negroes or recent immigrants. American negroes tend to score in the low 80s on tests of intelligence and achievement, though there are considerable geographic variations, and differences on different types of test. Moreover younger children perform better and show a cumulative deficit at later ages. Negroes are at least as handicapped in non-verbal or spatial tests as in verbal abilities, though relatively better in simple number and rote learning tests; and this may be attributable to familial factors such as the frequent absence of masculine identification models for boys. The interpretation and implications of observed differences in abilities have given rise to even more heated controversy in the USA. At the same time there have been valuable positive efforts to reduce the handicaps of 'disadvantaged' children by compensatory or introductory schooling, or by integrating schools of different ethnic composition. It is too early to say how successful these measures are in improving general intellectual growth and scholastic performance, or whether the effects of home upbringing and of intergroup suspicions are too strong (Chapter X and XI).

There is rather little evidence of the effects of different kinds of schooling, or of studying different subjects in different ways, on general mental growth. But it is clear that sheer amount of schooling, even – in backward countries – of low-quality education, helps to promote both school achievement and the kind of reasoning measured by non-verbal tests. Also if such schooling is unduly delayed, the possibilities of mental growth deteriorate. The acquisition of lower-order schemata opens up the way to higher-order thinking, but they can also become rigidified and block further progress. Likewise in western countries the level of adult intelligence depends on the kind and amount of intellectual stimulation provided by the adolescent's secondary schooling and occupation. The notion of optimal or critical periods for learning probably has less applicability to conceptual than to sensory-motor functions, and greater importance should be attached to motivational factors – to the maintenance or repression of curiosity, and to the child's or young adult's aspirations and prospects of advancement. In this sense growth depends on the future as well as on the past (Chapter XII).

Cultural groups and subgroups are exceedingly varied, and so also must be their effects on the intellectual growth of their members. A number of attempted classifications or typologies are examined, and it seems reasonable to regard the Puritan ethic of the western middle class as producing the greatest development of intelligence, in contrast both to western lower class and to the 'less civilised' cultures. The two latter differ in important respects, but the less civilised can be subdivided into hunting and agricultural types, which coincide rather closely with Witkin's field-independent and dependent; i.e. they are to some extent linked with the major group-factors of spatial and verbal abilities (Chapter XIII).

The evidence in the preceding Part that Intelligence B is built up in response to environmental stimulation and is therefore affected in many ways by cultural differences does not mean that tests constructed in western cultures are always worthless elsewhere. Despite the valuation of different skills in different ethnic groups, all groups have increasing need for complex, symbolic thinking. Researches in Africa and other countries in fact show that adaptations of western tests possess promising validity in assessing educational aptitudes and work effectiveness, though this may be partly because they are measuring language skills required for advanced schooling in the former situation, or acculturation and cooperativeness with white employers in the latter. Correlations with job efficiency assessments (which tend to be unreliable) are low, but this is true in western cultures also. However tests may often be inappropriate not so much because they do not measure useful abilities as because they are also greatly affected by unfamiliarity with the materials, or with the testing situation, or by other irrelevant 'extrinsic' factors.

Cross-cultural comparisons are unavoidable when members of different cultural groups or subgroups, who have very likely been reared under different conditions and are differently handicapped, are in competition for the same schooling or same jobs. Different regression equations, or different norms or cut-offs for acceptance, may be needed for such groups. Another legitimate cross-cultural application is for studying the effects of different background conditions on abilities, and this is the main aim in the present book (Chapter XIV).

Unsophisticated testees are handicapped in many ways by lack of relevant experience, failure to understand the instructions, and absence of the motivations and sets which sophisticated testees bring with them to the testing situation. However the distinction between these extrinsic factors, and intrinsic factors which affect the underlying ability, is only a relative one. Probably it is best defined in terms of how readily the handicap can be overcome, e.g. by better conditions of administration. A bimodal score distribution or the piling up of low scores among 'non-starters' is another useful indication of extrinsic difficulties. Also differences in the order of item difficulty may show that a test is measuring different things in different groups. However a number of investigations of practice effects among Africans indicate that these are not so large as is sometimes supposed, particularly when the testees have received some schooling. The results are comparable to those obtained with unsophisticated testees in the UK, and the same kind of measures used to familiarise British children with tests can be applied or extended. The suggestion that abilities should be judged from scores on several successive administrations, i.e. from learning curves, is technically unsound (Chapter XV).

It is obviously far more difficult to transfer western-type tests to relatively unacculturated groups, with little or no schooling, and the psychologist may have to confine himself to individual testing with specially constructed materials, under informal conditions. However Biesheuvel's work shows that it is possible to get across performance tests to groups of linguistically heterogeneous and illiterate adults; and Schwarz has formulated a series of useful principles for giving group tests, e.g. to applicants for technical training, which amount to teaching the testees beforehand precisely what they have to do. For most purposes it would be better to construct new tests based on materials and conditions appropriate to the culture concerned, than to adapt western ones, though this is difficult in view of the shortage of trained personnel. It is essential to validate old or new tests locally and to devise an appropriate system of norming.

In attempting to assess the educational potential of immigrant children, verbal tests are preferable to non-verbal or performance – either standard tests in English if they can communicate in it, or if not then similar tests in their own tongues. Alternatively a varied battery should be given and the results interpreted in the light of their educational, linguistic and social history, i.e. clinically. Objective tests of achievement are being produced in many developing countries and used on a large scale for secondary school selection. Less progress has been made with aptitude tests, e.g. for technical training, largely because, in the absence of suitable background experience, the skills needed for technical work are too undeveloped to provide a basis for worthwhile tests (Chapter XVI).

Part IV describes the present writer's investigations in which a battery of varied group and individual tests was applied to small groups of 10–12-year boys in England, Scotland (the Hebrides), Jamaica, Uganda and Canada (Indians and Eskimos). All the boys were being educated in the English medium. The chief aim was – not to show that some groups are more backward than others – but to link up patterns of scores on different types of tests with differences of background. No intelligence tests as such were used. The main categories were:

(a) Verbal and educational – arithmetic, silent reading and English, oral vocabulary, rote learning and learning of meaningful information.

(b) Induction – versions of the Shipley Abstraction and the Matrices test.

(c) Conceptual development – sorting and labelling, and a series of Piaget tasks dealing with conservation and other concepts.

(d) 'Creativity' tests of fluency and imagination.

(e) Perceptual and spatial tests, including Kohs Blocks, Embedded Figures, Bender-Gestalt, Porteus Mazes and Draw-a-Man.

In interpreting what the tests measure, reference is made to previous evidence of their validity, and to factorial analyses of the scores in several groups. The scores on each test were converted into Deviation Quotients or Standard Scores (similar to IQs), on the basis of the distributions in the English group, so that relative performance on different tests could be compared. Each boy was also interviewed, usually by a local teacher, to obtain information on his background, home, schooling, interests and vocational aspirations (Chapter XVII and XVIII).

Within the English group, the g factor, or general ability in all the tests, correlated highly with an assessment of Cultural Stimulus in the home, and to a lesser extent with Socioeconomic level and with Planfulness or Purposiveness of the home; but there was no correlation with Stable vs. Broken homes. The educational, verbal, perceptual and practical group factors, measured by particular groups of tests, also gave small correlations with several background conditions, though there was only limited support for the hypothesis that masculine dominance in the home and encouragement of initiative are associated with perceptual-spatial abilities.

Small groups of delinquent boys in an Approved School, and maladjusted children, gave unusual patterns of scores. The delinquents were very low in educational attainments, but also in the two Induction tests and certain perceptual tests. Their oral vocabulary, concept development and rote learning were rather better (quotients in the 80s); on some performance tests they scored in the 90s, and their performance on creativity tests was close to average. The maladjusted boys were specially backward in arithmetic, less so in verbal abilities; they were near average in concept development and in most spatial-perceptual tests and above average in creativity. The poor reasoning of the former, and the well-developed ability of the latter to deal with concrete notions of space, conservation, etc. – in contrast to their disturbed emotional and social relations – suggest that a wide-ranging battery of ability tests may be valuable diagnostically. In addition the Drawing and Creativity tests have projective possibilities. Socioeconomic level, Planfulness and Regular Schooling were found to correlate moderately with verbal and educational performance, but not Broken Home or Parental Tension. Patterns of family relationships, mother or father dominance and affection or rejection, together with neurotic, aggressive or other syndromes, seemed to be related to test scores, but in no clear-cut manner (Chapter XIX).

A group of Scottish Hebridean boys was tested in or near Stornoway, Isle of Lewis; half of them were from English-speaking, half from Gaelic-speaking, homes. Apart from the linguistic differences, both groups are of interest as growing up in a relatively isolated community, free from the rush of modern civilisation. There are strong traditions of responsible and provident living, of rather rigid upbringing, and respect for formal education. The Gaelic-background group was handicapped in oral vocabulary, the Sorting test and Piaget, but did not differ significantly from the English-background boys in other respects. Both were superior to English norms in scholastic achievement and learning tests, though there was some restriction in originality. The test correlations were unusual in showing no distinction between g and verbal abilities. This does not seem to be due so much to linguistic heterogeneity as to a strong contrast between the more culturally stimulating and sophisticated homes vs. the more traditional and restricted (Chapter XX).

Turning now in Part V to our deprived groups – two of African and two of indigenous Canadian origin: we will first summarise the cultural and other characteristics most likely to affect their ability development, and then compare and discuss the test results. Jamaica is a country in transition from a primitive agricultural to a technological economy, and the population ranges from extremely poor, largely illiterate and superstitious rural communities – descendents of African slaves – to a well-educated middle class, often of mixed descent. The sample of boys for testing was drawn from schools representing all levels. The mother tongue of the majority is a kind of pidgin English which considerably impedes education, and primary schooling tends to be irregular, of poor quality, and far too formal and repressive of initiative. Family life is apt to be unstable, female-dominated and likewise conformist and authoritarian (Chapter XXI).

Uganda is basically a rural subsistence economy, with a low standard of living and much malnutrition, though the writer's sample was derived mainly from urbanised East Africans living in or near to Kampala, i.e. a relatively acculturated group. As in many African countries there is a diversity of tribes with different dialects. Education is mainly conducted in English, though the language is seldom used by the children outside the classroom. Schooling is available only for about one third of this age group, but it is greatly prized. Because of the language difficulties (among teachers as well as pupils) and the strong motivation, and for historical reasons, education tends to be highly mechanical. But the major differences between African and western intelligences probably arise more from the emphasis on conformity and social integration as against individual responsibility and internal controls; and from the acceptance of magical beliefs which inhibit analytic perception and rational thinking (Chapter XXIII).

Canadian Indians and Eskimos are equally disadvantaged linguistically, though English has greater currency in transactions with the white culture, and is freely used by Eskimo boys in and outside school. The quality of schooling is good also, especially in our Eskimo sample, though attendance may be delayed or irregular. The majority of families live at a low economic and cultural level, and show the traditional improvidence, or generous sharing now, rather than planning for the future. Vocational prospects for the boys are poor, partly because of geographical difficulties and partly because of the reputation of the indigenes for shiftlessness; also because of the apathy and demoralisation consequent on the breakdown of the traditional hunting economies and, in the case of reservation Indians, their continued resentment and resistance to acculturation. At the same time, the traditional child-rearing practices and values mean that boys of 10–12 years are still trained for resourcefulness and show strong identification with hunting and other masculine pursuits. This was most marked among a sample of Eskimo boys boarding at a school hostel, whose families still tend to live on the land rather than in settlements (Chapter XXV).

Table 9 provides a crude summary of the main handicaps thought to operate in nine of the above groups or subgroups, together with the main features of their test score patterns. In the top half are listed assessments of environmental conditions, *relative to those of children in western cultures*. Inevitably these are somewhat subjective, though backed up by the descriptions of these groups in preceding chapters.*
Below, the groups are first graded on all-round ability, and then for *relatively* better or poorer performance on particular sets of tests, i.e.

---

* Perceptual-kinaesthetic stimulation is, perhaps, the most dubious. It is meant to refer to availability of toys, manipulable objects, and rich and varied non-verbal experiences. Clearly this is something which is lacking in African upbringing; but are not Eskimos, living in the Arctic, also deprived in this respect? And it hardly seems fair to equate the tranquillity of life in the Hebrides, and its somewhat reduced contacts with modern civilisation, with this type of deprivation.

they are *compared with their own means* rather than with English standards. All-round ability is roughly graded, a single minus indicating a mean quotient of about 87–93, a double minus about 80–85. It should be pointed out that most of these groups are *not* representative samples. They are drawn from school attenders only; some groups are a little

TABLE 9. *Environmental conditions and test score patterns in nine groups.*

Conditions	Maladj.	Delin.	Hebr. Engl.	Hebr. Gael.	Jamaica	Ugandan	Indian	Esk. Town	Esk. Host.
Socioeconomic level	—					—	—	—	—
Providence-planfulness		—	+	+			—	—	—
Cultural Stimulus		—	+		—	—	—	—	—
Language				—	—	—	—		
Adequacy of Schooling			+	+	—	—			
Progressive vs. formal	+		—	—					
Encouragement of initiative						—	—	+	+
Home security and stability	—	—				—	—		—
Perceptual-kinaesthetic stimulation			?—	?—	—	—			
Health, nutrition						—	—	—	—
Deficiencies in: All-round level	—	— —				— —	— —	—	—
Induction		—			—	—	—		+
School attainments	—	—	+	+			—	—	—
Oral English and comprehension					—	—	—	—	—
Conservation	+			—	+	—	—		
Memorising	—		+	+	+	+	—		
Fluency and originality	+	+				+		+	+
Practical-spatial	+		—	—	—	—		+	+
Perceptual			—	—	—	+			
Drawing		+			+	+	+	+	+

older than others; and the Ugandans, in particular, come mainly from urbanised families of above average socio-economic level.

Nevertheless there is clearly a general correspondence between the numbers of adverse conditions and overall performance: the main exceptions, who score lower than might be expected from their backgrounds, are the three most socially maladjusted groups – Maladjusted, Delinquents and Indians. It may be seen that the assessment of Cultural Stimulus is most diagnostic of all-round ability; most other variables overlap but show greater discrepancies (for example, Ugandans are among the lowest scorers though relatively high socioeconomically). Had we had a considerably larger number of groups and more objective techniques of comparing their relative standing on these environmental conditions, it would have been interesting to correlate each condition with the group scores.

Several other fairly close correspondences are apparent. Thus the language rating, based on lack of English in the home, is naturally related to deficiency in Oral English and Comprehension, though not so closely to School Attainments or to Fluency. Formality of schooling always tends to produce superior performance in Memorising (i.e. the Word Learning test + Spelling), but good School Attainments in English and arithmetic seems to be more related to the Providence or Planfulness rating of the average home. On the non-verbal side, the connections are less clear-cut, and give only limited support to the hypothesis that spatial ability is favoured by a hunting economy, or by cultures which train for initiative (cf. Fig. 3). Performance on the perceptual tests (mainly Embedded Figures, Design Reproduction and Mazes) does not correspond with any of the environmental variables. However practical-spatial ability (Kohs, Formboard and Picture Recognition) does tend to go with Encouragement of Initiative, and to some extent with Perceptual-Kinaesthetic Stimulation. Inductive ability also seems to be related to Initiative. What we can say is that there is a closer resemblance in test score patterns between Jamaicans (descended from West Africans) and East Africans, also between Indians and Eskimos, than across these two groups. Although our tests fail to pin down very clearly the essential ability factors in which they differ, Kohs Blocks – which mainly measures inductive + spatial ability – comes nearest to doing so. Thus 66 per cent of all the Jamaicans and (highly selected) Ugandans as against 22 per cent of Indians and Eskimos scored under 10 points on this test. In contrast the Jamaicans and Ugandans were much superior in Word Learning and Arithmetic despite roughly equivalent linguistic handicap.

The results of our enquiries show that we cannot afford to ignore the factor of general retardation. On the whole these groups and those individuals who are most backward in, say, linguistic tests also tend to be below average on all other types of tests. Nevertheless there are considerable irregularities in score patterns, and we have made a little, though not very much, progress in explaining why particular groups do some things much better than others.

Some of the main results in particular groups are as follows: the Jamaicans, in common with others, were noticeably more successful on standard classroom tests of English (including multiple-choice vocabulary) and arithmetic than on oral comprehension of language. Thus western tests of verbal intelligence and achievement are less unsuitable, e.g. for school selection purposes, than might be supposed, though naturally western norms are apt to be misleading. Much more striking is their deficiency on non-verbal materials such as Matrices, Kohs and Formboard (the latter test probably being additionally affected by conditions of health and nutrition), though relatively high on perceptual and drawing tests. They differ most markedly from Africans on the Piaget tasks, probably due to their greater sophistication, their many contacts with British and American cultures, the absence of tribalism and fewer magical beliefs. But there were big differences on most of the tests between the urban boys, who were within the normal English range (except in comprehension and induction) and the rural ones who are much less touched by modern civilisation. Somewhat as in the Hebridean groups, there was a closer correlation between verbal and other abilities than in English groups, suggesting that schooling and acculturation are necessary to development on the perceptual-spatial side. This may arise when many of the homes provide little stimulus to any kind of intellectual development, or even repress such development (Chapter XXII).

The Ugandan group was the most handicapped of any in oral vocabulary, although they were supposed to have been taught in English for five years. This seemed to be due, at least partly, to their unfamiliarity in analysing words out of context. But the effects of their very formal schooling were manifest in high spelling and rote memorising. A particular retardation was noted also in the conservation items of the Piaget tests, and in three-dimensional interpretation of pictures, both of which confirm previous observations of African abilities. On the other hand there was no general retardation on the spatial-perceptual side; Gottschaldt Figures, for example, Drawing and Mazes were within the normal range. The structuring of abilities differed markedly from that in other groups: instead of verbal abilities (in English) permeating intellectual development generally, they were relatively distinct from other types of ability – inductive, practical-perceptual and imaginative. There seems to be a clear need for greater integration of their learning of English with daily life, based on less mechanical, more active, methods; also for the introduction of greater opportunities for concrete, practical training to compensate for the inadequacies of psychomotor stimulation in the homes (Chapter XXIV).

The interests of the majority of Eskimo and Indian boys still lie mainly in hunting, trapping, fishing or riding and ice-hockey. But those who were tested were attending good schools, on the Canadian pattern, and had made some progress in classroom English, less in oral comprehension, in Piaget-type concepts or in arithmetic (where they are handicapped by 'the new' mathematics). In most other respects Eskimos who have had some exposure to schooling tend to score within the normal range, and are generally superior to the Indians, partly because of the greater apathy and uncooperativeness of most Indian families. Eskimo hostel boarders do better than those living in settlements on tests of induction and concept development, indicating that these abilities are promoted by the more resourceful and independent mode of existence. Indians are particularly restricted in imaginative ideas, i.e. they receive no encouragement to think 'divergently'. All groups are good at drawing, and their relatively high scores on spatial tests suggest mechanical potentialities. An unusual feature of the general factor in Eskimo test scores was that it does not correlate with cultural and economic characteristics of the homes, but does with amount of schooling. Probably therefore it is much less developed among the indigenous population who obtain less regular or no schooling. In the Indians, on the other hand, it correlated highly with an assessment of the initiative or morale vs. apathy of the boy and his family (Chapters XXVI and XXVII).

IMPLICATIONS

In summing up, it is desirable to stress once again that surveys of this kind are not very effective in pinning down the factors that underly any particular deficiency, or superiority, in an ability. In other words, our attributions are often speculative, though the fact that they are mostly based on the results of several tests, and on comparisons of several samples, gives them more substance. On the other hand, it should also be admitted that tests may measure rather different abilities in different groups, or be affected in different ways by what we have called extrinsic factors. Particularly non-verbal, spatial and perceptual tests are apt to show varied factor loadings (though this is no doubt partly due to the small sizes of the samples). Verbal and educational tests are more likely to measure the same thing in different contexts, since all our samples are being taught a similar body of knowledge and skills in English-medium schools. Hence, while our results on the whole justify quite widespread use of western-type tests across cultures (provided these are not too widely dissimilar), they also indicate the need for more intensive studies of particular aspects of mental development with locally constructed tests within non-western cultures.

Many psychologists might be inclined to banish further studies of 'intelligence' in non-western cultures on the grounds that it has no precise meaning or uniform content. While admitting its difficulties, the writer would point out that the same objection applies to any other more specialised abilities, e.g. perceptual discrimination, ideational fluency, problem solving, etc. not to speak of the American psychometrist's factors; since the structure and content of these are likely to be equally variable. Even if an investigator talked only in terms of performance on particular tests, e.g. Progressive Matrices or Kohs Blocks, he would still not be measuring the same ability, since the tests have to be given in different ways to, and have different meanings to, North American whites and, say, Africans. 'Intelligence' is justifiable in so far as it has been shown that a general factor always emerges from a wide range of varied tests, though one must be aware that it is culturally-loaded. What is important is that, in concentrating on abilities recognised by western culture, psychologists should not neglect special talents that might be more highly developed in other cultures. For example, in the writer's researches, little opportunity was provided for Eskimos to demonstrate their artistic and mechanical abilities, and none at all for Ugandans to display their auditory and rhythmic skills.

In the light of our surveys of four seriously handicapped groups, and of the literature summarised in earlier chapters, what are the main factors underlying poor performance on tests either of general intelligence or of more specialised mental faculties and educational or other attainments? A summary list will be useful, not only in considering how to help underdeveloped nations, but also in trying to diagnose the underlying handicaps of disadvantaged children, particularly immigrants, in our own culture. They are classified below under three or four main headings to correspond to our distinction between Intelligences A, B and C.

C. Extrinsic Handicaps

1. Unfamiliarity of testees with any test situation, and lack of motivation.

2. Difficulties due to particular form of items or materials (e.g. pictures), and conditions of testing (e.g. working at speed).

3. Anxiety, excitement, suspicion of tester.

4. Linguistic difficulties in understanding instructions or communicating responses.

B. Constitutional Handicaps

5. Brain damage due to pre- or post-natal malnutrition, maternal stress, or disease. Birth injury; later brain pathology and deterioration.

Positive Environmental Factors

6. Reasonable satisfaction of biological and social needs, including exercise and curiosity.

7. Perceptual and kinaesthetic experience; varied stimulation, encouragement of exploration, experiment and play.

8. Linguistic stimulation encouraging a 'formal code' and clarity of concepts.

9. 'Demanding' but 'democratic' family climate, emphasizing internal controls, responsibility, and interest in education.

10. Conceptual stimulation by varied environment, books, TV, travel, etc.

11. Absence of magical beliefs; tolerance of non-conformity in home and community.

12. Reinforcement of Nos 8 and 9 by school and peer group.

13. Regular and prolonged schooling, also demanding-democratic; emphasising discovery rather than rote learning only.

14. Appropriate methods to overcome language problems.

15. Positive self-concepts with realistic vocational aspirations.

16. Broad and deep cultural and other leisure interests.

A. Genetic Factors

17. General plasticity.
18. Genes relevant to special aptitudes.

Naturally many other classifications are possible, and some of the factors listed (e.g. B. 15 and 16) are less well attested than others. Note that socioeconomic status as such does not appear, though it is, of course, associated with Nos. 6–13; nor does emotional security or maternal warmth, except under No. 6. Ecological and climatic conditions might merit inclusion, but are probably covered by No. 7.

What can be done to improve these conditions? Economic progress within the developing nations, and technical assistance from abroad, will obviously impinge at some points, particularly in reducing malnutrition and disease, building up the educational system, and providing worthwhile occupational prospects for much larger numbers. Likewise reduction of unemployment and better housing among immigrants in

Britain should open the way to advance in many or most of the categories.

We would naturally expect the education system to provide the chief mode of attack on the syndrome of negative factors in a backward culture or subculture. Schooling is given by fairly small numbers of the more intelligent members of the population, who should be open to new ideas and who can be trained to follow new methods and aims; and they influence the minds of a large proportion or even the whole of the population over the period when concepts, skills and values are being built up. However the school is by no means as powerful an instrument in practice as in theory. Teachers are themselves so strongly imbued with the traditions of the old culture that they do not readily absorb or communicate the new; and the younger, more progressive, individuals cannot easily stand up to the entrenched beliefs of older, more conservative colleagues or of the community in which they work. And when they have charge of 30 to 60 and over, it is only the exceptional personality whose influence is sufficient to outweigh that of the home and the peer-group. They can get across 'peripheral' skills such as spelling and mechanical arithmetic fairly successfully, and therefore – in backward educational systems – tend to concentrate unduly on these. But it is far more difficult to develop logical reasoning, flexibility of mind, the use of 'formal' language, understanding of the world and society, initiative, responsibility, and democratic attitudes. The effects of peripheral training are easily forgotten and, of course have scarcely any transfer to the daily life of ex-pupils or to the bringing up of their children more intelligently. Nevertheless one should not be too pessimistic. When even a few in each school generation are helped to be more intelligent, they leaven the community.

The greatest promise of quick advance lies in the field of language-teaching, that is the spread of effective methods of acquiring a language which is suitable as a medium for advanced education, communication and thinking among children whose mother-tongue is ineffective for these purposes. This applies equally to dialect-speaking Africans, to Jamaicans in Jamaica or Britain, and to lower working-class or deprived children in any western nation whose natural speech is of the 'public' type. However it is not sufficient to teach the second language as a subject, i.e. peripherally. Our own results have shown that current techniques, not only in Jamaica and Uganda but even in Canada, produce some competence in written English tests but fail to develop English as a central tool of comprehension and thought. But linguistic and psychological research, together with the experiments under way in American introductory schools, in Kenya and elsewhere, offer prospects of a considerable breakthrough.

Whether it is realistic to advocate the extension of such methods to the complete populations of developing countries is a moot point, since the mother-tongues are adequate for the lives that the majority are going to live for generations to come, and much more useful types of education could be devised for them. But such a policy would involve a split between the minority educated in the foreign language and the rest; and even if this was not socially disastrous, how would the minority be chosen at a sufficiently early age?

Clearly the major barrier to the fuller realisation of human intellectual potential lies in the realm of adult values and child-rearing practices, and we have scarcely any assured techniques of modifying these. Changes are occurring all the time, but seldom as planned by the administrators; and although anthropological and psychological studies have greatly increased our understanding of the dynamic forces of social change, we are hardly in a position yet to offer much practical advice. (Psychological theories of crime and delinquency, for example, do not seem to have done anything to reduce the amount of social deviancy.) And yet it is not impossible to plan and to carry through radical changes – an outstanding example being supplied by Soviet Russia. There can be no doubt that over the past 50 years the average level of Intelligence B of the Russian population has been raised tremendously. Ruthless techniques may indeed have been applied which other countries would be loath to adopt, and they have not always achieved their purpose. But to a large extent they have succeeded in transforming a country which was as economically weak, as educationally backward, and as culturally and linguistically heterogeneous as many underdeveloped nations of today.

Among the more humane approaches are community development schemes where local or foreign teams persuade a backward community to cooperate in improved agricultural techniques, in an industrial or housing project, in health or child-care measures, or in local government. Usually these are small-scale, trial and error, ventures, and frequently they fail or have no lasting effects. But they can be conducted in the people's own language, be shown to have direct value to the community, and be integrated with, rather than destroying, the existent culture. Where they do take roots they are likely to spread geographically, and to affect many cultural elements beside the particular practices worked on.

More sure, perhaps, but slower is the traditional method of educating the upper strata of the population to a high level and encouraging their contacts with outside cultural groups. If they thereby acquire good intelligence and adopt some of the attitudes associated with it, they are better able to bridge the gulf between the old and the new. In so far as they achieve prestige positions, their influence tends to percolate and they make possible greater progress in subsequent generations. Admittedly this mode of attack does not always work; it seems to have broken down among Canadian indigenes, and it is clearly failing to meet the needs of American negroes. The more able and acculturated members of the relatively backward group often meet with rejection, either from their own or from the more advanced groups.

We return finally to the point that changes in material conditions, which the more favoured nations and subcultures are in a position to facilitate, are important, but not the whole answer. Even more important and vastly more difficult are changes in people's attitudes and ways of life. Developing nations often seem to be trying to bring about in a matter of years developments which, in Europe, took place over centuries. There are far more resources of technology, of communication, of intelligent and trained people anxious to help, in the world of today than ever before. But our knowledge of human individuals and societies and our control over our own prejudices and emotions are still so rudimentary that progress can only be fragmentary and disappointing.

STATISTICAL TABLES

TABLE 10. *Conversion tables for scores on certain tests to developmental quotients, for boys aged 11:0.*

Arithmetic		Terman Merrill Vocab.		Word Learning		Information Learning		Piaget Errors		Porteus Mazes		Draw-a-Man Goodenough	
Score	DQ	Score	DQ	Score	DQ	Score	DQ	Score	DQ	Score	DQ	Score	DQ
39	138	26	138	53	135	30	135	2	129	16	128	36	138
38	132	25	132	52	133	29	126	3	121	15½	121	35	135
37	127	24	127	51	132	28	120	4	117	15	116	34	132
36	123	23	123	50	130	27	116	5	113	14½	111	33	129
35	119	22	120	49	129	26	113	6	110	14	107	32	126
34	116	21	119	48	127	25	110	7	107	13½	104	31	123
33	113	20	117	47	126	24	107	8	104	13	100	30	119
32	110	19	115	46	124	23	104	9	102	12½	97	29	115
31	107	18	113	45	123	22	101	10	99	12	93	28	111
30	104	17	110	44	121	21	98	11	97	11½	90	27	107
29	102	16	105	43	119	20	96	12	95	11	86	26	104
28	101	15	100	42	118	19	94	13	93	10½	83	25	101
27	99	14	96	41	116	18	92	14	91	10	80	24	99
26	98	13	92	40	115	17	90	15	88	9½	76	23	96
25	96	12	89	39	113	16	88	16	86	9	73	22	94
24	95	11	85	38	112	15	86	17	84	8½	70	21	91
23	94	10	81	37	110	14	83	18	82	8	66	20	88
22	92	9	78	36	109	13	81	19	79	7½	63	19	86
21	91	8	74	35	107	12	79	20	77	7	59	18	83
20	89	7	70	34	106	11	77	21	75	6½	56	17	81
19	88	6	66	33	104	10	75	22	73			16	78
18	86	5	63	32	102	9	72	23	71	Draw-a-Man Witkin		15	75
17	85	4	59	31	101	8	70	24	68	Score	DQ	14	73
16	83	3	55	30	99	7	68	25	66			13	70
15	82	2	52	29	98	6	66	26	64	14	132	12	68
14	80	1	48	28	96	5	64	27	62	13	124	11	65
13	79			27	95	4	61	28	59	12	117	10	62
12	78			26	93	3	59			11	113		
11	76			25	92	2	57			10	108		
10	75			24	90					9	104		
9	73			23	89					8	101		
8	72			22	87					7	98		
7	70			21	85					6	94		
6	69			20	84					5	90		
5	68			19	82					4	86		
4	66			18	81					3	82		
3	65			17	79					2	78		
2	63			16	78					1	75		
1	62			15	76								
0	60			14	75								
				13	73								
				12	72								
				11	70								
				10	68								
				9	67								
				8	66								
				7	64								
				6	62								
				5	60								
				4	59								
				3	58								
				2	56								
				1	55								
				0	53								

TABLE II. *Ninetieth, fiftieth and tenth percentile developmental quotients for maladjusted, delinquent and Hebridean boys.*

N.B. In the English standardisation group, the 90th, 50th and 10th percentiles are 119, 100 and 81, respectively, for all tests.

	Maladjusted			Delinquent			Hebridean (English)			Hebridean (Gaelic)		
	90	50	10	90	50	10	90	50	10	90	50	10
Arithmetic	95	77	70	83	75	62	123	102	92	135	102	94
Spelling	112	85	77	84	75	62	120	105	94	128	111	93
English	103	89	72	90	72	60	117	103	96	117	99	85
Group Vocabulary	110	93	77	86	80	63	121	103	91	110	96	80
Terman Vocabulary	118	93	74	99	81	68	119	96	81	105	87	74
Word Learning	118	88	74	110	82	60	136	111	79	140	113	75
Information Learning	120	92	80	103	85	59	123	103	89	114	101	77
Sorting	116	97	81	108	81	58	111	98	84	106	88	72
Piaget	113	98	81	100	84	64	111	102	78	113	86	68
Abstraction	102	87	77	89	73	62	117	104	90	118	95	82
Matrices	113	93	73	93	75	63	113	97	84	106	93	77
Porteus Mazes	116	95	84	94	85	63	107	95	81	107	97	81
Kohs Blocks	115	101	80	104	81	61	114	95	74	111	95	79
Formboard	117	100	68	106	93	65	106	91	61	116	94	60
Picture Recognition	119	98	80	106	77	60	119	98	84	107	96	78
Gottschaldt Figures	114	95	76	103	80	54	104	93	77	109	90	72
Design Reproduction	115	95	76	102	90	72	126	103	89	113	100	82
Goodenough Man	107	88	74	106	93	62	121	94	76	117	99	79
Witkin Man	103	89	80	104	90	69	124	92	84	124	98	82
Fluency	118	106	92	115	99	79	118	100	80	120	105	79
Originality	123	108	84	111	96	75	116	101	80	114	97	75
Incomplete Drawings	123	105	82	114	96	79	103	88	72	100	79	67

TABLE 12. *Ninetieth, fiftieth and tenth percentile developmental quotients for overseas samples of boys*

	Jamaicans		
	90	50	10
Arithmetic	104	83	65
Spelling	111	92	75
English	103	81	69
Group Vocabulary	96	83	72
Terman Vocabulary	89	72	63
Word Learning	114	92	63
Information Learning	104	75	57
Sorting	97	92	78
Piaget	107	90	68
Matrices	91	75	63
Porteus Mazes	107	91	66
Kohs Blocks	96	75	68
Formboard	94	68	50
Gottschaldt Figures	104	88	65
Design Reproduction	113	89	74
Goodenough Man	127	91	68

	Ugandans			Eskimos (Hostel)			Eskimos (Town)			Indians		
	90	50	10	90	50	10	90	50	10	90	50	10
Arithmetic	95	86	78	96	75	62	88	78	66	84	76	65
Spelling	104	91	78	111	94	75	113	95	76	106	85	75
English	90	80	73	96	85	70	96	85	76	89	78	70
Group Vocabulary	—	—	—	96	86	72	95	87	74	90	79	71
Terman Vocabulary	68	57	48	89	76	52	89	74	64	83	70	63
Word Learning	115	94	66	125	87	61	106	86	67	100	75	56
Information Learning	94	78	66	107	82	59	110	83	59	94	72	55
Sorting	100	88	76	121	105	81	114	104	87	110	91	79
Piaget	96	73	64	102	85	64	96	77	66	94	73	62
Abstraction	94	84	71	106	93	74	106	89	74	93	82	72
Matrices	93	81	68	106	93	74	100	88	71	94	81	69
Porteus Mazes	111	99	80	116	93	73	116	97	76	106	98	80
Kohs Blocks	91	78	70	111	92	71	107	84	70	102	88	72
Formboard	98	80	54	109	80	66	112	92	65	104	85	64
Picture Recognition	95	79	66	107	95	80	110	95	77	104	91	80
Gottschaldt Figures	108	94	82	108	95	78	108	93	72	103	93	65
Design Reproduction	112	93	85	109	91	76	106	89	69	108	91	72
Goodenough Man	115	95	74	113	95	69	119	94	73	115	96	73
Witkin Man	124	97	80	117	106	86	117	98	78	117	101	86
Fluency	120	104	87	125	112	96	128	111	98	127	110	92
Originality	104	86	70	112	88	71	109	89	75	99	77	63
Incomplete Drawings	118	97	82	117	92	75	115	90	78	111	91	82

TABLE 13. *Group-factor analysis of all tests and environmental variables in Eskimo sample*

	g	v:ed	Fluency	k	Drawing	Conservation
Arithmetic	·79	·48				
English	·73	·63				
Spelling	·76	·52				
Word Learning	·62	·33				
Information Learning	·71	·54				·37
Group Vocabulary	·68	·64				
Terman Vocabulary	·71	·38				
Sorting	·46	·24	·28			
Abstraction	·88	·18				
Matrices	·84			·25		
Porteus Mazes	·66			·23		
Progressive Matrices '38	·74			·37		
SCRIT	·58			·44		
MacArthur Tests	·67	·20				
Lorge-Thorndike Nonverbal	·89					
Cattell Culture-Fair	·87					
Otis Beta	·57	·46				
Picture Recognition	·30	·24	·28		·28	·28
Gottschaldt Figures	·72			·36		
Design Reproduction	·66			·34		
Kohs Blocks	·68			·53		
Formboard	·53			·43		
Goodenough Man	·55			·37	·26	
Witkin Man	·53			·48	·45	
Piaget Total	·81	—	—	—	—	—
Time Concepts	·42	·13	·17			·16
Left and Right	·23	·27	·18			·30
Equidistant Counters	·22	·31	·12			
Logical Inclusion	—·12		·21			
Tilted Bottle	·60			·28		
Conservation of Liquid	·51					·46
Conservation of Plasticine	·32					·28
Insect Problem	·30				·41	·11
Number Concepts	·68	·14				·19
Conservation of Length	·48					·39
Reversed Dot	·47	·24				·39
Shadow	·34			·40		·09
Conservation of Area	·29					·60

	g	$v{:}ed$	Fluency	k	Drawing	Conservation
Rorschach N	·22		·37			
A%	·13	·35	−·26			
H%	−·23		−·28			
P%	−·29					
Dd%	−·10	−·12				
U%	·33	·14	·49		·39	
Incomplete Drawings U	·23		·21			
E	·41		·36		·49	
Wings N	·29	·51	·63			
p%	−·35	·14				
Ae%	·15	·21	·55			
Ahs%	·42		·29			
EU%	·33	·12	·08			
Tin Can N	·13	·22	·55			
P%	−·13					·47
U%	·25		·29			
Dog Story N	·23	·37	·41			
Activity %	·36	·16	·38			
Kind vs. Cruel	−·10		−·19	·36		
Delayed Gratification	−·02					
Age	·61	·30	·17			
School Grade	·73	·60				
Length of Schooling	·36	·65				
Regularity of Schooling	·04	·44				
Hostel Boarding vs. Own Home	·10	−·21				·42
Land vs. Town Dwelling	−·16	−·18				
Socioeconomic Level	−·04				·25	
Unbroken Home	·15	·20				
Linguistic Background	·23	·25				−·34
Cultural Stimulus	·00	·52	·15			
Initiative	·15		·37			
Planfulness	−·08					−·20
Health	·12		·24			

Bibliography

ABIOLA, E. T. (1965) 'The nature of intellectual development in Nigerian children', *Teacher Educ.*, **6**, 37–57.

ALBINO, R. C., and THOMPSON, V. J. (1956) 'The effects of sudden weaning on Zulu children', *Brit. J. med. Psychol.*, **29**, 177–210.

ALLISON, R. B. (1954) *Learning Measures as Predictors of Success in Torpedoman's Mates School.* Princeton, N.J.: Educational Testing Service, ONR Project 151–113.

ALLISON, R. B. (1956) *Learning Measures as Predictors of Success in Pipefitter and Metalsmith Schools.* Princeton, N.J.: Educational Testing Serivice, ONR Project 151–113.

ALLISON, R. B. (1960) *Learning Parameters and Human Abilities.* Princeton, N.J.: Educational Testing Service, Technical Report.

ALLPORT, G. W., and KRAMER, B. M. (1946) 'Some roots of prejudice', *J. Psychol.*, **22**, 9–39.

ALLPORT, G. W., and PETTIGREW, T. F. (1957) 'Cultural influence on the perception of movement: The trapezoidal illusion among the Zulus', *J. abn. soc. Psychol.*, **55**, 104–113.

ANASTASI, A. (1930) 'A group factor in immediate memory', *Arch. Psychol.*, No. 120.

ANASTASI, A. (1932) 'Further studies on the memory factor', *Arch. Psychol.*, No. 142.

ANASTASI, A. (1958) *Differential Psychology.* New York: Macmillan. Earlier edition (1949) by ANASTASI, A., and FOLEY, J. P.

ANDERSON, J. E. (1940) 'The prediction of terminal intelligence from infant and preschool tests', *Yrbk. Nat. Soc. Stud. Educ.*, **39** (1), 385–403.

ANNETT, M. (1959) 'The classification of instances of four common class concepts by children and adults', *Brit. J. educ. Psychol.*, **29**, 223–236.

AUSUBEL, D. P., and AUSUBEL, P. (1963) 'Ego development among segregated Negro children', in A. H. PASSOW, *Education in Depressed Areas.* New York: Teachers College Columbia Bureau of Publications, pp. 109–141.

BABCOCK, H. (1930) 'An experiment in the measurement of mental deterioration', *Arch. Psychol.*, No. 117.

BALDWIN, A. L., KALHORN, J., and BREESE, F. H. (1945) 'Patterns of parent behavior', *Psychol. Monogr.*, **58**, No. 268.

BARRY, H., CHILD, I., and BACON, M. K. (1959) 'Relation of child training to subsistence economy', *Amer. Anthropologist*, **61**, 51–63.

BERNARDONI, L. C. (1964) 'A culture fair intelligence test for the Ugh, No, and Oo-La-La cultures', *Personnel & Guid. J.*, **42**, 554–557.

BERNSTEIN, B. B. (1961) 'Social class and linguistic development: A theory of social learning', in A. H. HALSEY, *Education, Economy and Society*. Glencoe: The Free Press, pp. 288–314.

BERNSTEIN, B. B., and YOUNG, D. (1966) 'Some aspects of the relationships between communication and performance in tests', in J. E. MEADE and A. S. PARKES, *Genetic and Environmental Factors in Human Ability*. Edinburgh: Oliver and Boyd, pp. 15–23.

BERRY, J. W. (1966) 'Temne and Eskimo perceptual skills', *Intern. J. Psychol.*, **1**, 207–229.

BIESHEUVEL, S. (1949) 'Psychological tests and their application to non-European peoples', *Yrbk. Educ.* London: Evans Bros., pp. 87–126.

BIESHEUVEL, S. (1952) 'The study of African ability', *African Stud.*, **11**, 45–58, 105–117.

BIESHEUVEL, S. (1966) 'Some African acculturation problems, with special reference to perceptual and psychomotor skills', *Burg-Wartenstein Symposium* No. 33. New York: Wenner-Gren Foundation for Anthropological Research.

BIESHEUVEL, S., and LIDDICOAT, R. (1959) 'The effects of cultural factors on intelligence-test performance', *J. Nat. Inst. Personn. Res.*, **8**, 3–14.

BILLINGSLEA, F. Y. (1963) 'The Bender Gestalt: A review and perspective', *Psychol. Bull.*, **60**, 233–251.

BING, E. (1963) 'Effect of childrearing practices on development of differential cognitive abilities', *Child Devlpmt.*, **34**, 631–648.

BIRCH, H. G., and LEFFORD, A. (1963) 'Intersensory development in children', *Monogr. Soc. Res. Child Devlpmt.*, **28**, No. 89.

BLAKE, J. (1961) *Family Structure in Jamaica*. Glencoe: The Free Press.

BLISHEN, B. R. (1958) 'The construction and use of an occupational class scale', *Canad. J. Economics & pol. Sci.*, **24**, 519–531.

BLOOM, B. S. (1964) *Stability and Change in Human Characteristics*. New York: John Wiley.

BLOOM, B. S., DAVIS, A., and HESS, R. (1965) *Compensatory Education for Cultural Deprivation*. New York: Holt, Rinehart and Winston.

BOWLBY, J. et al. (1956) 'The effects of mother-child separation: A follow-up study', *Brit. J. med. Psychol.*, **29**, 211–247.

BRIMBLE, A. R. (1963) 'The construction of a non-verbal intelligence test in Northern Rhodesia', *Rhodes-Livingstone J.*, **34**, 23–35.

BRONFENBRENNER, U. (1962) 'Soviet methods of character education: Some implications for research', *Amer. Psychologist*, **17**, 550–564.

BRUNER, J. S. (1964) 'The course of cognitive growth', *Amer. Psychologist*, **19**, 1–15.

BRUNER, J. S. (1965) 'The growth of mind', *Amer. Psychologist*, **20**, 1007–1017.

BRUNER, J. S. *et al.* (1966) *Studies in Cognitive Growth.* New York: John Wiley.

BURT, C. L. (1935) *The Subnormal Mind.* London: Oxford University Press.

BURT, C. L. (1961) 'Intelligence and social mobility', *Brit. J. stat. Psychol.*, 14, 3–24.

BURT, C. L., and CONWAY, J. (1959) 'Class differences in general intelligence', *Brit. J. stat. Psychol.*, 12, 5–33.

CAROTHERS, J. C. (1953) *The African Mind in Health and Disease: A Study in Ethnopsychiatry.* Geneva: WHO.

CASTLE, E. B. (1966) *Growing Up in East Africa.* London: Oxford University Press.

CATTELL, R. B. (1949) 'The dimensions of culture patterns by factorization of national characters', *J. abn. soc. Psychol.*, 44, 443–469.

CATTELL, R. B. (1963) 'Theory of fluid and crystallized intelligence: A critical experiment', *J. educ. Psychol.*, 54, 1–22.

CLAIRMONT, D. J. H. (1963) 'Deviance among Indians and Eskimos in Aklavik, N.W.T.' Ottawa: *NCRC Rep.* 63–9.

CLARK, K. B. (1963) 'Educational stimulation of racially disadvantaged children', in A. H. PASSOW, *Education in Depressed Areas.* New York: Teachers College Columbia Bureau of Publications, pp. 142–162.

CLARKE, E. (1957) *My Mother Who Fathered Me.* London: Allen and Unwin.

CLOWARD, R. A., and OHLIN, L. E. (1960) *Delinquency and Opportunity.* Glencoe: The Free Press.

COLLINS, J. E. (1961) *The Effects of Remedial Education.* Edinburgh: Oliver and Boyd.

COWLEY, J. J., and MURRAY, M. (1962) 'Some aspects of the development of spatial concepts in Zulu children', *J. soc. Res.*, 13, 1–28.

COX, C. (1956) 'The impact of British education on the indigenous peoples of overseas territories', *Adv. Sci.*, 13, 125–136.

CRANE, A. R. (1959) 'An historical and critical account of the Accomplishment Quotient idea', *Brit. J. educ. Psychol.*, 29, 252–259.

CRAVIOTO, J., BIRCH, H. G. *et al.* (1967) 'The ecology of infant weight gain in a pre-industrial society', *Acta Paed. Scand.*, 56, 71–84.

DAVIDSON, M. A., MCINNES, R. G., and PARNELL, R. W. (1957) 'The distribution of personality traits in seven-year-old children', *Brit. J. educ. Psychol.*, 27, 48–61.

DAWSON, J. L. (1963) *Psychological Effects of Social Change in a West African Community.* Unpublished Ph.D. Thesis, Oxford University.

DENNIS, W. (1957) 'Performance of near Eastern children on the Draw-a-Man test', *Child Devlpmt.*, 28, 427–430.

DENNIS, W. (1960) 'The human figure drawings of Bedouins', *J. soc. Psychol.*, 52, 209–219.

DENNIS, W., and NARJARIAN, P. (1957) 'Infant development under environmental handicap', *Psychol. Monogr.*, 71, No. 436.

DEPARTMENT OF CITIZENSHIP AND IMMIGRATION: INDIAN AFFAIRS BRANCH (1962) *Indian Education.* Ottawa: Queen's Printer.

DEUTSCH, M. (1963) 'The disadvantaged child and the learning process', in A. H. PASSOW, *Education in Depressed Areas.* New York: Teachers College Columbia Bureau of Publications, pp. 163–179.

DEUTSCH, M. (1965) 'The role of social class in language development and cognition', *Amer. J. Orthopsychiat.*, 35, 78–88.

DOOB, L. W. (1960) *Becoming More Civilized.* New Haven: Yale University Press.

DOPPELT, J. E., and BENNETT, G. K. (1967) 'Testing job applicants from disadvantaged groups'. New York: Psychological Corporation, *Test Service Bulletin*, No. 57.

DOUGLAS, J. W. B. (1964). *The Home and the School.* London: McGibbon and Kee.

DOUGLAS, J. W. B., and ROSS, J. M. (1965) 'The effects of absence on primary school performance', *Brit. J. educ. Psychol.*, 35, 28–40.

DREGER, R. M., and MILLER, K. S. (1960) 'Comparative psychological studies of negroes and whites in the United States', *Psychol. Bull.*, 57, 361–402.

DUBREUIL, G., and BOISCLAIR, C. (1960) 'Le realisme enfantin à la Martinique et au Canada Francais: Etude genetique et experimentale', *Thought from the Learned Societies of Canada 1960.* Toronto: Gage, pp. 83–95.

DUCKWORTH, E. (1964) *Piaget Rediscovered.* Cornell University: School of Education.

ECKLAND, B. K. (1967) 'Genetics and sociology: A reconsideration', *Amer. sociol. Rev.*, 32, 173–194.

EELLS, K., DAVIS, A., and HAVIGHURST, R. J. *et al.* (1951) *Intelligence and Cultural Differences.* Chicago: University of Chicago Press.

ERIKSON, E. H. (1950) *Childhood and Society.* London: Imago.

EYSENCK, H. J. (1960) *The Structure of Human Personality* (2nd ed). London: Methuen.

FAHMY, M. (1964) 'Initial exploring of the intelligence of Skilluk children: Studies in Southern Sudan', *Vita Humana*, 7, 164–177.

FAVERGE, J. M., and FALMAGNE, J. C. (1962) 'On the interpretation of data in intercultural psychology', *Psychol. Africana.* 9, 22–36.

FERGUSON, G. A. (1954) 'On learning and human ability', *Canad. J. Psychol.*, 8, 95–112.

FERGUSON, J. D. (1961) 'The human ecology and social economic change in the community of Tuktoyaktuk N.W.T.' Ottawa: *NCRC Rep.*, 61–2.

FERRON, O. M. (1967) 'The linguistic factor in the test intelligence of West African children', *Educ. Res.*, 9, 113–121.

FLAVELL, J. H. (1963) *The Developmental Psychology of Jean Piaget.* Princeton, N.J.: Van Nostrand.

FLEISHMAN, E. A., and HEMPEL, W. E. (1954) 'Changes in factor structure of a complex psychomotor test as a function of practice', *Psychometr.*, **19**, 239–252.

FLEISHMAN, E. A., and HEMPEL, W. E. (1955) 'The relation between abilities and improvement with practice in a visual discrimination reaction task', *J. exper. Psychol.*, **49**, 301–312.

FRASER, E. (1959) *Home Environment and the School.* London: University of London Press.

FRENCH, C. L. (1962) *Social Class and Motivation among Metis of Alberta.* University of Alberta at Calgary: Unpublished report.

FURTH, H. G. (1964) 'Research with the deaf: Implications for language and cognition', *Psychol. Bull.*, **62**, 145–164.

GALAL, S. (1964) 'The effect of bilharziasis and other parasitical diseases on the intelligence and achievement of primary school children'. Cairo: *Nat. Rev. of Soc. Sci.*, **1**, 138–144.

GEBER, M. (1958) 'The psychomotor development of African children in the first year, and the influence of maternal behavior', *J. soc. Psychol.*, **47**, 185–195.

GLUECK, S., and GLUECK, E. (1950) *Unraveling Juvenile Delinquency.* New York: Commonwealth Fund.

GOLDMAN, R. J., and TAYLOR, F. M. (1966) 'Coloured immigrant children', *Educ. Res.*, **8**, 163–183.

GOLDSTEIN, K., and SCHEERER, M. (1941) 'Abstract and concrete behavior', *Psychol. Monogr.*, **53**, No. 239.

GOODNOW, J. J. (1962) 'A test of milieu effects with some of Piaget's tasks', *Psychol. Monogr.*, **76**, No. 555.

GORDON, H. (1923) *Mental and Scholastic Tests among Retarded Children.* London: H.M.S.O., Board of Education Pamphlet No. 44.

GRANT, G. V., and SCHEPERS, J. M. (1967) *An Exploratory Factor Analysis of Five New Cognitive Tests for Use on African Mineworkers.* Johannesburg: National Institute for Personnel Research.

GRAY, J. L. (1936) *The Nation's Intelligence.* London: Watts.

GREGOR, A. J., and MCPHERSON, D. A. (1965) 'A study of susceptibility to geometric illusions among cultural subgroups of Australian aborigines', *Psychol. Africana*, **11**, 1–13.

GRIEVE, D. W. (1964) *English Language Examining.* Lagos, Nigeria: African Universities Press.

GUILFORD, J. P. (1967) *The Nature of Human Intelligence.* New York: McGraw-Hill.

HAGGARD, E. A. (1954) 'Social-status and intelligence: An experimental study of certain cultural determinants of measured intelligence', *Genet. Psychol. Monogr.*, **49**, 141–186.

HALSEY, A. H. (1958) 'Genetics, social structure and intelligence', *Brit. J. Sociol.*, **9**, 15–28.

HARRELL, R. F., WOODYARD, E., and GATES, A. I. (1955) *The Effect of Mothers' Diet on the Intelligence of the Offspring.* New York: Teachers College Columbia Bureau of Publications.

HARRIS, D. B. (1963) *Children's Drawings as Measures of Intellectual Maturity.* New York: Harcourt Brace.

HAVIGHURST, R. J., GUNTHER, M. K., and PRATT, I. E. (1946) 'Environment and the Draw-a-Man test: The performance of Indian children', *J. abn. soc. Psychol.*, **41**, 50–63.

HELD, R., and HEIN, A. (1963) 'Movement-produced stimulation in the development of visually guided behavior', *J. comp. & physiol. Psychol.*, **56**, 872–876.

HENDRIKZ, E. (1966) *A Cross-cultural Investigation of the Number Concepts and Level of Number Development in Five-year-old Urban Shona and European Children in Southern Rhodesia.* University of London: M.A. Thesis.

HIGGINS, C., and SIVERS, C. H. (1958) 'A comparison of Stanford-Binet and Colored Raven Progressive Matrics IQs for children with low socioeconomic status', *J. consult. Psychol.*, **22**, 465–468.

HOBART, C. W., and BRANT, C. S. (1966) 'Eskimo education, Danish and Canadian: A comparison', *Canad. Rev. Sociol. Anthrop.*, **3**, 47–66.

HORN, J. L., and CATTELL, R. B. (1966) 'Refinement and test of the theory of fluid and crystallized general intelligences', *J. educ. Psychol.*, **57**, 253–270.

HOUGHTON, H. (1967) 'The effect of the population explosion on education', *Adv. Sci.*, **23**, 443–446.

HUDSON, L. (1966) *Contrary Imaginations.* London: Methuen.

HUDSON, W. (1960) 'Pictorial depth perception in sub-cultural groups in Africa', *J. soc. Psychol.*, **52**, 183–208.

HUDSON, W. (1962) 'Pictorial perception and educational adaptation in Africa', *Psychol. Africana*, **9**, 226–239.

HUDSON, W. (1967) 'The study of the problem of pictorial perception among unacculturated groups', *Intern. J. Psychol.*, **2**, 89–107.

HUDSON, W., ROBERTS, A. O. H., VAN HEERDEN, C. D., and MBAU, G. G. (1962) 'The usefulness of performance tests for the selection and classification of Bantu industrial workers', *Psychol. Africana*, **9**, 189–203.

HUNT, J. McV. (1961) *Intelligence and Experience.* New York: Ronald Press.

HUNTER, G. (1963) *Education for a Developing Region.* London: Allen and Unwin.

HUSÉN, T. (1951) 'The influence of schooling upon IQ', *Theoria*, **17**, 61–88.

HYDE, D. M. (1959) *An Investigation of Piaget's Theories of the Development of the Concept of Number.* University of London, Ph.D. Thesis.

INNER LONDON EDUCATION AUTHORITY (1967) *The Education of Immigrant Pupils in Primary Schools.* London, ILEA Report 959.

IRVINE, S. H. (1965) *Selection for Secondary Education in Southern Rhodesia.* Salisbury: University College of Rhodesia and Nyasaland.

IRVINE, S. H. (1966) 'Towards a rationale for testing attainments and abilities in Africa', *Brit. J. educ. Psychol.*, **36**, 24–32.

IRVINE, S. H. (1967) *How Fair is Culture? Factorial Studies of Raven's Progressive Matrices across Cultures in Africa.* University of Bristol, Institute of Education: Unpublished Report.

IRVINE, S. H. (1968) 'The factor analysis of African abilities and attainments across cultures', Princeton, N.J.: *Educ. Testing Service RB*, 68–14.

JAHODA, G. (1956) 'Assessment of abstract behavior in a non-western culture', *J. abn. soc. Psychol.*, **53**, 237–243.

JAHODA, G. (1964) 'Social class differentials in vocabulary expansion', *Brit. J. educ. Psychol.*, **34**, 321–323.

JAHODA, G. (1966) 'Geometric illusions and environment: A study in Ghana', *Brit. J. Psychol.*, **57**, 193–199.

JENNESS, D. (1963) *Indians of Canada* (6th ed). Ottawa: Queen's Printer.

JENNESS, D. (1964) *Eskimo Administration: II. Canada.* Montreal: Arctic Institute of N. America, Tech. Paper No. 14.

JENSEN, A. R. (1966) 'Social class and perceptual learning', *Ment. Hyg.*, **50**, 226–239.

JENSEN, A. R. (1967) 'The culturally disadvantaged: Psychological and educational aspects', *Educ. Res.*, **10**, 4–20.

KAGAN, J., MOSS, H. A., and SIGEL, I. E. (1963). 'Psychological significance of styles of conceptualization', *Monogr. Soc. Res. Child Devlpmt.*, **28**, No. 86.

KATZ, I. (1964) 'Review of evidence relating to effects of desegregation on the intellectual performance of negroes', *Amer. Psychologist*, **19**, 381–399.

KEMP, L. C. D. (1955) 'Environmental and other characteristics determining attainment in primary schools', *Brit. J. educ. Psychol.*, **25**, 67–77.

KENNEDY, W. A. and LINDNER, R. S. (1964) 'A normative study of the Goodenough Draw-a-Man test on Southeastern negro elementary school children', *Child Devlpmt.*, **35**, 33–62.

KENNEDY, W. A., VAN DE RIET, V., and WHITE, J. C. (1963) 'A normative sample of intelligence and achievement of negro elementary school children in the Southeastern United States', *Monogr. Soc. Res. Child Devlpmt.*, **28**, No. 90.

KENT, N. and DAVIS, D. R. (1957) 'Discipline in the home and intellectual development', *Brit. J. med. Psychol.*, **30**, 27–33.

KERR, M. (1952) *Personality and Conflict in Jamaica.* Liverpool: Liverpool University Press.

KLINGELHOFER, E. L. (1967) *A Bibliography of Psychological Research and Writings on Africa.* Uppsala: Scand. Inst. Afric. Stud.

KLUCKHOHN, F. R. (1950) 'Dominant and substitute profiles of cultural orientations: Their significance for the analysis of social stratification' *Soc. Forces,* **28,** 376–393.

KNILL, W. D., and DAVIS, A. K. (1963). *Provincial Education in Northern Saskatchewan: Progress and Bog-down 1944–1962.* University of Alberta at Calgary: Unpublished Report.

KORNRICH, M. (edit. 1965) *Under-Achievement.* Springfield, Ill.: Thomas.

LANGENHOVEN, H. P. (1963) *Intergroup Comparison in Psychological Measurement.* South Africa: Nat. Counc. Soc. Res.

LEHMANN, H. C. (1953) *Age and Achievement.* Princeton, N.J.: Princeton University Press.

LEVINE, S. (1960) 'Stimulation in infancy', *Scient. Amer.,* **202,** 80–86.

LEWIS, L. J. (1962) *Education and Political Independence in Africa.* Edinburgh: Nelson.

LEWIS, M. M. (1963) *Language, Thought and Personality.* London: Harrap.

LLOYD, F., and PIDGEON, D. A. (1961) 'An investigation into the effects of coaching on non-verbal test material with European, Indian and African children', *Brit. J. educ. Psychol.,* **31,** 145–151.

LORGE, I. (1945) 'Schooling makes a difference', *Teach. Coll. Rec.,* **46,** 483–492.

LOVELL, K. (1955) 'A study of the problem of intellectual deterioration in adolescents and young adults', *Brit. J. Psychol.,* **46,** 199–210.

LOVELL, K. (1961) *The Growth of Basic Mathematical and Scientific Concepts in Children.* London: University of London Press.

MacARTHUR, R. S. (1964) 'Intelligence tests for two samples of Metis and Indian children', *Alberta J. educ. Res.,* **10,** 17–27.

MacARTHUR, R. S. (1967) *Longitudinal Predictions of School Achievement for Metis and Eskimo Pupils.* Winnipeg: Conf. Canad. Counc. Res. Educ.

MacARTHUR, R. S., and ELLEY, W. B. (1963) 'The reduction of socio-economic bias in intelligence testing', *Brit. J. educ. Psychol.,* **33,** 107–119.

MacARTHUR, R. S., IRVINE, S. H., and BRIMBLE, A. R. (1964) *The Northern Rhodesian Mental Ability Survey 1963.* Lusaka: Rhodes-Livingstone Institute.

MCCONNELL, J. (1954) 'Abstract behavior among the Tepehuan', *J. abn. soc. Psychol.,* **49,** 109–110.

MacDONALD, A. (1944–5) *Reports on the Work of the Selection of Personnel Technical and Research Unit, M.E.F.* London: War Office Archives.

MCFIE, J. (1961a) 'Recent advances in phrenology', *The Lancet*, No. 7198, 360–363.

MCFIE, J. (1961) 'The effect of education on African performance on a group of intellectual tests', *Brit. J. educ. Psychol.*, **31**, 232–240.

MacGREGOR, G. (1946) *Warriors without Weapons*. Chicago: University of Chicago Press.

MACKAY, G. W. S. and VERNON, P. E. (1963) 'The measurement of learning ability', *Brit. J. educ. Psychol.*, **33**, 177–186.

MCNEMAR, Q. (1940) 'A critical examination of the University of Iowa studies of environmental influences upon the IQ', *Psychol. Bull.*, **37**, 63–92.

MANLEY, D. R. (1959) 'The West Indian background', in S. K. RUCK. *The West Indian Comes to England*. London: Routledge.

MANLEY, D. R. (1963) 'Mental ability in Jamaica', *Soc. & econ. Stud.*, University of the West Indies: Institute of Social and Economic Research.

MICHAEL, W. B. (1949) 'Factor analysis of tests and criteria: A comparative study of two AAF pilot populations', *Psychol. Monogr.*, **63**, No. 298.

MILLER, D. R., and SWANSON, G. E. (1960) *Inner Conflict and Defense*. New York: Holt.

MILLER, G. A., GALANTER, E., and PRIBRAM, K. H. (1960) *Plans and the Structure of Behavior*. New York: Holt.

MISCHEL, W. (1961) 'Father-absence and delay of gratification: Cross-cultural comparisons', *J. abn. soc. Psychol.*, **63**, 116–124.

MOLLENKOPF, W. G. (1957) *The Gear Assembly Test: Description and Preliminary Results*. Princeton, N.J.: Educational Testing Service, ONR Project NR 151–113.

MOSER, C. A. (1957) *The Measurement of Levels of Living with Special Reference to Jamaica*. London: H.M.S.O., Colonial Res. Stud., No. 24.

MUSGROVE, F. (1952) 'Uganda secondary school as a field of culture change', *Africa*, **22**, 234–249.

NEWSON, J. and NEWSON, E. (1963) *Infant Care in an Urban Community*. London: Allen and Unwin.

NISBET, J. D. (1953) 'Family environment and intelligence', *Eugen. Rev.*, **45**, 31–40.

NISSEN, H. W., MACHOVER, S., and KINDER, E. F. (1935) 'A study of performance tests given to a group of native African negro children', *Brit. J. Psychol.*, **25**, 308–355.

OLERON, P. (1957) *Récherches sur le Développement Mental des Sourds-Muets*. Paris: Centre National de la Récherche Scientifique.

OMBREDANE, A. (1951) 'Principes pour une étude psychologique des noires du Congo Belge', *L'Année Psychol.*, **50**, 521–547.

ORD, I. G. (1967) 'The New Guinea performance scale and its educational uses', *Papua and New Guinea J. Educ.*, **5**, 7–16.

ORLANSKY, H. (1949) 'Infant care and personality', *Psychol. Bull.*, **46**, 1-48.

ORTAR, C. R. (1960) 'Improving test validity by coaching', *Educ. Res.*, **2**, 137-142.

ORTAR, C. R. (1963) 'Is a verbal test cross-cultural?' *Scripta Hierosolymitana* (Publications of the Hebrew University, Jerusalem), **13**, 219-235.

OSTROVSKY, E. S. (1959) *Father to the Child*. New York: Putnam.

PASSOW, A. H. (1963) *Education in Depressed Areas*. New York: Teachers College Columbia Bureau of Publications.

PATERSON, D. G. (1930) *Physique and Intellect*. New York: Appleton-Century.

PIAGET, J. (1950) *The Psychology of Intelligence*. London: Routledge.

PRICE WILLIAMS, D. R. (1962) 'Abstract and concrete modes of classification in a primitive society', *Brit. J. educ. Psychol.*, **32**, 50-61.

PRICE WILLIAMS, D. R. (1966) 'Cross-cultural studies', in B. M. FOSS, *New Horizons in Psychology*. London: Penguin Books, pp. 396-416.

PROTHRO, E. T. (1955) 'An alternative approach in cross-cultural intelligence testing', *J. Psychol.*, **39**, 247-251.

RABIN, A. I. and GUERTIN, W. H. (1951) 'Research with the Wechsler-Bellevue test: 1945-1950', *Psychol. Bull.*, **48**, 211-248.

RAMPHAL, C. (1962) *A Study of Three Current Problems of Indian Education*. University of Natal: Unpublished Ph.D. Thesis.

REID, L. H. E. (1964) *The Effects of Family Pattern, Length of Schooling and other environmental factors on English and basic arithmetical attainments of Jamaican primary school children*. University of London: Unpublished Ph.D. Thesis.

RICHARDSON, S. A. (1964) 'The social environment and individual functioning', in H. G. BIRCH, *Brain Damage in Children: The Biological and Social Aspects*. Baltimore: Williams and Wilkins.

RIVERS, W. H. R. (1901) 'Vision', in A. C. HADDON, *Report of the Cambridge Anthropological Expedition to the Torres Straits*. Cambridge University Press.

SAPIR, E. (1956) 'Linguistics as a science', in D. G. MANDELBAUM, *Culture, Language and Personality*. Berkeley: University of California Press.

SCHAEFER, E. S. and BAYLEY, N. (1963) 'Maternal behavior, child behavior, and their intercorrelations from infancy through adolescence', *Monogr. Soc. Res. Child Devlpmt.*, **28**, No. 87.

SCHAFFER, H. R. (1965) 'Changes in developmental quotient under two conditions of maternal separation', *Brit. J. soc. clin. Psychol.*, **4**, 39-46.

SCHWARZ, P. A. (1961) *Aptitude Tests for Use in Developing Nations*. Pittsburgh: American Institute for Research.

SCHWITZGEBEL, R. (1962) 'The performance of Dutch and Zulu adults on selected perceptual tasks', *J. soc. Psychol.*, **57**, 73-77.

SCOTT, G. C. (1950) 'Measuring Sudanese intelligence', *Brit. J. educ. Psychol.*, **20**, 43–54.

SCOTTISH COUNCIL FOR RESEARCH IN EDUCATION (1961) *Gaelic-speaking Children in Highland Schools*. London: University of London Press.

SCRIMSHAW, N. S. (edit. 1968) *Malnutrition, Learning and Behavior*. Cambridge, Mass.: M.I.T. Press.

SEDER, J. A. (1957) *The Origin of Differences in Extent of Independence in Children: Developmental Factors in Perceptual Field Dependence*. Radcliffe College, Mass.: Unpublished Bachelor's Thesis.

SEGALL, M. H., CAMPBELL, D. I., and HERSKOVITS, M. J. (1963) 'Cultural differences in the perception of geometric illusions', *Science*, **139**, 769–771.

SEMLER, I. J., and ISCOE, I. (1963) 'Comparative and developmental study of the learning abilities of negro and white children under four conditions', *J. educ. Psychol.*, **54**, 38–44.

SEWELL, W. H. (1952) 'Infant training and the personality of the child', *Amer. sociol. Rev.*, **58**, 150–159.

SHAPIRO, M. B. (1960) 'The rotation of drawings by illiterate Africans', *J. soc. Psychol.*, **52**, 17–30.

SHIPLEY, W. C. (1940) 'A self-administering scale for measuring intellectual impairment and deterioration', *J. Psychol.*, **9**, 371–377.

SHUEY, A. M. (1958) *The Testing of Negro Intelligence*. Lynchburg, Virg.: J. P. Bell.

SILVEY, J. (1962) *Preliminary Thoughts on Aptitude Testing and Educational Selection in E. Africa*. Kampala, Makerere University College: EAISR Unpublished Report.

SILVEY, J. (1963) 'Aptitude testing and educational selection in Africa', *Rhodes Livingstone J.*, **34**, 9–22.

SKEELS, H. M. (1966) 'Adult status of children with contrasting early life experiences: A follow-up study', *Monogr. Soc. Res. Child. Devlpmt.*, **31**, No. 105.

SMITH, C. A., and LAWLEY, D. N. (1948) *Mental Testing of Hebridean Children in Gaelic and English*. London: University of London Press.

SMITH, I. MCF. (1964) *Spatal Ability: Its Educational and Social Significance*. London: University of London Press.

SMITH, M. G., and KRUIJER, G. J. (1957) *A Sociological Manual for Extension Workers in the Caribbean*. Kingston, Jamaica: University College of the West Indies.

SOMERSET, H. C. A. (1965) *Success and Failure in School Certificate*. Kampala, Makerere University College: Unpublished Report.

SONTAG, L. W., BAKER, C. T., and NELSON, V. L. (1958) 'Mental growth and personality development: A longitudinal study', *Monogr. Soc. Res. Child Devlpmt.*, **23**, No. 68.

STAKE, R. E. (1958) *Learning Parameters, Aptitudes and Achievements.* Princeton, N.J., Department of Psychology: ONR Project NR 150–088.

STOCH, M. B. (1967) 'The effect of undernutrition during infancy on subsequent brain growth and intellectual development', *S. Afric. med. J.*, 1027–1030.

STONE, L. J. (1954) 'A critique of studies of infant isolation', *Child Devlpmt.*, **25**, 9–20.

STOTT, D. H. (1960) 'Interaction of heredity and environment in regard to "Measured Intelligence" '. *Brit. J. educ. Psychol.*, **30**, 95–102.

TAYLOR, A. (1962) *Educational and Occupational Selection in West Africa.* London: Oxford University Press.

TEAHAN, J. E., and DREWS, E. M. (1962) 'A comparison of northern and southern negro children on the WISC', *J. consult. Psychol.*, **26**, 292.

TILTON, J. W. (1953) 'The intercorrelations between measures of school learning', *J. Psychol.*, **35**, 169–179.

TIZARD, J. (1967) *Survey and Experiment in Special Education.* London: Harrap.

TORRANCE, E. P. (1962) *Administration and Scoring Manual for Abbreviated Form VII Minnesota Tests of Creative Thinking.* University of Minnesota: Bureau of Educational Research.

TYLER, L. E. (1956) *The Psychology of Human Differences.* New York: Appleton-Century.

VALLEE, F. G. (1962) 'Kabloona and Eskimo in the Central Keewatin', Ottawa: *NCRC Rep.*, 62–2.

VERHAEGEN, P. and LAROCHE, J. L. (1958) 'Some methodological considerations concerning the study of aptitudes and the elaboration of psychological tests for African natives', *J. soc. Psychol.*, **47**, 249–256.

VERNON, P. E. (1949) *Graded Arithmetic-Mathematics Tests.* London: University of London Press.

VERNON, P. E. (1951) 'Recent investigations of intelligence and its measurement', *Eugen. Rev.*, **43**, 125–137.

VERNON, P. E. (1955) 'The assessment of children'. University of London, Institute of Education, *Studies in Education*, **7**, 189–215.

VERNON, P. E. (1957a) 'Intelligence and intellectual stimulation during adolescence', *Indian Psychol. Bull.*, **2**, 1–6.

VERNON, P. E. (edit. 1957b) *Secondary School Selection.* London: Methuen.

VERNON, P. E. (1958) 'The relation of intelligence to educational backwardness', *Educ. Rev.*, **11**, 7–15.

VERNON, P. E. (1960) *Intelligence and Attainment Tests.* London: University of London Press.

VERNON, P. E. (1961a) *The Structure of Human Abilities.* London: Methuen.

VERNON, P. E. (1961b) *Selection for Secondary Education in Jamaica.* Kingston, Jamaica: Government Printer.

VERNON, P. E. (1962) 'The determinants of reading comprehension', *Educ. psychol. Measmt.*, **22**, 269–286.

VERNON, P. E. (1964) *Personality Assessment – A Critical Survey.* London: Methuen.

VERNON, P. E. (1965a) 'Environmental handicaps and intellectual development', *Brit. J. educ. Psychol.*, **35**, 9–20, 117–126.

VERNON, P. E. (1965b) 'Ability factors and environmental influences', *Amer. Psychologist*, **20**, 723–733.

VERNON, P. E. (1966a) 'Educational and intellectual development among Canadian Indians and Eskimos', *Educ. Rev.*, **18**, 79–91, 186–195.

VERNON, P. E. (1966b) 'A cross-cultural study of "creativity tests" with 11-year boys', *New Res. in Educ.*, **1**, 135–146.

VERNON, P. E. (1967a) 'Administration of group intelligence tests to East African pupils', *Brit. J. educ. Psychol.*, **37**, 282–291.

VERNON, P. E. (1967b) 'Abilities and educational attainments in an East African environment', *J. spec. Educ.*, **4**, 335–345.

VERNON, P. E., and PARRY, J. B. (1949) *Personnel Selection in the British Forces.* London: University of London Press.

WALKER, A. S. (1955) *Pupils' School Records.* London: Newnes.

WALLACH, M. A., and KOGAN, N. (1965) *Modes of Thinking in Young Children: A Study of the Creativity-Intelligence Distinction.* New York: Holt, Rinehart and Winston.

WALTERS, E. (1958) *Learning to Read in Jamaica.* Kingston, Jamaica: U.C.W.I. Centre for the Study of Education.

WARBURTON, F. W. (1951) 'The ability of the Gurkha recruit', *Brit. J. Psychol.*, **42**, 123–133.

WEIL, P. G. (1958) 'Influence du milieu sur le dévellopement mental', *Enfance*, **2**, 151–160.

WELFORD, A. T. (1958) *Ageing and Human Skill.* London: Oxford University Press.

WERNER, H. (1940) *Comparative Psychology of Mental Development.* New York: Follett.

WHITING, J. W. M., and CHILD, I. L. (1953) *Child Training and Personality: A Cross-Cultural Study.* New Haven: Yale University Press.

WHITING, J. W. M., and WHITING, B. B. (1961) 'Contributions of anthropology to the methods of studying child rearing', in P. H. MUSSEN, *Handbook of Research Methods in Child Development.* New York: John Wiley, pp. 918–944.

WILLMOTT, W. E. (1961) 'The Eskimo community at Port Harrison P.Q.' Ottawa: *NCRC Rep.*, 61–1.

WINTER, W. (1963) 'The perception of safety posters by Bantu industrial workers', *Psychol. Africana*, **10**, 127–135.

WISEMAN, S. (1964) *Education and Environment*. Manchester University Press.

WISEMAN, S. (1966) 'Environmental and innate factors and educational attainment', in J. E. MEADE and A. S. PARKES, *Genetic and Environmental Factors in Human Ability*. Edinburgh: Oliver and Boyd, pp. 64–80.

WISEMAN, S., and WRIGLEY, J. (1953) 'The comparative effects of coaching and practice on the results of verbal intelligence tests', *Brit. J. Psychol.*, 44, 83–94.

WITKIN, H. A., and DYK, R. B. *et al.* (1962) *Psychological Differentiation*: *Studies of Development*. New York: John Wiley.

WOBER, M. (1967a) 'Notes on administering psychological tests in Africa', *Bull. Brit. Psychol. Soc.*, 20, No. 68, 25–34.

WOBER, M. (1967b) 'Adapting Witkin's field independence theory to accommodate new information from Africa', *Brit. J. Psychol.*, 58, 29–38.

WOODROW, H. (1938) 'The relation between abilities and improvement with practice', *J. educ. Psychol.*, 29, 215–230.

WOODROW, H. (1939) 'Factors in improvement with practice', *J. Psychol.*, 7, 55–70.

YARROW, L. J. (1961) 'Maternal deprivation: Toward an empirical and conceptual re-evaluation', *Psychol. Bull.*, 58, 459–490.

ZENTNER, H. (1963a) 'Parental behavior and student attitudes towards further training among Indian and non-Indian students in Oregon and Alberta', *Alberta J. educ. Res.*, 9, 22–30.

ZENTNER, H. (1963b) 'Factors in the social pathology of a North American Indian society', *Anthropologica*, 5, 119–130.

ZENTNER, H. (1964) *The Pre-Neolithic Ethic – Avenue or Barrier to Assimilation*. University of Alberta at Calgary: Unpublished Report.

Author Index

Subject Index

(N.B. Most tests are listed here under their authors' names.)